Eyes are Watching, Ears are Listening

Eyes are Watching, Ears are Listening

Growing up in Nazi Germany
1933-1946

A Memoir

Eycke Strickland

iUniverse, Inc.
New York Lincoln Shanghai

Eyes are Watching, Ears are Listening
Growing up in Nazi Germany 1933-1946

iUniverse books may be ordered through booksellers or by contacting:

iUniverse
2021 Pine Lake Road, Suite 100
Lincoln, NE 68512
www.iuniverse.com
1-800-Authors (1-800-288-4677)

Because of the dynamic nature of the Internet, any Web addresses or links contained in this book may have changed since publication and may no longer be valid.

ISBN: 978-0-595-44704-6 (pbk)
ISBN: 978-0-595-70046-2 (cloth)
ISBN: 978-0-595-89025-5 (ebk)

Printed in the United States of America

An abbreviated version of "Watching the Old Fox" appeared in *Tidepools*, The Olympic Peninsula Arts and Literary Magazine, 40th Anniversary Issue, 2004.
Through the Eyes of a Child, a series of seven sawdust-fired clay tablets, exhibited at the Schatten Gallery, Emory University, Atlanta, Georgia in 1999, contains excerpts from an earlier version of the manuscript.

In Memory of My Father and Mother

Karl and Auguste Viktoria Laabs

Only guard yourself and guard your soul carefully lest you forget the things your eyes saw, and lest these things depart your heart all the days of your life. And you shall make them known to your children, and to your children's children.

—Deuteronomy 4:9

Contents

Part II
Witnessing the Holocaust
Krenau, Poland
1942–1945

Illustrations

1. The author's father Karl, and his siblings Otto and Toni Laabs. Göttingen, 1900.

2. The author's maternal grandparents Gustav and Lisette Wallbach, with their seven children (the author's mother second from the left), shortly before Gustav left for Flanders, where he was killed in battle ten days later. Kassel, summer, 1914.

3. The author's father (first row on the right) during World War I, taken days after his brother Otto was killed in battle. Langemarck, Flanders, summer, 1915.

4. Ludwigstein Castle. Werra Valley.

5. The author's mother. Ludwigstein Castle, 1920s.

6. The author in the arms of her mother. Kassel, December, 1933.

7. The author with her mother at her baptism. Kassel, March, 1934.

8. The author learning how to walk, holding the hand of her father. Glider camp, Staufenberg Hill near Kassel, summer, 1934.

9. The author on an outing with her brother Sven. Wilhelmhausen, winter, 1935–36.

10. The author with her brother Sven. Spa Graal on the Baltic Sea, summer, 1936.

11. The author's aunt Marianne with brother Sven. Wilhelmshausen, summer, 1936.

12. The author with her brother Frank. Wilhelmshausen, summer, 1937.

13. The author schmoozing with her favorite uncle Wütt, with a family friend looking on. Wilhelmshausen, summer, 1937.

14. The author in the arms of her father. Wilhelmhausen, summer, 1938.

15. The author with her brothers Sven and Frank and her mother and sister Ute. Wilhelmshausen, Christmas, 1938.

16. View of Vaake/Weserbergland, with the author's home in the foreground on the right, winter, 1941.

17. The author on the first day of school, carrying a *Zuckertüte* filled with sweets and fruit. Vaake, March, 1940.

18. The author with her brothers Sven and Frank and sister Ute, one month before Ute's death. Vaake, summer, 1940.

19. The author in the garden. Vaake, summer, 1941.

20. "The Lair of the Fox." Auschwitzer Strasse 36b, the author's family residence, became a safe haven and temporary hiding place for Jews between 1941 and 1943. Krenau, Poland. In January, 1945, during the family's flight from Poland, much of their luggage was stolen at the end of their journey. After rifling through the content, the thief threw one of the cases into the Werra River. A kind soul fished it out and restored the waterlogged papers and photos to the family. The photo above is one of those saved.

21. The author's mother. Krenau, summer, 1941.

22. The cottage on Auschwitzer Strasse 36b before renovation. Krenau, summer, 1941.

23. The rear entrance to the cottage on Auschwitzer Strasse 36b before renovation. Krenau, 1941. On the right is the corner of the hay barn, one of the two barns where the author's father hid over one hundred Jews during a night in the early spring, 1943. In the summer of 1944, it served as a shelter for the author and her siblings, during an air raid.

24. Auschwitzer Strasse 36b during renovation. Krenau, winter, 1941–42.

25. Auschwitzer Strasse 36b. Krenau, winter, 1942–43.

26. Anita Tudela Crespo with the author's sister Dagmar. Krenau, summer, 1942.

27. The author with brothers Sven and Frank and Maria Crespo. Krenau, summer, 1942.

28. The author's hiding place, the linden tree, in the garden at Auschwitzer Strasse 36b. Krenau.

29. Madam Chicowa, Gela, and Ivan making hay. Krenau, summer, 1944.

30. The author (front row right) with a small group of her fourth-grade class. Jürgen Helms on the far right. Krenau, 1942.

31. The author's father, Karl Laabs, in Luftwaffe uniform, 1943 or 1944. During the spring of 1943, shortly after he saved over one hundred Jews from Auschwitz, he was indicted for conduct unbecoming a German civil servant. He was fired from his job as County Architect by his Nazi bosses, drafted into the Luftwaffe, and narrowly escaped arrest by the Gestapo.

32. The author's mother with her four children. Krenau, summer, 1943 or 1944.

33. The author trying out wings. Libiaz Glider Camp near Auschwitz, October, 1944.

34. Map "Norddeutschland," Diercke Schulatlas für höhere Lehranstalten, Grosse Ausgabe, 81. Auflage, Westermann Verlag, 1942, pp. 153–154. The map shows the annexed territories and extended borders of the German Reich under the Nazis. It is reprinted here with permission (Nr. F072-40) from the Schulbuchverlag Westermann Schroedel, Braunschweig, Germany, with the specific stipulation that it not be used for Nazi propaganda, which is against the law in the Federal Republic of Germany. Marked in black is the route the author's family traveled during their

xviii   Eyes are Watching, Ears are Listening

flight from the advancing Russian army from Poland in the east to central Germany in the west, between January and April of 1945.

35. Vaake/Weserbergland, Hesse, Germany.

36. The parish house where the author's family found refuge and awaited the end of World War II. Vaake.

37. On Pentecost, the author's family and friends celebrated her brother Björn's baptism at the parish house. Vaake, May, 1945.

38. The *Evangelische Kirche* in Vaake, dating back to the eleventh century, where the author's brother Björn, was baptized and the author confirmed.

39. In 1946, the author's parents purchased land in Vaake on a hill covered with heather. On it, they built a small cottage with their own hands and named it *Haus am Heidehügel.*

40. The family home that the author's father designed and built in the late 1960s on the site of the cottage *Heidehügel.* Vaake.

41. President Gustav Heinemann awarded the author's father the *Verdienstkreuz Erster Klasse,* Cross of Merit, First Class, for rescuing Jews during the Holocaust and for helping rebuild a democratic Germany after World War II. Kassel, 1974.

42. The author's parents. Vaake, summer, 1978, one year before her father's death in March, 1979, at the age of eighty-three.

43. The *Diplome d'Honneur,* issued by Yad Vashem, the Holocaust Memorial for the Martyrs' and Heroes' Remembrance Authority. It "conveys upon Karl Laabs, who, at the risk of his own life saved persecuted Jews during the Holocaust in Europe, the honor of the Award for the Righteous among the Nations, and authorizes the planting of a tree in his name on the Avenue of the Righteous on the Mountain of Remembrance in Jerusalem. January 6, 1981."

44. The author planting a tree in her father's honor on the Avenue of the Righteous. Yad Vashem, Jerusalem, Israel, May, 1983.

45. The author's mother reading and critiquing the unabridged manuscript of *Eyes are Watching, Ears are Listening*. Berlin, Germany, summer, 2000, four years before her death, at the age of one hundred.

Prologue

Adolf Hitler's rise to power at the end of January, 1933, set Germany on a course that would eventually draw the world into the bloody maelstrom of World War II. I was born into this world nine months later, in Kassel, a city in northern Hesse in the heart of Germany. I survived the first thirteen years of my life, guided by Divine Providence, and strengthened by the courage of my parents and the compassion of strangers. My parents, Auguste Viktoria Wallbach and Karl Laabs, named me, their first-born, Eycke. The day after I was born, my father wrote my mother, "I am very happy that the child of our deep, beautiful and wild love is finally here." My mother wrote in her diary, "When I hold your small body to my breast, I am filled with happiness and a deep awareness of the miracle of your being."

My parents' extraordinary and unconventional relationship began in March, 1929. My mother, twenty-five years old and a virgin, took my father, nine years her senior and a married man, as her lover. For most of their lives together they loved and quarreled passionately. As I was growing up, their quarrels troubled me deeply. At the same time, their love sustained me. My parents opposed Hitler's fascist regime, and when the dark shadow of Nazi brutality began to touch our lives, they tried to shield my siblings and me from the evil that surrounded us. During World War II, my father kept his rescue activities a secret to protect us. But I watched and listened. What I saw with my own eyes, heard with my own ears, and felt in every cell of my body, I shall remember as long as I live.

Like all Germans of that generation, my parents were deeply affected by World War I. In 1914, at the age of eighteen, my father interrupted his architectural studies and volunteered for the Kaiser's Army. A year later, his older brother Otto was killed next to him at Langemarck in Flanders. After that, my father suffered and fought three more years in the trenches of Flanders and France until he was wounded in 1918. He returned home to a shattered and demoralized Germany.

My mother was ten years old, when, in 1914, her father, Gustav Wallbach, volunteered to fight in the war, leaving behind his wife and seven children. An aunt had promised my mother that if she prayed hard her father would come back alive. Ten days later, after he said good-bye to his family, my grandfather was killed at the first battle of Langemarck. When the news of his death arrived, my mother stopped praying for a long, long time. Widowed at the age of thirty-five, my grandmother Karoline Lisette, was ill-equipped to raise seven children, who were between the ages of five months and twelve years. Her youngest son, weakened by malnutrition, died before his second birthday. However, by drawing on inner strength, my grandmother managed, with determination, grace, and the help of her parents, to raise the remaining children.

It was the *Wandervogel*, a German youth movement founded at the turn of the century, which brought my parents together and shaped their values. My father joined the *Wandervogel* during the years before the war. He was drawn by the movement's idealism and egalitarianism, by its protest against Victorian morals and mores, and by its love of nature, hiking, folk music, and dance. After the war, he completed his study of architecture and upon graduation joined an architectural firm in Kassel. He resumed his activities in the *Wandervogel*, where he and his first wife rose to leadership positions. From 1920 until 1930, my father played an important part in the restoration of a medieval castle called Burg Ludwigstein, which crowned a wooded hill high above the Werra River in northern Hesse. The *Wandervogel* restored the ruin, dedicated it to the members who had fallen in Flanders' fields during World War I, and used it as a gathering place for *Wandervogel* groups.

At the age of seventeen, in 1921, my mother also joined the *Wandervogel*. She attended business school, but was totally unsuited for office work. Her passion was reading and writing poetry. She worked at Ludwigstein Castle between 1923 and 1926, and she graduated from nursing school in 1929. She returned to Ludwigstein for one more year until 1930. Her happiest years were those spent at Ludwigstein. She glowed when she talked about living with writers, poets, and musicians. She recalled that the rewards for their hard work were glorious evenings of conversation, music, and reading poetry by Rilke, Hölderlin, Goethe, and George. She cherished the memory of being loved, respected, and treated like a sister by the young men of the *Wandervogel*. It was at Ludwigstein that she first took notice of my father, and he, of her.

By 1930, my father's first marriage was falling apart, and in the spring of 1931, he and my mother moved from Kassel to Frankfurt. My father enrolled at the Goethe University to study economics and social sciences on a scholarship from the Social Democratic Party. On the day in 1933 that Adolf Hitler became chancellor of Germany, my father wrote on the blackboard of a lecture hall, *30. Januar—Beginn der Fastnacht*, January 30—when fools begin to rule. Nazi faculty members saw this act as a provocation, and they barred him from completing his doctorate, so he left Frankfurt in the spring of 1933 with a degree in voca-tional education in his pocket. That same year Hitler banned the *Wandervogel.*

My father took a job as an architect in his hometown, Hannoversch Münden, while my mother, pregnant with me, returned to live with her siblings in Kassel until I was one year old. My father finally divorced his first wife. On December 1, 1934, my parents married. A few days before Christmas, my mother and I left her family to live with my father in Wilhelmshausen. My mother wrote in her diary, "That night the stars were so radiant that it seemed as if they were lighting the way to our first home with their brilliance." Wilhelmshausen was a small village in the Fulda River Valley, five miles north of Kassel, and four miles south of Münden. It was in those surroundings that my earliest memories emerged, and my own story begins.

PART I
In The Heart of Germany
1933–1942

Papa has Wings

My earliest memory is of white-winged objects slowly turning circles in a deep blue sky above me. I felt warm and safe in the arms of my mother, who pointed to the sky and whispered, "Papa, Papa." I echoed, "Papa, Papa," the first words I spoke. Years later, my mother—I called her Mutti—explained to me that the white objects were gliders and that my father was piloting one of them as he soared on warm currents rising from the earth. She also told me that while she was pregnant with me and even after I was born we accompanied Papa on sunny weekends to Staufenberg Hill in the rolling countryside near Kassel. There we watched Papa get into the cockpit of a glider, wave to us, and climb toward the sun, where he soared on fragile wings until the air cooled in the early evening.

The second letter my father wrote to my mother and me floated down from one of those gliders. Children playing in a meadow nearby found it and brought it to my mother. The envelope had a long red ribbon attached to it, and the letter said that Papa loved us both and would visit us soon. My mother told me that I adored my father, and when I could speak in sentences I proclaimed, "Papa has wings."

Three months before I was born, my mother's sister Marianne, accompanied my mother and father to Staufenberg Hill to watch my father complete a series of glider qualification flights. During the night, while camped near a grove of trees on the side of the mountain, my mother suffered a hemorrhage. My father made his way to the next village and persuaded a doctor to return with him. In the meantime, my aunt gathered enough wood to start a roaring fire to help guide the doctor and my father to their campsite. The doctor ordered my mother to be admitted to a hospital. My mother refused. Under Marianne's care, my mother spent the next three months confined to her bed. She worked on a layette and a blue quilt for my playpen, on which she appliquéd in bright yellow the sun, the moon, and stars. She read poetry and started a diary, in which she recorded her thoughts, including my development, until I was fourteen months old.

When I was three months old she wrote, "I am filled with longing and anticipation for the arrival of spring. For the first time you will look upon the sun, behold the blue sky, the flowers, birds, and butterflies. My dearest, this world is filled with breathtaking beauty to those who open their eyes and hearts to the wonders of nature." A few months later, she wrote, "It is summertime, my love. We spent the day outside, where you lay in a meadow of fragrant clover. Your hands reached for the blossoms, and your eyes took in the thousand miracles of this earth. Tonight, I held you in my arms, and we listened to the evening song of the birds. I prayed that God would grant you a gentle life, and that you would never lose the trust and sweet faith of childhood."

A year after I was born, my parents married and followed the Fulda River north to make their first home in Wilhelmshausen, a small village nestled between the river and the hills that were covered with spruce forest. For the next five years, our family occupied the second floor of a half-timbered farmhouse. Here, my godmother Marianne attended my mother at the births of brothers Sven and Frank and sister Ute. Marianne and her husband Wütt were unable to have children of their own. They visited us every weekend and showered us with tenderness, toys, and exquisite clothes. They read to us, took us for walks and drives in the countryside, and to the seaside on holidays.

My mother wrote in her diary that I had a hard time moving from Kassel to Wilhelmshausen. After Sven was born, I became listless and lost my appetite. She thought that I missed Marianne and Wütt, who had doted on me since the day I was born. I got tired of competing with my siblings for my mother's attention and was overjoyed when Marianne and Wütt took me home with them. I reveled in their undivided attention, unconditional love, and devotion. My aunt affectionately called me *Mäuschen*, little mouse. I walked on tiptoes and kissed my uncle every time he called me *mein Schätzchen*, my little treasure. There were times when I wanted to stay with my aunt and uncle instead of going home. I felt torn between them and my parents, but, as I grew older, I realized that I was fortunate to have been nurtured by two sets of parents.

My siblings and I grew up without grandparents. My mother's parents died before I was born. My paternal grandparents did not approve of my mother. As a result, my siblings and I never knew my father's father, who died in 1942. We did not get to meet my father's mother until 1943. We were fortunate, however, to have inherited the Wallbach clan, my mother's boisterous brothers and sisters, who since the death of their parents had clung to each other like burrs. They gathered around us on holidays, teased and argued with each other, laughed and played with us.

Our great-aunt Gustchen Wallbach was the only surviving member of her generation. She visited us often, arriving every Tuesday morning on the nine o'clock train from Kassel. On the day she was expected, my brothers and I watched impatiently from our living room window as the train, billowing clouds of smoke, whistled and puffed around the bend high on the bluff across the Fulda River. I thought I recognized my mother's aunt at a distance, as she walked down the hill toward the ferry. The ferryman had to pull the flat, wooden raft by a rope attached to a heavy steel cable, which stretched across the river, and it seemed like an eternity until Tante Gustchen turned the corner into Holzhäuser Strasse. She passed Müller's farmhouse on the left and the meadow on the right, where a gaggle of snowy white geese honked at her, but she seemed unafraid of the big gander who was my foe. Every morning, as I walked by to get the milk, he chased me, hissed, and nipped at my legs. The day I stopped being afraid of that beady-eyed monster was when I took a long stick and chased after him.

When Tante Gustchen walked through the front gate, the first thing she asked was, "What have you little rascals been up to?" as she bent down to hug each one of us. I blushed and hoped that the time I snitched fruit salad didn't make me undeserving. I also prayed that Mutti wouldn't tell her that I had broken Sven's red toy dog on purpose and let him take the blame.

Tante Gustchen's eyes twinkled in her wrinkled face, and she smiled as she pulled fruit and chocolate from her plum-colored velvet bag. I detected the smell of lavender about her, and the folds of her ankle-length gray skirt rustled as she walked toward the house, with the three of us in tow.

During most of the day, my great-aunt sat in an easy chair next to the window. She wore a black shawl wrapped around her shoulders. With her head bent low, she knitted and mended socks, and sewed and embroidered my dresses. She radiated warmth like a big rock heated by the sun. I circled around her like a kitten, hoping for her smile and the gentle touch of her soft hand. She called me her *"Schmusekätzchen,"* and her caresses warmed me and made me feel like dancing.

When I was five, she brought a ball of wool and some needles, and patiently began teaching me how to knit. I dropped many a stitch, but I liked the feel of the soft wool sliding through my fingers and the clicking of the needles. "Knit one, pearl one," my great-aunt sang, and at the end of the year, I finished a misshapen scarf, which I proudly presented to my mother at Christmas time.

I cherished Tante Gustchen's quiet and gentle presence and wished that she could live with us. She told us stories and was patient when Mutti was harried and impatient. Tante Gustchen consoled me after Mutti scolded me for getting in the way of the road repair crew, who sprayed me with tar. "I look like *Pechmarie*," I wailed, "and I so much want to be *Goldmarie*." In the fairy tale "Mother Holle," *Goldmarie* is rewarded with a shower of gold for her good deeds, whereas *Pechmarie* is showered with pitch for being an uncaring and lazy girl.

In the evening, my great-aunt would put on her big black hat with the faded yellow rose and leave. I watched as she walked down the street, turning every once in a while and giving a short wave. I lost sight of her when she disappeared around the corner on her way to the ferry but then again had a glimpse of her when she got off the ferry on the other side. I imagined that I saw her wave one more time before she disappeared from my sight in a cloud of steam from the train engine. That is when I began pestering Mutti to teach me to count the days until Tante Gustchen would return to us.

A long time passed, and I asked Mutti why Tante Gustchen had not been visiting. She replied that Tante Gustchen was ill. Months later, when I asked once again, Mutti answered that Tante Gustchen wouldn't be coming back. I asked, "Why not?" She explained that Tante Gustchen was in heaven with God. Yet, the train that had brought us Tante Gustchen continued to billow clouds of smoke, whistle, and puff around the bend high up on the bluff across the Fulda River. In spite of what Mutti had said, I expected the train to bring my great-aunt back to us any day.

Praying and Working

Our landlords, the Schäfers, were a hard-working, pious couple who occupied the downstairs apartment of their farmhouse. We called the tall, skinny, old man Opa, and his wife Oma, although they were not related to us. Each time the church bells echoed through the valley, Oma and Opa answered them by proclaiming in their *Plattdeutsch* dialect to anyone who would listen, "*beten und arbeten*," pray and work. When they didn't work, they prayed, and when they didn't pray, they argued. One of them spoke in a deep voice *mumumum* and the other one a high voice *yakyakyak*. We couldn't believe it when we found out that Opa had the high voice and Oma the deep one. From then on, Sven and I amused our visitors by imitating the old couple arguing with each other.

The Schäfers kept livestock and cultivated a vegetable and flower garden, which Oma believed in fertilizing in a unique way. She, like the other old village women, wore long skirts over layers of petticoats. When Oma got the urge to urinate, she walked into her garden, stepped on top of one of the well-tended beds, lifted her petticoats and skirt ever so slightly, spread her legs, and let go of a stream of steaming urine, a smile of contentment on her face.

I was duly impressed and amazed at her expertise in relieving herself, having tried to imitate it and having failed. It puzzled me how she managed to pee without pulling down her pants and squatting, until one washday I saw her snow-white linen drawers fluttering on the clothesline. Oma's bloomers were slit open at the crotch. That was her secret to successful urination while standing over her garden plots. My mother laughed when I asked her to cut holes in my drawers so that I could pee the way Oma did.

The only time Oma Schäfer smiled was when she greeted my brother Sven. With a calloused hand, she patted him on his blond head, cooed and tickled his chin, and let me know what a sweet boy my brother was. She even invited him into her kitchen and fed him slices of fatback and hard sausage. I wondered why, no matter how many times I chased the chickens out of her garden plot, she never gave me a treat or said a kind word to me. Instead, she cackled like one of her chickens and fussed at me for running up and down the stairs, shook a knobby finger in my face, and inquired sharply, "Have you said your prayers today?"

"No," I replied, as I breezed past her with my nose up in the air and snapped, "but I did my chores."

In the evenings, after my brothers and I were in bed, Oma Schäfer appeared at our door, walked in without saying a word, made herself comfortable in an easy chair, and read the newspaper until Papa came home late at night. When I asked Mutti why Oma came to our apartment to read the paper every night, she told me that it was because Opa was a cheapskate who didn't believe in turning on the electric lights.

*   *   *

One day, I overheard Papa telling Mutti that a war was coming and because it was too dangerous living near the Rotwesten Airfield, we would have to move. That was the first time I heard the word "war." All I understood was that it was something to be afraid of. The second time the subject of war came up was when I met Enid. I noticed whenever Enid was around, she made Mutti happy, and that is how I could tell that they were friends. Enid lived in a large house between Wilhelmshausen and Münden. It was perched on a hilltop overlooking the river. I stared at the strange things that decorated her walls: scary masks, drums, and spears with feathers. She explained that they came from a faraway place called South Africa, where she was born, and that her father was German and her mother English. I didn't know much about the English, except that soon their planes might come to bomb us. When I asked her if her mother had any bombs, she replied that she didn't think the English were going to harm us. She showed me a book with pictures of a girl with long curly hair named Alice, who followed a rabbit down a hole, where she drank tea with a bunch of strange-looking characters. Enid explained that the book was written in English, and that one day I would learn how to read it. I had the feeling that Enid was worried about Mutti, because each time before Enid said goodbye, she made me promise that I would mind Mutti and help her take care of my siblings.

Every morning I kissed Papa goodbye before he drove the three miles to his job in Münden. My mother told me that I waited for him and greeted him with my biggest smiles when he came home for lunch every day. I stood at the gate and waved when he went back to work, and I complained that I didn't get to see him when he returned in the evenings after we were asleep. When I asked him what he did when he was away from home, he answered that he was an architect and a glider pilot in charge of a glider camp. When I wanted to know what an architect did, Papa explained that he drew pictures of houses and took care that they were built properly. And when I asked him if he would teach me how, he grinned and answered, "Maybe, when you're older."

*　　　　*　　　　*

Decades later, I explored some of the attractive *Siedlungen*, clusters of white stucco houses with high-gabled, red-tiled roofs, which my father designed between World War I and World War II. These neighborhoods were made up of modestly priced, one-family houses, each with its own garden. They were a manifestation of the socialist dream of humane, affordable housing for workers, who lived in crowded tenements.

*　　　　*　　　　*

The day Papa, Mutti, my siblings and I left Wilhelmshausen, Oma Schäfer indicated that I was crazy by tapping her finger to her temple when I begged her to tell Tante Gustchen our new address when she came looking for us. The journey to our new home took us ten miles downriver past Münden, where the Fulda merged into the Weser River. From there, we followed the course of the Weser.

The Trouble with Adolf

In August, 1939, we arrived in Vaake, a small village in the northern part of Hesse. For centuries its inhabitants had made their living cutting timber, making barrels, burning charcoal, fishing, and farming. They lived in half-timbered houses built along the main road, which ran north and parallel to the Weser River. Another road led west into the hilly forest called the Reinhardswald, and ended at a small coal mine, which straddled the Gahrenberg. Two valleys with crystal clear rivulets cut through fields and meadows that clustered around the village like a colorful patchwork.

The white stucco house on 170 Mündener Strasse to the south of the village had a pointed gable, a red tile roof, two stories, and seven rooms. And, just as Papa had promised, there was a large garden, surrounded by a tall hedge for privacy. Papa seemed to know that bad times were coming and that we would need to grow some of our own food. Soon after we moved in, we started preparing the ground for planting in the spring.

A month later, after German troops attacked Poland, World War II broke out. The grown-ups wrung their hands and whispered about the trouble a man named Adolf was getting us into. Nobody explained to me who Adolf was, but I decided that it had to be his fault when, at the end of October, Papa closed his architectural firm in Münden. I cried when he kissed us goodbye and walked out the gate, carrying a suitcase, and his *Aktentasche,* briefcase. The night before he left, my parents had a heated argument behind closed doors, which left me bewildered and frightened. I asked Mutti how come Papa had to go away, and she burst into tears. When I asked her to explain, she told me that because of the war he had been drafted to build airfield installations on the Island of Sylt, in the North Sea.

Around that time—I don't remember exactly when—my mother went away without telling us where she was going. She left us in the care of Annemarie, a maid who had recently come to live with us. I hoped that Mutti hadn't gone away because we had been naughty. I was so relieved when she returned a few days later that I tried to please her in every way I could think of. For a few days I even succeeded in getting along with my brothers.

*   *   *

Sixty years passed before I learned that my mother had been hauled into court. She had been tried for "insulting a member of the National Socialist Party" when she protested my father's being drafted to do civilian duty for the Luftwaffe. Her argument had been that other men his age, who had served in World War I and were the heads of large families, were exempt from the draft. My mother never talked about the incident, which leaves me to wonder if the court had warned her, fined her, or merely given her a suspended sentence.

The Call of the Hawk

"Here I am," announced my mother's oldest sister Addie, with her son Uwe, in tow. She breezed through the door, spread her arms, and gave each one of us a wet kiss on the mouth. Mutti seemed especially glad to see her. The two of them spoke in hushed tones, and then they shut the living room door and left us standing in the hallway.

Shortly after Addie's arrival, Mutti began to drag herself around, looking sick and flushed. I didn't know what to do, so I busied myself in the playhouse Mutti had built for us. With its three walls, a roof, a table, and benches, it was a good place to share my worries with my dolls. But nothing I did made me feel better. The next day, when Mutti did not get out of bed, Addie informed me that Mutti was not well. She ordered me to go outside and to watch my sister Ute. A while later a white van, its side painted with a red cross, stopped at the gate. Two men in white coats, carrying a litter between them, entered through the gate and walked up to the house. A lump formed in my throat and my legs felt wobbly. I wanted to run and see what was wrong, but instead I remained frozen in place and prayed to God over and over, "Please, *lieber Gott*, do not let Mutti die." When I saw the men put my mother in the ambulance and close the doors, I ran to the gate and watched the ambulance disappear in the distance, its horn blasting *tatee tata tatee tata* until the sound was lost in the distance, like the shrill call of the chicken hawk vanishing over the pine ridge above.

It was only then that I realized I had forgotten all about my sister, who had been playing in the sand box. I gathered her into my arms and rushed into the house. "Tante Addie," I choked out, "what's the matter with Mutti?" She looked at me from behind her thick glasses, her head bent slightly to one side. She brushed back her hair, cleared her throat, and told me that Mutti had been taken to the hospital in Münden. When I asked her what was wrong, she shrugged her shoulders and hesitated before reassuring me that she believed the doctors would make Mutti well. Addie didn't sound very convincing, and I had the sense that she knew more than she was telling me.

The house seemed empty now that both Papa and Mutti were gone. A sense of doom had slowly been building up and weighed on us like a heavy blanket. My brothers, our cousin, and I played listlessly. The boys watched as military trucks rolled along the road in front of our house, and columns of soldiers marched by. Our squabbles were subdued. I continued praying, "Please, *lieber Gott*, don't let Mutti die."

Mutti returned a month later, looking pale and weak. She hugged each one of us and went straight to bed. After Mutti had regained her strength, Addie and her son returned to their home in Hamburg.

Years later, when I was a young adult, my mother confided in me that one reason for her despair was the fact that she discovered Papa had been having an affair. The second reason was a miscarriage, which had resulted in systemic puerperal septicemia. Her fever rose to 105 degrees, her heart stopped, and the doctor had to administer an injection directly into her heart to revive her. Before she returned home, he told her that she had been clinically dead and that her recovery was a miracle.

Elisabeth

Elisabeth Niemeyer was my first friend. She was a year younger than I and a head taller, had a round face, big brown eyes, and wore her dark brown hair in a short pageboy, with neatly cut bangs. Like all of the village girls, she wore a big white ribbon on top of her head and a pinafore over her dresses. She lived across the road on the banks of the Weser River with her younger brother August, her parents, and her grandparents, Oma and Opa Söder.

Elisabeth liked coming over to my house to play, and I liked being around this gentle girl with the funny voice. We pushed my sister Ute in her carriage and played with my dolls. "Does your mother allow you to play with your dolls any time you want?" Elisabeth asked.

"Of course, that's what they're for." Elisabeth seemed surprised, and when I invited her into our living room to meet my mother, she stood at the door, opened her mouth and forgot to close it. She took in the bright, sunny room with its eggshell wallpaper, the cherry furniture, and the vase of wild flowers on the table. Mutti, who was drinking her afternoon tea, invited us to come in. Elisabeth checked her shoes for dirt before she tiptoed across the white hand-woven rug to curtsey and shake my mother's hand.

"And what is your name?" Mutti asked kindly.

"Elisabeth Niemeyer," she croaked her eyes on the floor.

"I am glad to meet you. I talked to your grandmother, who shared her gardening secrets with me. You are welcome any time." Elisabeth smiled shyly and scratched her leg. Year-round she wore long, woolen stockings her grandmother knitted for her. She complained that they made her hot and that they itched, and she wondered aloud why I didn't have to wear them.

After meeting Mutti, Elisabeth remarked, "Your mother is nice ... only everything is so different at your house."

"What do you mean?"

"Don't know, just different," she replied timidly and shrugged her shoulders. Sometimes I had trouble understanding Elisabeth when she slipped into her *Plattdeutsch* dialect, as happened when we put on a play on my sixth birthday. We couldn't understand Elisabeth's muffled *"Eck dümpe, eck dümpe,"* when she got stuck in her fairy godmother costume. Mutti helped pull the dress over her head. We apologized and comforted her as she lay gasping for air in the grass.

"The poor girl was trying to tell you that she couldn't breathe," Mutti scolded. But as soon as Mutti served lemonade and the *Gugelhopf* birthday cake, Elisabeth looked like she had forgotten all about the mishap.

On a chilly November afternoon, Elisabeth arrived out of breath at our house to invite me for an early dinner. Mutti sent me off with a bouquet of the last purple asters from the garden. Elisabeth and I entered their kitchen through the back door and I curtsied. "There you are." Oma Söder's smile made her bright blue eyes almost disappear in her wrinkled face. A tempting aroma came from the steaming iron pot she stirred on her large wood stove. "I hope you like *Eintopf*," she said as she wiped her hand on her apron before she accepted the bouquet and shook my hand. I was grateful when she spoke to me in High German instead of *Plattdeutsch*.

A shaded lamp hung low over the bare kitchen table, casting a warm glow. Oma Söder saw me run my hand over the surface of the tabletop. She explained that the heavy pine table had belonged to her great-grandmother. To keep its surface smooth and white, Oma scoured it with sand every day of the week except on the Lord's Day, of course. Elisabeth and I set the table with deep soup plates, spoons, knives, and strange-looking forks, with three sharp tines on wooden handles. My mouth watered as I inhaled the delicious smells from the simmering soup, and I was glad when Opa and Elisabeth's mother came in, carrying buckets of creamy milk. We washed up quickly and sat down at the table. "Wishing everybody a good evening," Elisabeth's grandfather said solemnly, as he slowly let himself onto his chair. *"Feierabend,"* he sighed, inviting us to celebrate the end of the workday.

Frau Niemeyer greeted me. Oma poured milk—still warm from the cow—into a saucer for her husband and into beakers for us. She ladled the steaming stew onto our plates and offered thick slices of dark rye bread from a wooden bowl. "Home-baked," she said proudly, and set a lump of butter in the middle of the table. Opa, who sat at the head of the table, nodded at Oma. We bowed our heads and folded our hands as Oma prayed, *"Komm, Herr Jesus, sei unser Gast und segne was Du uns bescheret hast,"* Come, Lord Jesus, be our guest and bless the food you have bestowed upon us.

"Amen," we replied, and, without another word, we savored the stew of homemade sausages and vegetables, covered with big yellow eyes of fat, and we chewed the coarse rye bread, slathered with glistening, freshly churned butter. After dinner, Elisabeth asked her mother for permission to show me her doll.

"Go ahead, but, remember, don't touch anything."

A musty odor greeted us when Elisabeth opened the door to the parlor. "This is our *gute Stube*," she whispered. White lace curtains framed by heavy velvet drapes covered the windows. The drapes were tied with golden cords, ending in intricate tassels. A collection of tiny gold-rimmed mocha cups and crystal goblets sparkled behind glass in an ornately carved china cabinet. Against the opposite wall stood a sofa upholstered in green velvet. Lacy doilies covered small tables and chairs, which were grouped in the corners of the room. The heavy, dark furniture and the navy blue wallpaper, decorated with golden flowers, gave the room a solemn air. Elisabeth must have read my mind when she explained, "We only use this room for special occasions, like Christmas, christenings, confirmations, weddings, and funerals. I'm not allowed to play in here."

"Why not?"

"Because my Oma and Mama say so," she answered in a matter-of-fact tone.

I gazed at a painting of an enormous fourteen-point buck. His head was thrown back, his mouth wide open, and he was exhaling a white cloud. Elisabeth showed me the faded photographs of women in white wedding gowns and men dressed in black suits, stiff collars, and top hats. "These are my great-grandparents and my grandparents, and this is a picture of my parents on their wedding day," Elisabeth explained.

I pointed to two glass cases in which rested silver and golden wreaths. Anticipating my question, Elisabeth said, "My grandmother wore them in her hair for her silver and her golden anniversaries."

"What are anniversaries?"

"My Mama said that couples who have been married for twenty-five years celebrate their silver anniversary, and when they have been married fifty years they celebrate their golden anniversary."

Tucked in a corner of the parlor stood an old-fashioned wicker doll carriage on metal wheels. Propped up between white cushions sat a beautiful doll in a yellow gown. "This is my doll. My mother lets me play with her sometimes. Her head is made of china, and her eyes are real. Look." Elisabeth glanced over her shoulder at the door, pulled back the cover, and tilted her doll backwards. "See, she can open and close her eyes." Elisabeth quickly put her doll back and smoothed out the coverlet. "We'd better go, or Mama will think we are up to no good."

Elisabeth and I tiptoed out of the parlor back into the cozy kitchen, where Opa Söder sat, his glasses perched on the end of his nose. He was reading from the Bible to Oma, who sat by the kitchen stove, knitting a long black stocking. I bid everyone a good night and thanked Oma for supper.

"Did you have a good time?" Mutti asked when I returned home.

I nodded and told Mutti about the dinner, Elisabeth's fancy parlor, and her doll. "Did you know that she is not allowed to play with it except with permission from her mother? They only use their parlor on special occasions. Why don't we have a parlor?"

Mutti shook her head and replied, "I guess the Söders are old-fashioned. They still live the way my parents and grandparents did." I described the wedding pictures and shiny wreaths on their walls and asked why Mutti had never shown me her wedding picture.

"Because we didn't have one taken," she answered and quickly changed the subject. "It's way past your bedtime. Get ready, and I'll be up to hear your prayers and tuck you in."

I thought about Papa, and I prayed for his safety that night. I knew that there was trouble in the world, and that German U-boats were prowling the seas and sinking enemy ships. And I wondered why.

Kräuterlieschen

Around that time, Mutti befriended an old crone, who was the guardian of age-old secrets about the healing powers of plants. She learned from her that one has to harvest the herbs in the morning when their fragrance is at their peak, to tie them together, suspend them upside down, and dry them in a dark place. She learned how to cure our colds with chamomile by pouring boiling water over the dried chamomile. After it had steeped, Mutti put a towel over our heads and had us breathe in the healing steam. She rinsed my hair with water infused with chamomile to make it shine like gold. The old woman stopped by our house from time to time and seemed happy that anyone would listen. "My own daughter doesn't hold much with old-timey cures," she sighed. "Tincture of arnica is good for sensitive and chapped skin, you know, and you can use comfrey in poultices for cuts and bruises." Pointing in my direction, she advised, "Saint John's Wort will do the same for that scrape on your knee. In the springtime, you can make a tonic from the new leaves of the sticky goose grass. You can pick nettle shoots and sorrel to make delicious soups. Tender dandelion leaves make a good salad, too, and dried, they help cure rheumatism." *Kräuterlieschen*—as I called her—rubbed her knees under her long homespun skirts and turned to my mother, "Wild primula, which is said to have sprung where Peter dropped his golden key to heaven, will calm your nerves after a long day chasing little ones, and the leaves of the great mullein will help you sleep."

Whenever she had our attention, the old woman's deeply wrinkled face took on a glow. She spoke of the fruit of the briar rose, which, dried and steeped in hot water, makes a fine tea, and of elderberries which, when boiled down to a syrup with sugar, are good for treating colds and influenza. She mentioned that hawthorn blossoms can strengthen a failing heart. From then on, each fall we began collecting and drying rosehips to make "red tea," picked elderberries, and turned them into delicious jams and syrup.

The next spring *Kräuterlieschen* presented Mutti with small packets of seeds neatly folded and wrapped in newspaper. She brought different roots and tubers and advised her which plants to set during a certain cycle of the moon. "These are lemon balm seeds," she explained. "Tea made from its leaves drives away sad thoughts, and this is mint to freshen the breath and the spirit." She recommended sorrel, chopped parsley, dill, chives, cucumbery borage and salad burnet for *Grüne Sosse*, a zesty sauce made with sour cream, enriched with chopped eggs, and served over boiled potatoes. As she sifted through her treasures, she talked about burning rosemary to chase away diseased air. With a nod in my direction, she added, "A sprig of it tucked under your pillow will banish evil spirits and nightmares. *Ja, ja,* those are things my dear grandmother taught me." Once she took me along to gather Waldmeister, the sweet woodruff, which grows in shady spots at the edge of the woods. Mutti used its leaves to flavor a wine punch for a special celebration. When I came down with a sore throat, *Kräuterlieschen* recommended, "sage tea laced with honey will sooth your inflamed throat and lower the fever." I didn't much like the treatment, for the tea was bitter in spite of the honey that Mutti used to sweeten it.

Sitting at *Kräuterlieschen's* feet I learned to appreciate the wisdom of an old woman.

Growing Up Too Fast

Toward the end of March, 1940, Mutti presented me with a satchel. I inhaled its pungent new-leather odor. I practiced opening and closing the small wooden case, which held sharpened slate styluses, and traced the bright red poppies and sky-blue bachelor buttons on its cover with my finger. I put the satchel on my back, danced, and sang, "I'm going to school." I didn't know what to think when I heard Mutti muttering to herself, "Why do they have to grow up so fast?" The day she helped me try on my new school outfit, she couldn't hide her tears. I wondered what made her so sad. I loved my new outfit: a gray pleated skirt, white blouse, beige coat with the neat white collar, brand new shoes, and a white beret. It didn't bother me that the shoes were too large. "Big enough to grow into," the shoe salesman had said. I had to wear a pair of heavy woolen socks over my white knee socks for the shoes to fit.

My mother reminded me of a hen who clucked at her chicks from the moment they strayed too far from her. She wasn't happy until she had them tucked safely back under her wings. Perhaps that was the reason why my first day of school turned out to be so distressing. The moment my mother and I walked through the entrance to the school, tears started streaming down my cheeks. When I saw the unfamiliar faces of the teacher, the other children, and their mothers, I broke down sobbing. I noticed that, like me, every child carried a *Zuckertüte*, a large cardboard cone decorated with pictures of flowers and filled with candy, fruit, and nuts. Mutti tried to comfort me, "*Schätzchen*, don't cry." She pulled out a handkerchiefs, dried my tears, retied and fluffed the ribbons on my braids, and assured me that once I got used to school I would like it. I hugged her tightly, not intending to let go. She pried my arms loose and reminded me, "You are a big girl now." I didn't want to hear how big I was, nor any of her promises. What I wanted was to go home with her, right then and there.

When the parents left, I resumed my sobbing, punctuated by an occasional hiccup. The teacher ignored me, my classmates stared, but I didn't care. The teacher instructed us to hang our coats on hooks, and then she assigned desks. I kept my eyes on the floor and put my *Zuckertüte* at my feet, crushing the delicate snowdrops Mutti had lovingly fastened to it. When everybody was seated, the teacher greeted the class, "Good morning, children." I lifted my tear-stained face. "My name is Fräulein Alles, and I am your teacher," she announced primly, as she made sure that not a single hair had escaped from the tight bun at her nape. She smoothed out her navy blue skirt, adjusted the collar of her starched white blouse, and added, "What do you say?"

"Good morning, Fräulein Alles," the other students replied, as loud sobs escaped my mouth. First, Fräulein Alles went around the room to check our hands, necks, and behind our ears for dirt. She asked those who did not pass the inspection to wash at the sink. Only then did she ask us to say our name, address, place and date of birth, religious affiliation, father's name and occupation. Relieved that I was prepared, I answered with a trembling voice, "My name is Eycke Laabs."

A girl behind me sniggered. "What a funny name."

"Shut your mouth!" Fräulein Alles chided.

A bit unnerved, I continued, "I live at 72 Mündener Strasse." I mentioned the place and date of my birth and added, "I am Protestant, and my father is Karl Laabs, and he is an architect."

"Well done," the teacher said. When I heard her admonish those who couldn't introduce themselves properly, I couldn't help being pleased.

Next, Fräulein Alles had us take the slates and styluses out of our satchels and copy the vertical lines she drew on the blackboard. The room filled with the sounds of squeaking and scratching of styluses on slate, and I watched the boy next to me spit on the sharp end of his stylus. After a while, I stopped crying and concentrated on making my lines stand up straight like fence posts. When the bell rang for recess, I watched everyone grab their snack pouches and head for the door. I followed my classmates reluctantly and watched them walk off in groups of twos and threes. They were eating their sandwiches, talking, running, and chasing each other, while I sat on the schoolhouse steps and moped. I strained to listen for familiar words as the children chattered with each other. During class, they had to speak High German, but on the playground and the moment school let out, they reverted to *Plattdeutsch*. Two older girls put their heads together, looked at me, and pointed. I recognized the word *Fremde*, and understood that I was a stranger.

After recess, each teacher made her class line up until the headmaster, Herr Braun, rang a bell, the signal for the groups to return to their classrooms. Margret Tichy, a slender girl with long braids, shyly paired up with me. The teacher showed us how to wipe and dry our slates. The chalk scraped and scratched, as she continued drawing letters she called "vowels" on the blackboard. When the last bell rang and everyone jumped up, Fräulein Alles made us sit back down. "Class, after we stand up, we say, 'Auf Wiedersehen' before leaving the classroom."

"Auf Wiedersehen, Fräulein Alles," we sing-songed obediently. Then followed the sounds of shoving and rustling as the pupils packed up. I quickly put my things into my satchel, picked up my Zuckertüte, grabbed my coat off the hook on the wall, and left the school behind without looking back.

With my satchel bouncing on my shoulders, and my braids flying, it took me all of fifteen minutes to run home. I arrived out of breath at the garden gate, sat down on the ground, and caught my breath. Then I burst into the house and called out, "Mutti, I'm home." There was no answer.

Sven saw me come in. "How was school?" he asked, as he glanced at my Zuckertüte.

"You don't want to know," I replied, and, without taking off my coat, I sat on the stairs and opened up my Zuckertüte. Sven joined me, and we devoured sweets by the handful until Mutti discovered us.

She didn't sound too stern when she scolded, "You are going to spoil your Mittagessen."

After crying and sobbing during my first day of school, I slowly became accustomed to being among strangers. What helped me more than anything else was that I liked the idea of learning new things. I liked sitting at my desk and watching Fräulein Alles show us how to put what looked like simple lines and loops together to form letters, eventually turn letters into words, and a string of words into sentences. I listened with awe as the second graders—who occupied half of the classroom—read short stories they had written on their slates. I watched with amazement as they drew numbers on the blackboard, connected them with something called pluses and minuses, and came up with different numbers. I believed that Fräulein Alles was teaching magic, and I wanted nothing more than to be able to write stories, to read, and play with numbers. I couldn't get home fast enough to do my assignments. I wrote my letters as nicely as I could. When they didn't look quite right, I washed and wiped my slate clean and practiced until I was satisfied. When the teacher was pleased with my work, she put the number "one" at the bottom of my slate. She explained, "A 'one' is the best grade one can receive; then comes a 'two', followed by a 'three', 'four', 'five', and 'six.' You don't ever want to get anything lower than a 'three'." I planned to tell Sven, so that he would know all about these things when he started school next spring.

During recess, I watched the games the girls played in the courtyard. I liked especially well the one they called Dornröschen. When Margret and Brigitte Blankenburg smiled at me and waved for me to come on over, I joined them. One girl was chosen to be Sleeping Beauty, a second girl the Good Fairy, and a third the

Bad Fairy. The rest of us formed a large circle surrounding the princess and sang as we slowly rotated around her, *"Dornröschen war ein schönes Kind,"* Sleeping Beauty was a lovely girl. During the second verse, the mood of the song changed when the Bad Fairy forced her way into the circle, as we sang, *"Da kam die böse Fee herein."* The Bad Fairy sang, *"Dornröschen, du sollst sterben,"* Sleeping Beauty, you must die. But then, the Good Fairy promised the princess that she would sleep one hundred years, until a prince would awaken her with a kiss. Herr Braun rang his bell, ending recess and breaking the spell.

I had heard scary stories about Herr Braun. Teachers sent unruly and lazy children to his office. There he beat them on their bottoms and hands with a bamboo rod until they cried for mercy and returned sobbing to their classrooms. When I asked Mutti how come parents allowed Herr Braun to beat their children, she explained that their parents didn't mind. In fact, they approved of it. That's the way it had always been in the village. Having experienced only a light slap on my backside when I misbehaved, I couldn't believe what I had heard, and I asked my mother, "Why?" She explained that the children in our valley finish school at the age of fourteen, and then begin an apprenticeship. When I asked, "What's an apprenticeship?" Mutti explained that during the four years following graduation from elementary school, most girls and boys learn a trade while practicing under a master.

Mutti tried to make me understand that the parents of my fellow students received the same rough treatment from Herr Braun when they went to school years ago. They believed that he knew what he was doing. She said that it was important to them that, by the time their children left school, they would have learned how to read, to write, and to do their times tables. She finished with "I have heard people say, 'If old Braun has to beat it into them, so be it.'"

Frightened, I looked to my mother for reassurance, "You don't believe that, do you?"

Mutti stroked my hair, "Of course not, dear. Stop worrying." I didn't stop worrying, and I fervently prayed that I wouldn't get into trouble.

Fräulein Alles hadn't sent any of the first and second graders to Herr Braun's office yet. She smacked one boy every time he tried to write with his left hand, until he finally gave it up. She boxed the shoulders and ears of the children who didn't write their letters well, or couldn't get their sums right. She humiliated them by making them sit on the *Eselsbank,* the donkey bench. Every morning, she made the biggest boy in our class—nicknamed *Schnuttkaka*—go to the sink and wash his face, neck, and hands in front of everyone. On the days when the school superintendent visited, she made *Schnuttkaka* stay home. The children called him "Snotshit" because his nose ran all the time. They whispered that he was repeating the first grade for the second or third time, and that he lived in an old tumbled-down farmhouse with his mother, who was one hundred years old and looked like a witch. I remembered what the witch did to Hänsel and Gretel, and I felt sorry for the boy, but didn't have the courage to speak to him.

After I finished my homework, I organized a school of my own at home, with my brothers as pupils and me as the teacher. In the beginning, the boys seemed willing enough. When they had to sit still while I made them practice letters on their slates until they got it right, they quickly lost interest. "Mutti," they complained, "we don't want to play school. It's no fun. Eycke isn't the boss of us, is she?" To my disappointment, Mutti agreed and told me to leave the boys alone.

Ute Dies

At the beginning of July, 1940, the doctor ordered a rest for Mutti. While she visited Papa on the island of Sylt, Tante Addie helped take care of us. Shortly after Mutti left, I started feeling sick. "It looks like you've got the measles," Addie announced, when she discovered red spots on me. To make sure, she called the doctor, who came to the house to examine me. A while later, my brothers and Ute became sick. The diagnosis was the same. Addie, assisted by our maid, Anne-marie, put all our beds against the walls of the nursery and pulled the shades. She got the household organized and donned her nurse's uniform. "Listen up, kids. You want to get well, right?" Sven, Frank and I nodded respectfully. We knew from experience that Addie could be a lot of fun, but that she did not tolerate disobedience. Morning, noon, and night she called out cheerfully, "I want to see some fannies," before she took our temperature. The first week we were too sick to think up trouble. Later, we started feeling better and got bored after we had looked at all the picture books we owned. Frank was only too happy to entertain us. He puckered up his lips, hunkered down, scratched himself, and made monkey noises, until we squealed with laughter. We scratched ourselves and threw pillows at each other. When we got too noisy, Addie threatened to separate us. When Frank got tired, he crawled into Ute's bed, where they played and napped together.

The doctor visited. He poked, prodded, listened to our hearts and breathing, and thumped on our chests. We got over our bout with the measles, but, before long, we became ill once again. Sven cried because his ears hurt. Addie poured warm oil into his ears and plugged them up with cotton. Frank suffered wheezing attacks, which the doctor diagnosed as asthma. Addie tore open a window to let in fresh air to help him breathe. When I complained about bellyaches, the doctor poked, prodded, and told Addie something was wrong with my pancreas and to put me on a bland diet. When I asked my aunt what a pancreas was, she replied irritably that it was a part of my body, to stay in bed, and stop asking so many questions.

Mutti returned from her visit with Papa just before Ute took a turn for the worse. The little one coughed all day and all night. Mutti rocked and sang to her:

Schlaf, Utelein, schlaf.	Sleep, little Ute, sleep.
Dein Vater hüt' die Schaf.	Your father guards the sheep.
Deine Mutter schüttelt's Bäumelein,	Your mother shakes a little tree,
Da fällt herab ein Träumelein.	Down glides a dream for thee.
So schläft das kleine Utelein ein.	And little Ute falls asleep.
Schlaf, Kindchen, schlaf.	Sleep, my little one sleep.

By the end of July, Ute had developed pleurisy. Mutti had to take her to the children's hospital in Kassel and stay with her. I prayed, *"Bitte, lieber Gott,* don't let Ute die." Frank climbed into Ute's empty crib, where he rocked back and forth, wheezed, and cried himself to sleep every night.

One day, Addie announced, "Your mother and sister are coming home tomorrow." I felt well enough to help Annemarie bake a cake to celebrate. In the meadow next to our house, I picked daisies, delicate harebells, and foamflowers. We waited. Mutti and Ute did not come home. Two days passed. Tante Addie got tired of our questions, but, on August 24, she spoke to me, "Eycke, I'm sorry, but your little sister died last night."

"Why?" I asked. "God let Mutti live when I prayed to Him." Without saying a word, Tante Addie, who smelled of cigarette smoke and disinfectant, pulled me to her bosom, where her tears mingled with mine.

"Your mother is with Tante Marianne in Kassel. Marianne is coming to get you this afternoon."

When Marianne arrived, I ran into her arms. She kissed me and wiped away my tears. She looked lovely in a white suit, hat, and gloves. My uncle was waiting for us at his car, with the motor running. As I climbed into the back seat, he smiled, threw me a kiss, and off we went. Just then, I wished for one of his big hugs and needed to hear him say the words of which I never tired, "You are *mein Schätzchen.*"

Marianne explained that my mother hadn't left her room since Ute died. She hadn't slept and hadn't eaten. At first, she couldn't stop crying. Now, all she did was sit and stare. When we arrived at Marianne's house, I ran up the stairs, careful not to slip on the polished wooden steps. I knocked on Mutti's bedroom door. There was no answer. Mutti did not notice my presence when I entered the room. She sat on her bed and stared into the distance, her eyes surrounded by dark circles. She looked so much smaller than I remembered her. I knelt down before her and looked into her empty eyes. I stroked her cool, sunken cheeks with both of my hands. "I'm so sorry that Ute died," I sobbed. But at that moment, even more than feeling Ute's loss, I was afraid that Mutti was going to die, too. "Mutti, please." I gently shook her shoulders and kissed her dry cheeks. "Did you only love Ute?" For the first time since I entered the room, she stirred, blinked, and focused her eyes on me.

"What did you say?" she whispered hoarsely.

"I repeated, "Did you only love Ute?"

"Child," she cried, "I do love you." I held her to keep her from crumbling in my arms. I asked her what had happened. She motioned for me to sit down and explained between sobs that the doctors told her a week ago that Ute was well enough to be released. She blamed herself for not having taken her home that day, because that night, while the air raid sirens wailed, the hospital rushed all the children, including the contagious, into one bomb shelter. As she continued weeping, she added, "Ute became infected with diphtheria. I held her until her heart stopped beating. And it is all my fault." The talk had exhausted Mutti.

"No, it isn't. You take good care of us," I replied, as I helped her lie down. I pulled a blanket over her and wondered why Mutti continued to blame herself for Ute's death. Papa is coming, I thought. He'll know what to do.

Later that day, the doorbell rang. It was Papa. He looked pale under his suntan, yet handsome and dashing in his white suit and hat. My heartbeat quickened, and I greeted him with a big smile. "Papa, you came!" He smelled of fresh air. I hadn't noticed until then that it was a beautiful summer day. Papa gave me a quick hug, did not smile back, and handed Marianne his hat and jacket. I felt tears welling up and turned away, trying hard not to let Papa see my disappointment that he did not appear to be glad to see me, too.

Looking over my head, Papa asked my aunt, "Where is she?"

"Upstairs. She is devastated."

Papa bounded up the stairs, two at a time, and rushed in to see Mutti. Later that night, I saw them sitting on the couch in the living room, holding each other tightly. Both of them were crying. They did not notice my standing there.

Ute's funeral was the next morning. My parents did not allow me to attend the funeral. Instead, I had to stay home with my aunt's housekeeper, Frau Gonnerman. When I asked her why they hadn't let me attend, she answered that funerals weren't for children. She patted me on the back and dried my tears with the corner of her starched white apron, after which she continued polishing the floors with vigorous strokes of a heavy brush. Papa, wearing a black armband to show that he was in mourning, returned to the island of Sylt that afternoon. He had been with us for 24 hours and had hardly said a word to me the whole time.

Mutti and I went back home to Vaake a day later, but Mutti had changed. In the middle of a chore, my mother would stop and stare into space. She looked like she was lost somewhere, a place where I could not follow to console her. I reasoned that if I were good, she'd feel better. I did all my chores without being reminded. I brought her bouquets of wild flowers, and I even tried not to fight with my brothers. Mutti did not seem to notice. A new mother's helper, Gretel, took care of us. I didn't realize then that it would take a long time before Mutti would be her old self again.

Mutti did not wear black from head to toe during the year of mourning, as was the custom of the village women. Instead, like Papa, she wore a black armband. As the number of men killed in the war increased, so did the number of women wearing black dresses, and the men wearing black armbands. On All Saints Day, a brass band of men wearing black suits and top hats solemnly marched from the village past our house. They were playing mournful music on their way to the *Kriegerdenkmal*, the war memorial on the hill above.

I kept thinking of my sister Ute. I remembered how she had climbed on a chair, and from there onto the table, where she looked at me expectantly, while I ate my lunch. She had opened her mouth wide, and I had let her eat from my spoon. She'd squeal, clap her hands and asked for more. I missed her.

Although he had been told time and time again that Ute was an angel in heaven, Frank did not believe it. "I am going to find her, I am," he said as he traipsed around the house looking under the stairs and in closets. He insisted on sleeping in Ute's empty crib. Sven did not mention Ute's name again.

Once, while poking my nose into my mother's nightstand, I came upon a photo of our dead sister. The picture showed Ute dressed in white, surrounded by flowers. Her skin was translucent, and her closed eyes were sunken into deep dark circles. My sister's death left me sad and bewildered, and I wished somebody would explain to me why people, especially little children, had to die.

Deutschland über Alles

On January 30, 1941, Fräulein Alles asked our class if any of us knew why we celebrated this day as a national holiday. I promptly lifted my hand and, when asked
to rise, spoke in a clear voice: "We celebrate this day because it is my father's
birthday." Duly impressed, my classmates looked at me in astonishment. But it
was Fräulein Alles who surprised me when she burst out laughing. In the past, I
had seen only the slightest of smiles appear on her lips, and even that had disappeared as quickly as the sun hides behind a cloud. But this time, she laughed so
hard at my answer that she had to take off her glasses and wipe her eyes. "No,
Eycke," she said, after she had composed herself. "We celebrate this day in honor
of our Führer, Adolf Hitler, who became the chancellor of our country eight
years ago."

Later that day, the school assembled in the hall decorated with fir branches
and red and white flags. Fräulein Alles had explained that the black cross in the
middle of the flags is called a *Hakenkreuz*, a swastika. I don't remember much
about the speech Herr Braun made on the occasion. When we returned to the
classroom, Fräulein Alles announced that she expected us to learn all the verses of
Deutschland, Deutschland über Alles, so that, during the next assembly, she could
be proud of her first and second graders.

After Easter, Sven entered first grade, and I advanced to second grade. I had
learned to form words with letters and was writing little stories for which Fräulein
Alles gave me coveted "ones." On Sven's first day, he didn't cry the way I had,
but I could tell that he didn't like going to school. He had a hard time writing his
letters neatly. This displeased Fräulein Alles so much, that every time his work
was not to her liking, she punched him in the shoulder or boxed his ears. Sven
hung his head, and his face would turn red, but he never cried. Instead, I was the
one who burst into tears every time it happened. I loathed Fräulein Alles for what
she was doing to my brother and the other children. I wished that I were big
enough to give her a piece of my mind. I imagined telling her that writing and
doing numbers is hard for some children. Hitting them and making them sit on
the bench for donkeys didn't help either.

On our way home, I mentioned to Sven that I thought Fräulein Alles was unjust. He shook his head. I knew this meant that he didn't want to talk about it. We walked home in silence, until we came to our front gate, when he spit out, "I'll never, ever play your dumb school game again. I hate it. I hate everything about school."

"I don't blame you," I replied. "I think teachers are cruel. Anyway, I have changed my mind about becoming a teacher when I grow up."

Dagmar is Born

While Papa was away on the island of Sylt, he wrote a poem for Mutti in anticipation of the birth of their fifth child:

Was Du empfangen in süsser Lust,	The child you conceived in sweet bliss,
Nun bald du legst an Deine Brust.	You shall soon hold at your breast.
Was Göttliche Liebe gegeben, Schenkst Du Leben.	What divine love gave to us, You shall give life.
Meinem lieben Weib.	To my beloved wife.

On May 24, 1941, nine months after Ute's funeral, Mutti disappeared once
again. A week later, Gretel told us that Mutti had given birth to another daughter. By that time, Gretel, the pretty girl with blue eyes, two long braids, a ready
smile, and a lot of tolerance for our antics, had become part of our family. Gretel
was fulfilling her *Pflichtjahr*. Under the Third Reich, all single women under the
age of twenty-five had to serve the state for one year before they were permitted
to continue their education. During that year, the women were expected to work
for some social agency, on a farm, in a hospital, or in a large family. Since our
family was *kinderreich*, rich with children, we qualified for such help.

The following week, Gretel took us on the bus to Münden. There we visited
Mutti and our baby sister at the house of the midwife, who had brought Sven,
Frank and Ute into the world. I asked Gretel why Mutti had the baby in Münden
instead of at home. Gretel answered that she couldn't take care of Mutti and the
new baby and keep track of us rascals. I prattled on about Sven, Frank, and Ute
having been born at home. I told Gretel that Mutti said Frank wasn't happy
when he was born, that he came out bottom first, had the cord wrapped around
his neck twice and wasn't breathing. The midwife, Frau Henze, the doctor, and
Mutti's friend, Lischen Köhler, had to work long and hard to get him to breathe.

"Didn't want to breathe, eh? Made trouble from the start," Sven said, nudging Frank with his elbow.

"I do, too, know how to breathe," countered Frank.

"You learned how," I added, feeling guilty for bringing up the subject. "And you were cute. Wasn't he, Sven?"

Sven ignored me, but Gretel gave Frank a hug. "You still are," she said, as she tousled his hair.

The midwife, Frau Henze, led us into Mutti's room. Everything was white: the walls, the bed, the armoire, the changing table, the bassinet, and Frau Henze in her starchy uniform. The odor of disinfectant permeated the air, but when I kissed Mutti, I detected the scent of lilies of the valley from the bouquet on her nightstand. Mutti was happy to see us and asked Gretel if we had given her any trouble.

"No, they haven't," Gretel lied. I loved her for it.

The baby lay in a canopied wicker bassinet, which was bedecked with a lacy skirt. Her eyes were closed. Her skin looked silky, soft, and rosy, as she sucked on her fingers. Looking at her, I secretly wished that I could be small and in her place. I, too, longed to be loved, cuddled, and fussed over by everyone.

We are Different

The summer of 1941 was hot and carefree for my siblings and me. I was unaware that Germany had widened the war by invading Russia and was set on conquering its capital, Moscow.

Addie was relaxing on a lounge chair in the shade. She was sipping a glass of raspberry juice while she watched my brothers and me. We cavorted naked, splashing each other, squealing, and hopping in and out of a tub filled with water warmed by the sun. Mutti and her sisters believed in lots of fresh air and sunshine for healthy bodies. They encouraged us to run naked during the short summer season. We heard Sven call from the back of the garden, "Tante Addie, Frau Schmidt is calling for you from behind the hedge."

Addie reluctantly got out of her chair and investigated. "Where aaaare you, Frau Schmidt?" she called out, pretending to play a game of hide and seek. "I'm over here," came the crabby reply. We followed Addie and found the woman on the other side of the hedge, pushing apart two shrubs. "Frau Lamprecht," she said in a huff. "It's disgraceful the way you and your sister allow those children to run around like little heathens, and you, and you ..." She pointed a finger at our aunt's two-piece bathing suit and sputtered indignantly as she lifted herself up another inch to get a better look. "As for you, Frau Lamprecht, I never, ever would be seen in such a skimpy outfit. You should be ashamed of yourself. And those children, those poor, poor children ..." Dressed in heavy boots, an ankle-length skirt, blouse, sweater, and a black kerchief, she wiped the perspiration from her face with the corner of her apron.

With a chuckle, my aunt countered, "If I were you, Frau Schmidt, I wouldn't be seen like this either, and a good day to you, too."

We heard the woman inhale and huff, "I never," as she turned and disappeared from our view. Addie gave one of her throaty laughs and herded us back toward the tub.

"Why did she say that we are poor children?" I asked.

"Yeah, why did she? We aren't poor, are we?" Sven piped up. Our aunt gave Sven a pat on his bare bottom, "Of course not. Don't mind the old biddy. You're different, that's all. Go, run along, and play."

Waiting for Mutti to come and say *Gute Nacht,* I remembered what Addie had said about being different. We spoke, dressed, and acted differently than the people around us. Mutti didn't spend time looking out a window, while resting her arms on a featherbed, to gossip with the neighbors. On Sunday mornings, we didn't join the villagers, who left their houses when the church bells rang through the valley fifteen minutes before services. I don't remember praying before and after dinner. Although each one of us children helped around the house and garden, we didn't have to work in the fields or muck out barns. Most of the time, I didn't mind not fitting in. At other times, when the village children called me a stranger, threw rocks at my brothers, when old women fussed at us for playing naked in the privacy of our own garden, or when I couldn't understand the local dialect, it didn't feel good at all.

Anita Tudela Crespo

Mutti's brother, Willi, was a naval communications officer. During the Spanish Civil War, he was stationed in Balboa, a port city on the northern coast of Spain, where it was his mission to guide German ships into the harbor in secrecy. There, he had met and fallen in love with a Cuban beauty named Anita Tudela Crespo. She had been married to a Spanish soldier who was killed during the Spanish Civil War. Willi brought Anita and her six-year-old daughter Maria to Germany and, now that the war was over, he hoped to get permission to marry her. Anita and Maria had stayed with Tante Marianne for a time, but Marianne and Anita didn't get along too well.

In the fall of 1941, Anita arrived at our house with a pile of luggage, including one entire suitcase full of "green" coffee beans. Anita was stunningly beautiful. She was in her mid-twenties, slender, with brown skin and jet-black hair piled high on her head. She wore a fashionable print frock with padded shoulders that reached just above her knees. Anita walked like a queen on her high-heeled cork wedgies, fully aware of her beauty. She held her head high, turning it slowly to observe the house, the garden, and each one of us. My brothers and I stared with our mouths open. I was in awe of her.

Close behind Anita walked her daughter Maria. Every once in a while Anita turned around and talked to Maria in a language I did not understand. Maria hurried to catch up with her mother. With a smile, Mutti descended the front steps to welcome our guests in Spanish. Our mother loved foreign languages, had learned English and French in school, and, anticipating the arrival of our guests, had memorized a few sentences of Spanish. Anita took Mutti's outstretched hand, returned her greetings, and, without looking behind her, grabbed her daughter by the neck and pushed her toward Mutti. Her eyes downcast, Maria approached Mutti. Maria did a quick curtsy. Mutti bent down, embraced her, whispered something into her ear, and waved us over. "Come, say hello to our guests." Mutti introduced us and asked us to show Maria around before she and Anita disappeared into the house.

To my delight, Maria spoke a little German. I was happy to have a new play-mate, and I knew right from the start that we were going to be friends. For the most part, even Sven and Frank got along with her. Maria lost her shyness quickly and became a part of our family. She shared her mother's effervescence, but not her hot temper. Anita had dyed Maria's black hair blond in an attempt to make her look Nordic. Once her hair grew out, she no longer looked like a canary. It was amazing how fast Maria's German improved. By the time she and her mother returned to Spain, she spoke it like a native.

Within a short time, Mutti rolled her R's, dropped the J's, and "grated" the G's like a proper Spaniard. Anita had a long list of complaints. They were laced with well-chosen expletives, which Mutti committed to memory. Papa used salty language with gusto, but to my surprise and secret delight, Mutti, who never spoke a profane word, began to use a few choice words in Spanish. We children caught on quickly. We were not supposed to use profanity, but were glad that nobody fussed at us when we declared this or that to be "*mierde*."

Tante Anita—as we children called her—remained aloof. She refused to learn German and slept until noon. She and her daughter occupied one of the four bedrooms, which Anita kept spotless. She did her own laundry, but I never saw her help with any other housework, like cooking or washing dishes. During the time she lived with us, the only times I knew I could find her in the kitchen was when I detected a strong aroma of coffee wafting through the house. Anita stood next to the wood stove. She held the handle of a heavy iron pot, which she shook quickly back and forth over the fire. Making a rattling noise, the green coffee beans danced and roasted to a deep, dark brown. From time to time Anita lifted the lid and checked to see if the beans were dark enough. When she had roasted them to perfection, they had to cool before they were ready to be ground up.

When I was given permission to help, I poured the beans through a hole in the wooden coffee grinder. Not a single spilled bean was allowed to escape. It was hunted down and added to the rest. I turned the handle until the small drawer in the bottom of the grinder was filled. Anita spooned the coffee into the bottom of a pot and added boiling water. After it steeped for a few minutes, it was ready to be served. I was not permitted to drink the steaming dark liquid, but a small taste, less than a teaspoon, convinced me that the coffee did not taste as good as its fragrance had promised. For their afternoon coffee hour, Mutti and Anita retired to the living room, or, in the summer, to a table and chairs in the garden. They enjoyed their cup of "genuine" bean coffee, which had become a rare commodity during the war, and each smoked one cigarette. Anita joined Mutti for meals, took Dagmar for walks in the village, and, during warm weather, sunbathed nude in the rear of the garden among the tall horseradish leaves. Her skin turned a light chocolate brown making her look exotic.

Anita had a hot temper, and most of the time it was Maria who served as her lightning rod. I asked Maria what *"que trompe la cabesa"* meant. She whispered in my ear that her mother threatened to bash her head in. I was speechless. I cried every time Papa scolded or shouted at me, and I felt sorry for Maria. To make her feel better, I tried to be funny and suggested that in a contest with Papa her Mama would win hands down in a shouting match. Maria responded with a giggle.

During the first winter that Anita and Maria were in Germany, Maria was ecstatic. "Eycke," she squealed. "What's that white stuff coming out of the sky?"

"Haven't you ever seen snow before?"

Maria shook her head. We quickly put on our warm clothes and ran outside, caught snowflakes with our tongues, made angels in the snow, and threw snowballs at each other. "Let's see if there's ice on the creek," suggested Sven, after we had finished building a snowman with two coals for eyes and a carrot for a nose. We followed Sven to the creek. Stepping lightly, we tested the ice and slid along its smooth surface with abandon. "We'd better be careful," I warned. Too late! Maria came to a thin spot, and, with a sickening crunch, broke through the ice. Fortunately, the creek wasn't too deep. Maria surfaced quickly, sputtering and crying. We pulled her out and hurried home. While Mutti fussed at us, she undressed the sobbing bundle of misery, warmed her in a tub filled with lukewarm water and rubbed her with towels until she turned pink. All hell broke loose when Anita found out what had happened. She hurled one of her highheeled shoes at Maria's head. Blood splattered against the wall, as a gash opened on Maria's scalp. Mutti got between Anita and Maria, shielding the child from further violence and stopped the bleeding by applying pressure to the wound. She yelled back at Anita. I thought I recognized a few choice words. Anita raged on. My brothers and I watched until Mutti chased us out of the kitchen. From that day on, I tried to stay out of Anita's way, which, I noticed, suited her just fine.

*   *   *

I wondered why Anita was so unhappy and who besides Maria made her so angry. Years later, after a bit of prompting, Mutti, with a gleam in her eye, would imitate Anita's litany of grievances in Spanish. I got a kick out of watching Mutti prepare herself for a proper delivery by pulling herself up to her entire five feet. She inhaled, and in a voice deeper than her own, let fly on a cushion of air Anita's list of complaints. After Mutti had run out of air, she took another deep breath and smiled broadly. I asked Mutti to translate Anita's outburst. She explained, "It was directed at your uncle Willi, of course. Anita was tired of sitting around and waiting for him. The permission to marry was never given. The Nazis didn't look kindly upon marriages between German officers and foreigners, you know. Anita sensed that Willi's ardor had cooled. So, from time to time, she gave vent to her rage. Loosely translated, here is what she said: 'Men, those lying, cheating, good-for-nothing bastards.'" Here, Mutti hesitated for a few seconds. "'One day they declare their undying love, the next day they're gone. Here I am, no country, no man, no money, nothing, except my poor little girl. If I find out Willi is fooling around, I'll kill him. Swine are running things, *No tengo gusto Alemania.* I don't like Germany. I have had it. One of these days I'm getting out of here.'" Mutti added, "I sympathized with her, especially during those times when your father and I were having problems. Enough said."

When Mary Walked Through a Forest of Thorns

It was the beginning of December, 1941, the third winter of the war and only days before the Japanese would attack Pearl Harbor, and less than two weeks before Germany would declare war on the United States. I knew that German soldiers were fighting on the Russian front and in North Africa. The name of Field Marshall Rommel, the commander of the Afrika Korps, was on everyone's lips. What I did not know was that the war had spread to countries all around the world.

We were looking forward to Papa coming home for Christmas. I had not seen him since March, when he rushed through Vaake on his way to Poland. He was being sent there, against his wishes, after he completed building the airfields on the island of Sylt.

Advent was near, and it had snowed the night before when Mutti announced one afternoon that we were going to cut pine branches for our Advent wreath. Anita did not mind telling us that we were *"loco."* She refused to take one step out the door in that kind of weather and did not allow Maria to accompany us. Sven and I pulled on our winter clothes and dashed out the door. We plopped on our backs and winged two perfect snow angels. Sven wrote into the snow, *Eycke ist doof,* Eycke is stupid. I countered, *Sven ist noch blöder,* Sven is even more stupid.

We threw snowballs at each other before we headed for the shed to retrieve our sleds and Mutti's skis. Mutti wrapped Dagmar in blankets and placed her on Papa's old sled. Sven was the first out of the gate, pulling Dagmar up the steep road to the pine grove above. Mutti hoisted her wooden skies and bamboo poles over her shoulder, and, pulling another sled, followed Sven. Frank and I brought up the rear with a third sled. The village below appeared to be asleep under a thick blanket of snow. The waterwheel on Wallbach's *Mühle* continued to turn, as it had done for the past 250 years. All sounds were muffled as if in a dream. It felt like we were moving in space.

On top of the ridge, we followed rabbit, fox, and deer tracks into a thicket, while Mutti cut snow-laden branches. We helped pile the greenery on one of the sleds and tied the three sleds together. Mutti strapped the leather bindings to her boots. Off she glided with elegant Telemark flourishes and stopped down below with her "poles up." We clapped our hands, hopped on our sleds, and hurtled down the hill, with the heady fragrance of freshly cut evergreens in our nostrils. Laughing and teasing each other, we returned home, where we unpeeled our suits and boots and rubbed our hands warm near the wood stove.

Now came the work only Mutti could do. She used a metal ring the size of a small wagon wheel, around which she wired pine branches until she had finished a wreath. To the wreath she attached four red candles and four red ribbons. She climbed on top of a chair, and, with Gretel's help, she lifted the heavy wreath toward the ceiling, where she attached it to a strong hook over the center of the dining room table. For days the kitchen had been a busy place. Gretel hummed as she kneaded the fruit and nut-laden dough for *Stollen*. I helped roll out dough and cut bell, star, and moon shapes for *Spekulatius* cookies. The fragrance of Christmas bread and cookies baking in the wood stove wafted through the house. With it were mixed the aromas of roasting apples and spiced fruit punch simmering on the stovetop. Altogether, these smells ushered in the Advent season.

After the winter sun disappeared behind the forest, and dusk settled gently over the valley, Mutti lit the first candle on the Advent wreath. We slurped hot, spiced cider and munched cookies. She tuned her guitar and wrapped us in her magic. Each one of us got to choose a Christmas carol, and then she sang her favorite, "*Maria durch ein' Dornwald ging.*"

Maria durch ein' Dornwald ging, When Mary walked through a forest of thorns,
Kyrieleison! Kyrieleison!
Der hat in sieben Jahrn kein Laub getragen! That seven years no bloom had born!
Kyrieleison! Kyrieleison!

Was trug Maria unter ihrem Herzen! What did Mary carry under her heart!
Kyrieleison! Kyrieleison!
Ein kleines Kindlein ohne Schmerzen, A little child without much pain,
Das trug Maria unter ihrem Herzen! that's what Mary carried under her heart!
Kyrieleison! Kyrieleison!

Da hab'n die Dornen Rosen getragen.	Red roses on the thorns appeared.
Kyrieleison!	Kyrieleison!
Als das Kindlein durch den Wald getragen,	As she carried the little child through the forest,
Da hab'n die Dornen Rosen getragen.	red roses on the thorns appeared.
Kyrieleison!	Kyrieleison!

Three weeks later Papa came home, and we celebrated Christmas together. Papa and Mutti talked about our having to pack up the household and move to Poland in the spring. Apparently, they weren't given a choice in the matter. Then Papa was gone again, and this time he took Frank with him. I asked Mutti why Frank was allowed to go with Papa and not me. She replied that Frank was sick. Since we didn't have any medicine to treat his asthma, the doctor believed that a change of air would do him good. Two months later, Frank returned home with a rucksack full of wild stories about escaping a fire, a nanny who locked him in the coal cellar, and a bloody ax.

The Move to Poland

In March, 1942, as German troops attempted to gain back the ground they had lost during their push toward Moscow and the war continued to rage in countless other places around the world, we had to leave Germany and move to Poland. We traveled from Vaake to Münden along the Weser River in the back of the yellow *Postauto*, the bus that carried passengers and mail up and down the river valley. As we neared the train station in Münden, Mutti addressed Sven, Frank, and me in her "this is important and serious business" tone. She explained that we would soon transfer to a train, which would take us to Poland. She added that she expected us to hold hands and take care of each other during the journey. Sven asked what kind of a place Poland was. I paid close attention when she answered that it was a country approximately 700 miles east of us, and it was going to take us at least two days to get there. When I asked if she was sure that Papa was going to be waiting for us, a broad smile lit up her face, "Yes, dear. After all these years we are finally going to be together again."

I remembered that when Papa and Mutti had objected to moving the family to Poland, the authorities had informed them that it was our duty "to settle the East where good Germans were needed to straighten out the mess." I was curious about what kind of mess we were going to have to straighten out, and who the authorities were who told Papa what to do. I couldn't imagine anybody telling my father what to do. He was usually the one who was doing the telling. Could the authorities be the people Papa disdainfully called *Bonzen*? Could they be the petty bureaucrats at the *Bürgermeisteramt*, the mayor's office, the ones who jerked their right arms into the air and shouted "*Heil Hitler*" every chance they got? One of them had barked at me recently and asked if I were too ignorant to know the proper German greeting. I blushed and did as I was told, but I couldn't think of one good reason why friendly *Guten Tag* and *Auf Wiedersehen* weren't good enough any more. And, why, I asked myself, is it that some grownups have to be so rude when they are teaching us children new things? When Mutti told me that we were going to move to Poland, my first thought was, "what? move again?" I whined and went on and on about how I liked our garden and the playhouse, about hating to leave the friends I had made. I decided that next time Papa started cursing those "damn authorities," I intended to join him.

*   *   *

As our train rushed east, it made a rhythmic, clacking sound. The rocking of the carriage from side to side lulled and pacified me. It was a beautiful day. Mutti called the blue skies and sunshine *Kaiserwetter.* She took us back to her childhood, when her family got dressed up to welcome their beloved Kaiser Wilhelm II and his family, flanked by flamboyant Hussars, to their summer palace in her hometown, Kassel. Like many Germans of their generation, my mother's grandparents and parents were *"kaisertreu."* Devoted to the empire, they gave five of their seven children royal names. My mother, their second oldest daughter, they named Auguste Viktoria Louise Adelheid, but nicknamed her Tutti.

We settled into one of the comfortable compartments. It had upholstered seats that faced each other, with a small table between them underneath the window. We stored our suitcases and a basket with food in nets above our seats. A sliding glass door, curtained for privacy, separated us from a long corridor, which ran along the length of the car. The locomotive at the head of the train pulled a dozen or more passenger and baggage cars.

Anxious and curious about what Poland would be like, I begged Mutti to tell us about her visit with Papa the previous summer. As Dagmar slept peacefully, Mutti recalled carrying her two-and-one-half-month-old daughter in a padded potato basket. Mutti told of being surprised by the gray poverty of Poland. I asked if the cottage I had seen in one of Papa's photographs was going to be our new home. Mutti explained that, while the cottage was being gutted, and a second floor and a new roof added, we would live in a small apartment nearby. I had seen photos of the cottage, the trees, ponds, and fields. In one of them Mutti, looked especially lovely reclining in her dressing gown. The light reflected off the silvery ripples on the surface of a pond, hinting at the beauty of the place we would soon call home. But I kept thinking aloud, "How am I going to like the new school? The teachers? Am I going to make new friends?" I was trying hard to imagine all this, but fear and uncertainty paralyzed me and kept me from drawing pictures in my mind. I couldn't help but feel that my family did not belong anywhere. I remembered that my mother and I had lived in Kassel with Marianne and Wütt for one year, in Wilhelmshausen for five, and in Vaake for two and one-half years. To shake off the mood, I turned back to looking out the window of the moving train as the trees, fields, villages, and towns flew by.

I thought about how apprehensive I had been last summer, as I waited for Mutti to return from Poland. Instead, Papa had arrived unexpectedly by himself in search of Mutti and Dagmar. He and Addie had had one of their fierce arguments. She accused him of breaking Mutti's heart, which really set Papa off. He told her to mind her own business, stop flirting with soldiers, and tend to his children instead. Papa and my aunt reminded me of a dog and a cat snarling and hissing at each other. I wished that I could persuade them to get along. I knew, however, that if I said anything to either of them, they would scold me for eavesdropping and remind me that children did not interfere in the business of grown-ups.

Soon after the argument between Addie and Papa, Papa left. A week later, Mutti and Dagmar returned home. When I asked why she had been gone so long, Mutti hesitated for a minute before she replied. "After Dagmar and I visited Papa in Poland, we spent time with my friend Li in Hamburg." Mutti and Li Rosenkranz had met when they were in their early twenties, and they had remained close friends. Throughout the years, Li had sent Mutti letters and photos of herself and her friends from exotic places. Li looked and lived like a diva. She was childless, divorced, glamorous, and in love with a wealthy man from South America named Carlos.

*   *   *

The reason why Mutti was gone so long that summer remained a mystery until I asked her years later. As Mutti told it, at first she and Papa had had a wonderful time until, at one point during the visit, Mutti had become aware that Papa had been having an affair with Frau Knöpfler, a woman who stayed at the same hotel where Papa was living. Deeply wounded, Mutti left Poland and returned to Germany. Without telling Papa, she and Dagmar changed trains en route and traveled to Hamburg to stay with Li, instead of returning home. When Papa did not hear from Mutti, he became alarmed. Tante Addie divulged the whereabouts of Mutti and Dagmar. Papa followed them to Hamburg, where he and Mutti once again reconciled.

*   *   *

Since I didn't know what to make of all the troubles between the grown-ups, most of the time I immersed myself in reading fairy tales, writing stories, and daydreaming and talking to my dolls. That is what I did during our train trip.

Frank sat drawing pictures at the table near the open window until a speck of cinder got into his eye. Sven pulled wooden horses from his knapsack and made them gallop and whinny up and down his seat. Mutti had finished nursing Dagmar and was dozing. We were on a fast train, which stopped only in the big cities. When I asked Mutti if we were still in Germany, she nodded. From time to time the train stopped in the middle of nowhere and sat on a sidetrack until another train would thunder past us. Sven and Frank shouted and pointed to the soldiers, trucks, tanks, and cannons. We jostled for position to watch farmers follow their teams, pushing their plows into rich soil and sculpting it into shiny clods. When the sun hit the steel blades just right, they yielded a bright flash. Mutti hummed the melody to: *"Im Märzen der Bauer die Pferde einspannt,"* in March the farmer harnesses his horses. We sang along. Sven pressed his nose against the window and bragged that he knew all about horses and farming. Although we were not farmers, we grew up among fields, meadows, and forests. Back home, farmer Wallbach, who plowed and tilled next to our house, had allowed Sven to walk behind his horses as he worked his fields. Farmer Wallbach had shared his bread, spread with *Schmand* that was made from rich, fermented cream. From the train window, I watched a wall of clouds, dark, and threatening, on the eastern horizon. With their heads bowed low and backs straining, farmers continued to crack their whips and carve up the soil in straight furrows without heeding the approaching storm.

As the train rushed on, it pulled me away from all that was familiar. I felt cut loose, as if I were floating on the wind like a balloon torn from the hand of its owner. One moment I felt sad, scared, and my stomach hurt. The next moment I was filled with excitement. Everything was moving too fast. My body was with me, but it seemed that a part of me wasn't catching up.

Groups of Hitler Youth, police, and men in gray, green, black, and brown uniforms milled about the railroad stations. Flags with the black swastikas were on display everywhere. Disembodied voices announced the coming and going of trains. On one occasion we heard military marching songs blare from loudspeakers, as travelers in civilian clothes and uniforms pushed and shoved each other on and off trains and platforms.

At first I had enjoyed the exhilaration of the trip. I liked my new clothes, the luggage piled around us, the good wishes, hugs, and kisses from friends and family. "Be sure to write," they had pleaded, and I had promised to do so. I had looked forward to the adventure, but now I wished I were back home. Anita had refused to move to Poland with us, which didn't upset me, but the fact that Maria stayed behind made me sad.

About two days or so after we left Vaake—I don't remember exactly—we reached the railroad station outside of Chrzanow, a small town in the southwest corner of Poland, which the Germans had renamed Krenau after the abundant horseradish that grew in its environs. Papa was waiting for us at the railroad station. I was happy to see him and delighted with his surprise—a ride in a horse-drawn carriage into town.

I couldn't believe it when Mutti told me years later that, aside from asking hundreds of times, "When will we get there?" we children had been perfect angels during the trip.

The author's father Karl, and his siblings Otto and Toni Laabs. Göttingen, 1900.

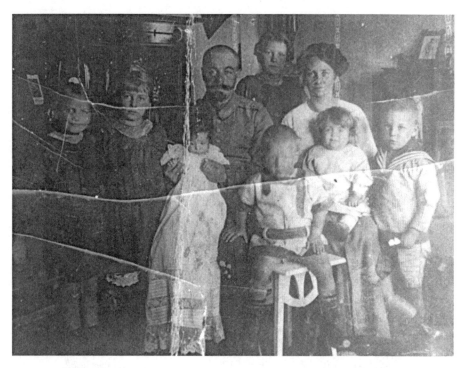

The author's maternal grandparents, Gustav and Lisette Wallbach, with their seven children (the author's mother second from the left), shortly before Gustav left for Flanders, where he was killed in battle ten days later. Kassel, summer, 1914.

The author's father (first row on the right) during World War I, taken days after his brother Otto was killed in battle. Langemarck, Flanders, summer, 1915.

Ludwigstein Castle. Werra Valley.

The author's mother. Ludwigstein Castle, 1920s.

The author in the arms of her mother. Kassel. December, 1933.

The author with her mother at her baptism. Kassel, March, 1934.

The author learning how to walk holding the hand of her father.
Glider camp, Staufenberg Hill near Kassel, summer, 1934.

The author on an outing with her brother Sven. Wilhelmshausen, winter, 1935–
36.

The author with her brother Sven. Spa Graal on the Baltic Sea, summer, 1936.

The author's aunt Marianne with brother Sven. Wilhelmshausen, summer, 1936.

The author with her brother Frank. Wilhelmshausen, summer, 1937.

The author schmoozing with her favorite uncle, Wütt, with a family friend looking on.
Wilhelmshausen, summer, 1937.

The author in the arms of her father. Wilhelmhausen, summer, 1938.

The author with her brothers Sven and Frank and her mother and sister Ute.
Wilhelmshausen, Christmas, 1938.

View of Vaake/Weserbergland, with the author's home in the foreground on the right, winter, 1941.

The author on her first day of school, carrying a *Zuckertüte* filled with sweets and fruit. Vaake, March, 1940.

The author with her brothers Sven and Frank and sister Ute, one month before
Ute's death.
Vaake, summer, 1940.

The author in the garden. Vaake, summer, 1941.

PART II
Witnessing the Holocaust
Krenau, Poland
1942–1945

No Cross for her Grave

My father had been living and working in Krenau as County Architect since March of 1941. When he arrived, he was unprepared for the violence he witnessed. The Nazis were using their power to brutally repress and persecute the Polish population. Twelve Polish construction workers who had left a small fire unattended were arrested and accused of arson. The Gestapo had planned to make an example of these men by convicting them of sabotage and hanging them. Papa testified before the court that the workers had intended no harm and that no damage was done, thus saving their lives, but in the process, attracting the attention of the Gestapo. He also saw the Jewish population being intimidated, harassed, and beaten in the streets. When a few German soldiers and civilians objected to this brutality, the public abuse stopped for a while. Before long, the persecutions resumed and began to take on monstrous proportions.

Shortly after my father arrived in Krenau, he met a young Jewish man, nineteen-year-old Mordecai Hartmann (his and the names of his family have been changed at their request to protect their privacy). Mordecai worked as a stoker in Papa's office building. His family owned a leather shop located on the ground floor of their house on the south side of the marketplace in the heart of Krenau. Since fresh food supplies were scarce, Papa turned to Mordecai for help. At the time, Jews were not yet forbidden to do business with Germans. Mordecai suggested that Papa talk to his sister, Fanny, who assisted her mother in managing their leather business. When Papa walked into the shop, Fanny stood behind the counter. As Fanny recalled their first meeting, the appearance of a German in the store caused her to tremble with fear, but she remembered his first words to her, *"Haben Sie keine Angst, Fräulein,"* do not be afraid, Fräulein. Papa admired the fine quality of the leather goods on display, made a purchase, and asked Fanny if she knew where he could buy fresh eggs. He offered to pay triple the going rate for anything she could provide. Fanny promised to see what she could do.

Later, Papa became acquainted with Fanny's mother, whose husband had died before the war, leaving her to care for her children—Shmuel, Fanny, Esther, Hava, Mordecai, and David. In time, Fanny and her family began to trust Papa. Gradually, he learned firsthand what it was like to be a Jew under the Nazis. The

Hartmanns informed him that the Jewish population of the town and surrounding area lived in terror of the Gestapo, SS, and the German and the Jewish police. They told of a massacre that had taken place in a neighboring village of Trzebinia the year before. Dozens of Jews were shot and buried in a mass grave. Sensing what was in store for his people, the eldest Hartmann son, Shmuel, had fled Poland on foot in the direction of Russia.

First, the Nazis rounded up the old, the young, the sick, and those whom they considered incorrigible. The Nazis transported them on trucks or forced them to walk the eleven miles to Auschwitz. David Hartmann, who was deaf and considered unfit for work, was the first to perish there. When the Nazis decided that they had use for Jewish labor, they set quotas and evicted the Jews from their homes. The Jews were rounded up, separated by age and sex, and herded onto trucks and trains to be deported to slave labor camps.

When her mother's health began to fail, Fanny tried desperately to keep the rest of her family together. She came to our house, pleaded with Papa for help, and cried on his shoulder. Many years later, she would remember that "Baurat Laabs was like a ray of sunshine in the darkness." On one occasion, she deliberately injured her eye by rubbing dirt into it so that she would not be sent off to a labor camp. Papa provided Mordecai, Fanny, Esther, and their friends with work permits, which allowed them to move about the town, and kept them from being deported. But when the Nazis began to arrest even those in the possession of permits, Fanny built a secret room for her family and friends in the basement of their home.

One day, Papa asked Mordecai to pick Frank up from school. On their way home, the boys walked along the dark, narrow, cobblestoned streets of the old town where years ago mildewed and sooty stucco had peeled off houses and fallen to the ground. They came upon houses with doors wide open, windows bashed in, and curtains billowing in the wind. It seemed as if the occupants had been swept away by a malevolent storm. After they rounded a corner of Krakauer Strasse, they noticed Jewish policemen and an SS *Sonderkommando* pounding on closed doors with their rifle butts and ordering the people to get out, shouting, "*Raus! Raus!*" Mordecai shuddered and pulled up his shoulders, tightened his grip on Frank's hand, and hurried down an empty street toward the marketplace. Frank cried out that he was scared and that he wanted his Papa. Mordecai looked over his shoulder as he placed his hand over the yellow star on his coat. Frank wailed that Mordecai was running too fast and that Mordecai was hurting his arm. They came to a place where they noticed bodies dangling on ropes. Frank tore away from Mordecai's hold to get a closer look. Mordecai caught up with him and dragged him away. They dashed across Auschwitzer Strasse and plopped on the ground behind a decrepit fence. Both were breathing hard. When they heard dogs barking, they peered from between broken slats. What they saw were armed soldiers and their dogs guarding a long column of marchers. One of the soldiers carried a pack from which a long antenna protruded. The antenna slowly swayed back and forth as he walked. "Radio man," Mordecai whispered into Frank's ear.

Among the marchers were children, men, and women. Many of them were old and frail. Suitcases and bundles weighed them down. Frank pointed to a man carrying a birdcage and whispered back that he had had a bird once. When the bird stopped moving, his mother told him that it was dead. And when his sister went to the hospital and didn't come back, his mother told him that she'd died and gone to heaven. Just then, an old woman hobbled into a ditch to relieve herself. A soldier followed her, pushed and prodded her with his rifle, and shouted, "*Schnell! Schnell! Du alte Judensau.*" When she did not get up, he raised his rifle, aimed, and fired three short bursts, causing her body to jerk, slump, and lie still. Startled, Frank jumped to his feet. Mordecai grabbed his arm and pulled him down. They watched as the soldier kicked the body, mumbled something, and turned to rejoin the line of marchers who slowly dragged themselves in the direction of Auschwitz.

Frank and Mordecai shivered in hiding until the last of the marchers had passed. They glanced around to make sure that nobody was watching, crawled from behind the fence, and approached the body. Frank asked if she was asleep. Mordecai pointed to the blood seeping onto the ground and shook his head. He then lifted his hands, closed his eyes, rocked back and forth, and moaned.

Frank pulled Mordecai's sleeve, "Is she dead like my bird and my sister?" Mordecai nodded once again. Frank told Mordecai how he and his siblings had buried the bird, made a cross with sticks, put flowers on the grave and said a prayer. Then he asked Mordecai, "When are we going to bury the old Oma?" Mordecai shook his head and took Frank's hand. Frank pulled back and protested that they had to bury her and put a cross on her grave.

Mordecai replied, "No cross for her grave."

"Why not?"

"Because ..." Mordecai answered, "she's Jewish."

Auschwitzer Strasse 36b

When our family arrived in Krenau in March of 1942, the house on Auschwitzer Strasse was not ready to be occupied. Instead, we moved into a bedbug-infested apartment on the corner of Auschwitzer Strasse and Schul Strasse. The next day Sven and I joined Frank in exploring our new neighborhood and the construction site of our future home. First, Frank took us up the street to the Hotel Deutsches Haus, where he had lived with Papa during the previous winter. There we met the friendly owner, Frau Seif, an elegant brunette with a Bavarian accent. Although Sven and I suspected that some of Frank's stories were the product of amazing and bizarre fantasies, we hung on every word. He chattered on about having to stay in a hotel room, where he cut out paper dolls and watched endless columns of army tanks and trucks go by. With a broad grin, he bragged about the hotel cook getting mad at him and chasing him around the kitchen with a meat hook. Sven responded, "The poor woman had to defend herself." But when Frank mentioned seeing Papa naked in bed with Frau Knöpfler, I called him a liar. Frank swore that he was telling the truth. Why else had Mutti gotten so upset when he had told her about it? What I didn't know was that Frank was telling the truth. Mutti had found out about Papa's affair with Frau Knöpfler the year before.

When I asked Sven if he believed Frank, he shook his head, gave his brother a shove and declared, "I don't believe a word he says." Nonetheless, we listened wide-eyed as Frank described riding in a sleigh with Papa and watching hundreds of hunters pounding pots and pans, scaring rabbits out of their burrows, shooting them and making their blood run onto the snow. We accused Frank of making up gruesome stories, but had to take it back when Mutti confirmed that he was telling the truth.

There were more stories. At some point, Papa and Frank had moved from the hotel to the decrepit cottage on Auschwitzer Strasse. It was during that time that Papa hired Maria, a former nun, as Frank's nanny. The first thing she did was light a fire in the stove and lock him into a room. Clothes left to dry near the stove caught on fire. When Frank beat on the door, nobody came to his rescue, and when he couldn't open the window, he smashed the glass with his toy horse and climbed out. "*Junge, Junge*, you're the king of the liars," Sven countered.

"I'm not."

"Yes, you are."

"No, I'm not. When Maria locked me up in the coal cellar, I tried to climb out through the coal chute." Remembering what had happened, he began breathing hard and ended up having a coughing fit. To prove his point, Frank led us into the cellar. There, Sven, who was a head taller and stronger than his brother, tried to crawl up the chute. When that didn't work, he tried to run up it. The third time, he got all the way to the top, but no matter how hard he tried, he was unable to open the trap door, which led to the outside. Sven and I stood by with our mouths open as Frank continued, "Papa made Maria leave after I hit her with an ax." Frank scrunched up his face and balled up his fists. "I snuck up behind her and hit her in the leg. There was blood all over. She went crying to Papa, who didn't believe her until I told him that I had done it because she had locked me in my room and in the coal cellar. Papa made her leave, and soon after, he took me back home to Vaake."

The first time my mother walked into the kitchen at Auschwitzer Strasse, she fell through the floor. This happened during her visit to Poland in the summer of 1941. Papa helped her pull her foot out from between the rotten floorboards. When she opened the cupboard, an army of cockroaches scurried into a hole in the wall. She jumped back, shuddered and demanded that before she and the children moved in, the kitchen floor be repaired and the vermin removed. When Mutti checked out the adobe hearth, which looked like it had been in use for one hundred years, she threw up her hands. She was mollified when Papa assured her that he would have a tile stove built by the time they planned to move in.

Around the end of April, two trucks finally arrived with all our furniture and household goods, and we moved into the house. White birch and chestnut trees shaded the long driveway, which led to the compound from the main road between Krakau to the east and Auschwitz to the west. The driveway curved around a meadow and ended at the garden gate. The property became a paradise for my siblings and me, with its house, a blooming jasmine bush at the gate, its sprawling outbuildings including a hay barn and a barn for livestock, its large weed-choked garden, its poplars, linden, birch and fruit trees and its three ponds. Parts of the house were still under construction. The place had been fumigated three times. As Papa had promised, in one corner of the kitchen stood an enormous wood stove made of firebricks and light green ceramic tile.

Mutti immediately began a ritual I had seen her engage in since I was little. She scrunched up some paper, criss-crossed kindling on top and pulled open the damper at the base of the chimney. She lit a match. The paper ignited. Sparks popped. She inhaled deeply and blew into the fire until the flames licked the wood, danced, and crackled. My mother smiled and stepped back, "Good draft," she said approvingly, added a few pieces of wood, and closed the door. Then she sent Sven and me into the garden to gather apples. An hour later the sweet aroma of baking apples wafted through the house, and I began to feel at home.

One day, Anita and Maria arrived. Anita had changed her mind and decided that Poland couldn't be much worse than the incessant bombing raids back in the *Reich*. Anita moved into one of the bedrooms. I remained leery of Anita, but loved having Maria join me in my room.

Once we settled in, Mutti launched her plan for the weeding and cultivation of the approximately seven acres surrounding the house and barns. Papa bought turkeys, chickens, ducks, and geese. After he inspected the new fence he announced, "It'll keep the children and our feathered friends in, and keep the troublemakers out." I understood about the children and feathered friends, but at that time, I had no idea who the troublemakers might be.

Service to the Earth

From the time I was six, my mother and I had shared a love for tending growing things. She called her care, *Dienst an der Erde*, service to the earth. When we moved to Auschwitzer Strasse, my parents decided that we would have to become self-sufficient within a year. Papa hired Ignaz and Hania, a young Polish couple, to help in the garden. The trouble was that, as soon as Mutti went into the house, they chased each other into the bushes or into the barn. We could hear her calling out, "Ignaaaaz" and his answer, "Haaaaniaa." From then on, we called the game of hide-and-seek "playing Hania and Ignaz."

One could see that they liked each other, when they sat shoulder to shoulder at the edge of the pond. They were both holding fishing poles, but what puzzled me was that we never saw them catch a single fish. Eventually, with a little help from Hania and Ignaz and a lot of help from Mordecai and Madame Chicowa, an old Polish peasant who lived nearby, we cleared the land of thick weeds, spaded it, and got it ready for planting. Mutti asked me to join her in the garden on the morning I noticed the first *Gänseblümchen* blooming in the meadow. She breathed in the sweet, cool air, and I followed her example. She bent down and scooped up a handful of soil, crumbled it, brought it up to her nose, and proclaimed, "We begin today."

"You're not going to put it on your tongue for a taste, the way Oma Schäfer did?" Mutti chuckled and shook her head. She knew nothing about gardening until we moved to Wilhelmshausen. There, we watched Oma Schäfer, as each spring, she carefully measured and laid out her vegetable and flower beds. She spaded, raked, and stretched a long string between two wooden stakes. She then used a stick to draw shallow grooves parallel to the string. Into these grooves, she spread the seeds and covered them with a thin layer of loamy soil. She watered, hoed, and weeded the tender plants. She fertilized with compost, manure, and an occasional sprinkling of urine.

Together, Mutti and I measured out the beds the way Oma had done. During the following days, we prepared nine more beds. When we were finished, Mutti got up, straightened her back, wiped her dirty hands on her pants, and mopped the perspiration from her brow. "We're going to need more help."

Maria, a sturdy young girl with short straw blond hair and a big smile whom the labor exchange sent us along with a number of other young women to help with the housework and the gardening, didn't stay long. She was good at carrying armfuls of wood and raising clouds of dust when she swept the yard with a birch broom but not much else. The reason Mutti had to let her go was because she persisted in hanging her behind out of a window instead of using the toilet. It was useless trying to persuade her that she wouldn't go straight to hell when she flushed the toilet. Maria stomped her feet, shook her head, and moaned. She crossed herself and insisted, "I don't want no trouble with the devil," and then she fled the scene. Other young women, whose names I do not remember, came to help with the work in the house garden, but none of them stayed long.

We continued to depend on Mordecai and Madam Chicowa. They helped us plant ever-bearing strawberries and seed a field with poppies. We removed the weeds by hoeing, and spread straw under each strawberry plant to keep the berries from touching the ground and rotting. As the summer progressed, we cut the runners from the mother plants. Our reward was the taste of the juicy fruit. Sven and I ate as many strawberries as we put into our pails. The rest we enjoyed with milk and on tarts for Sunday afternoon tea. What was left, the maids turned into jam and jelly.

During the early summer, Papa hired a man to cut the grass in the meadow. We watched him swing his scythe from left to right, cutting as he slowly made his way across the meadow. When I look at photos of Sven and me standing clad in baggy shorts, wooden rakes in hand, I recall that hot and muggy day. For hours we crossed the meadow, swinging our rakes from right to left, turning the drying hay, row after row. My back ached and my sweaty skin itched. Afterwards, Mordecai's sisters Esther and Fanny, Madam Chicowa, Sven and I cooled our bare feet in the creek. Later we rested in the shade of a chestnut tree and refreshed ourselves with blackberry juice and rye bread with strawberry jam.

Toward the end of August, my secret pleasure was to sneak into our poppy field once the scarlet blossoms had dropped off and their seedpods had dried. I snapped off a bouquet of them and, hidden under the protecting branches of the linden tree, rattled each seedpod before I twisted off the crown. I threw my head back and shook the tiny black seeds into my mouth. I chewed, crunched, and savored their nutty taste until I had my fill. This I did in spite of the fact that Mutti had warned, "Poppy seeds are bad for children." I reasoned that if Mutti allowed us to eat the poppy seed cakes our new maid Gela baked for Sunday afternoon coffee, the few seeds I enjoyed couldn't hurt me.

When Papa ordered the duck pond drained, he left it up to Mutti to plan and supervise the operation. We watched Mordecai straddle a narrow catwalk above the spillway on the east side of the pond, as he slowly pulled up a wooden board to allow the pond to drain.

Each spring, we watched as tiny yellow ducklings paddled behind their mother in a perfect row to disappear among the reeds and cattails. Papa, with a grin on his face, confided in us that he had taught the ducks how to say our last name. He slid his glasses to the tip of his nose and to our delight imitated the ducks' call: "Laabs, Laabs, Laabs, Laabs."

The day we invaded the ducks' sanctuary and drained the pond, they set up a racket, took to their wings, and left behind ripples and fluffy white feathers floating on the water. Our shouts and the clanking of metal tubs and buckets added to the din. Frightened frogs left the high grass where they had hunted bugs and plopped into the dark waters below. Sven and Frank prowled the bushes on the far side of the pond and flushed out a rabbit, which made a high jump into the water, and, to our amazement, came up paddling. We shouted, "Go, rabbit, go," and watched it safely reach the other side and disappear. As the water receded, it left a ring of smelly slate-gray muck, and uncovered dented buckets, pots with holes, broken dishes, and old bottles. Finally, when only a small pool was left in the center of the pond, fat golden carp and small silvery fish appeared in the shallow waters. In one hand, the maids carried nets fashioned from chicken wire, and they held up their skirts with the other. They screeched as their feet, ankles, and finally their knees disappeared into the muck. When they netted dozens of fish, Mutti instructed them to throw the fish onto the grass. There the slimy catch flopped until we pounced and wrestled with them. We wrapped rags around our hands to get a better grip and carried them to tubs and buckets filled with water. When the pond was almost dry, we watched the tip of a mud-covered object emerge from the slime.

"What is it?" Mutti called out.

The maids shrugged their shoulders. "Don't know, Frau Baurat." Mutti's demeanor suddenly changed. Although there were more fish to be caught, Mutti ordered everyone except Mordecai to stop working and to return to the house. I sensed from the edge in her voice that something was amiss. When I lingered, she shooed me off, like one would an errant goose.

*   *   *

After the war, when I asked Mutti why she had chased everybody except Mordecai away that day, she replied that the object at the bottom of the pond turned out to be a shortwave radio, which, she presumed, had belonged to the previous owners, the Christofoskis. After we disappeared into the house, she had Mordecai bury it in the garden and swore him to secrecy.

*   *   *

We shared the catch with the workers, our friends, and Frau Seif at the hotel. That evening Mutti simmered carp with aromatic vegetables and herbs, drizzled vinegar over it, and served it as *Karpfen blau*. For days Mutti fried, sautéed, baked, smoked and salted down a barrel full of fish. The maids pickled them in vinegar, onions, and dill and stored them in the basement in gray salt-glazed pottery jars.

I never did understand why Papa made us drain that pond before refilling it. Was it because it was easier than catching fish with a hook or was it because the stagnant water needed refreshing? For months Hania and Ignaz had been trying to catch fish. Sven, Frank, Maria, and I had tried our luck, but we were unable to sit quietly for more than five minutes. If Papa thought that Hania and Ignaz whisked the fish they caught off the property without anybody's noticing, he never confronted them. I heard him tell Mutti, "Poaching and pilfering is a time-honored tradition in these parts."

We had been eating fish during our main meal at noon and in the evenings as *Abendbrot* for days when Sven pronounced, "If I eat one more fish, I'm going to grow gills and go live in a pond!" Frank and I nodded in agreement.

Mutti overheard our conversation. She said, "It would have been better if we could have had a few fish at a time, but each day I have enough food to fill everybody's stomach, I thank God."

Mutti struggled to feed more than a dozen people, including long-term houseguests like Anita and Maria, as well as daily dinner guests. With ration stamps, we bought staples, but without the food we raised or foraged, we would have had scant supply. We planted, tended the garden, harvested, and preserved the crops. We fed, guarded, and chased the turkeys, chickens, geese, and ducks. Madam Chicowa greeted our flocks early each morning by cackling and quacking as she cast handfuls of golden maize kernels from the deep folds of her apron. In the fall, Madam Chicowa began catching and dragging the geese by their wings to a stump. There she plunked herself on her behind, spread her legs and clamped one goose after another between her knees. Following time-honored Polish custom, she stuffed small sausages made of ground-up grain down their necks to fatten them up for the holidays.

Madam Chicowa

Wednesdays the government designated as *Eintopftag*, a day when all housewives were expected to prepare soup for dinner as a rationing measure. For a simple but nourishing meal, Mutti browned diced onions, to which she added potatoes, beans, peas, and carrots—and whatever was in season or stored in the root cellar. Depending on how many mouths she had to feed that day, she added water to the pot and moved it to the back of the stove, where it simmered until the flavors were blended.

One day, I happened to be in the kitchen when our maid Lucie bustled through the door. She smoothed out her apron and brushed back her thin mousy hair. "Frau Baurat," she said in a low, conspiratorial voice, "I must tell you something."

Mutti, who had become used to Lucie's awkward attempts to ingratiate herself, asked, "What is it now?"

Lucie spit out, "Madam Chicowa is a thief."

"What makes you think so?" Mutti replied casually, without looking up from her chores.

Lucie describe how Madam Chicowa hid "tons" of chicken feed in the large pockets sewn into her petticoats and carried them home at the end of each day. Madam Chicowa—we children called her Damsche Kova—was the Polish peasant who started working for us when we moved to Auschwitzer Strasse. Her kindly face looked like that of a shriveled apple. Her deep sunken eyes sparkled when she flashed a toothless smile. She covered her head with a black kerchief, and throughout most of the year she walked barefoot on scarred and dirty feet. Until Mutti gave her a pair of rubber boots, she wrapped rags around her feet when it snowed. Mutti had wondered why Madam Chicowa walked so slowly and looked more rotund in her long, voluminous skirts when she returned to her hut in the evenings. Lucie pointed out, "Stealing is against the law, isn't it?"

Mutti continued stirring a pot of soup, "Don't worry about it, Lucie. I'll take care of it." Clearly disappointed, Lucie turned her back on Mutti and me and left the kitchen in a huff. Mutti sighed, "I wish that Lucie would do her work as diligently as she does her tattling and sniffing around." I asked Mutti why Lucie acted the way she did, and why she had such a strange accent. Mutti answered that she was an ethnic German born in Czechoslovakia. When I asked Mutti what an ethnic German was, she explained that ethnic Germans, also called *Volksdeutsche,* are people of German descent who were born outside Germany. She added that they have a particularly difficult life. "Some of them do not know where they belong. Around here they are not accepted by the Poles, but neither are they accepted by the Germans."

The employment office, which had sent Lucie, had informed my mother that Lucie had a criminal record. When Mutti asked Lucie directly about it, Lucie wouldn't say what she had done, but she didn't mind talking about her incarceration in Auschwitz before it became a concentration camp. What surprised and puzzled my mother was that Lucie had not minded being a prisoner in Auschwitz where, although expected to work hard, she had eaten white bread for the first time in her life. Soon thereafter, I overheard a conversation between Papa and Mutti about the possibility that Lucie had been sent to spy on us. From that time on, Mutti had to be careful what she said and did around Lucie. This was the case when a young woman arrived at our gate one afternoon, asking for Mordecai's sister Fanny. Mutti knew right away that the woman, who was carrying a baby under her coat, was Jewish, and that she was looking for a place to hide. In broad daylight, with Lucie watching, Mutti couldn't invite her in. Instead, she let her know that the gate would be left open for her and her baby that night.

I asked Mutti what she was going to do about Madam Chicowa. She replied that she'd have to think about it. The situation reminded her of her mother's stealing food to feed her seven children, after her husband was killed during World War I. My grandmother was unaccustomed to poverty and deprivation, having lived a comfortable life before the war. In spite of being unprepared, she reached deep within herself and, with a small widow's pension and help from her parents, took care of her children best as she could. When she offered the owner of a cabbage field near their home money for his produce and he refused, she sneaked into his field under cover of darkness and cut off several cabbages. She left a note with "I OWE YOU" pinned to the stem of a cabbage head.

Mutti did not confront Madam Chicowa and accuse her of stealing. Instead, she decided to tell her that if ever she needed something, Mutti would be glad to share. Madam Chicowa bowed her head and bent down to kiss the hem of Mutti's dress. She murmured, "God's blessings on you and your family, Frau Baurat." Mutti's face flushed when she told the old woman, "Please, you mustn't." Madam Chicowa never did ask for food or anything else. Mutti concluded that asking for anything might be too humiliating for Madam Chicowa, reasoning that it was probably by pilfering that she had survived during hard times, and that she preferred it to begging.

Madam Chicowa lived in a tiny straw-thatched hut five minutes from our house. One entered her cottage through a low opening, covered with sackcloth, and then stepped onto a dirt floor. The small windows and the flickering flame from the open fireplace barely illuminated the single room. To one side was a pallet with a straw mattress. The pallet was covered with blankets and a ratty, moth-eaten fur. Clothing hung on pegs along the walls. At the other end of the room, stood a cupboard and a table with two chairs. Above it, next to a crucifix, hung a picture of a haloed Jesus Christ pointing to his bleeding heart.

One day Madam Chicowa invited me to come in. "Come see," she smiled, and led me to a box in which a dozen chicks cuddled to keep warm. She allowed me to touch their downy fuzz. A week later, one of our hens, which Madam Chicowa had tended to so skillfully, scratched around the barnyard, surrounded by a flock of golden chicks. We children cried bitterly when we found their dead bodies scattered around the barnyard after a heavy downpour.

Eyes are Watching, Ears are Listening

I was happy every time I had my father's undivided attention. A ride in an open buggy, the horses' rhythmic clip-clopping, the tinkling of bells, and the swishing of their tails made me giddy with delight. At the end of the ride, the driver turned onto our sun-dappled driveway and passed underneath the ancient chestnut trees in bloom. I beamed. "Thank you, Papa." He nodded absentmindedly. "I like riding in a buggy better than in a car," I chattered, trying my best to let him know how much I appreciated our time together. Since only the military, high Nazi officials, and wealthy people with connections were permitted to drive automobiles during the war, Papa had anticipated that his Ford would be confiscated. He had concealed it under the hay in a neighbor's barn back in Vaake. In Poland, when we wished to get to places we couldn't reach by walking, we hired a *Droschke*, a horse-drawn buggy. During the winter, we rode in a *Schlitten*, a horse-drawn sleigh.

"I wonder who that is?" Papa muttered, when he noticed a man walking toward the house.

The driver pulled at the reigns and signaled the horses to stop by making a vibrating sound with his lips. A gentleman in a neat black suit stopped, doffed his hat, and bowed, "Good day, Herr Baurat."

"Good day. What can I do for you, Herr Goldmann?" Papa replied, doffing his hat.

Herr Goldmann stepped up to the cab, his face lit by a broad smile, and in broken German he said, "I would like to present this to your *schöne, kleine Mädchen*." He nodded in my direction and offered me a beautiful baby doll. I stifled a shout of delight when I saw in his arms a Käthe Kruse doll. These dolls were made by hand and much loved by little girls and collectors alike.

I was just about to reach for it when Papa's words burned in my ears, "You know we cannot accept your gift. Goodbye, Herr Goldmann." I turned in time to see that Herr Goldmann's smile had disappeared, his jaw had dropped, and the sparkle in his eyes had been replaced with a look of incomprehension. He withdrew the gift, dropped his head, and turned to leave. Stunned, I glanced at Papa, who stared straight ahead. He motioned toward the driver and whispered, "Eyes are watching, ears are listening."

I jumped out of the cab when it stopped at the gate. I ran into the garden and hid under the branches of the linden tree, where I sobbed and pondered how Papa could be so rude and mean. After I calmed down, I wondered what could have prompted my father to react in such a peculiar way. It led me to suspect that our family, but especially Papa, was in some unnamed danger. I didn't say anything to my mother about the doll and forgot all about it until I saw it in Dagmar's arms the following Christmas. Hey, I thought, that doll was supposed to be mine. Later I happened to hear my mother telling a friend that she had found the doll sitting on a fence post near the gate.

*   *   *

What I did not know is that Papa had reason to be cautious. As Kreisbaurat, County Architect, he was in a unique position to issue permits for different public work details to hundreds of Jews. The department he worked for, the Kreisbauamt, the County Building Commission, needed workers to complete municipal projects. Papa made up a list of names, issued work permits to Jews, signed passes and stamped them. He saw to it that the workers were given food and pay. With special passes, some of them could move about freely and even take care of their own business. However, the passes afforded the holder only limited protection during general *"Aktionen,"* roundups, when the Nazis needed to fill quotas for labor, or for extermination camps. Whenever Papa got wind of an *Aktion,* he put his list in his pocket and rushed to the *Sammelplatz,* an assembly place at the market, or at the old school.

As my father remembered thirty-five years later: "With the inspectors from the Bauamt in tow, I arrived at the old school where the selection process was already under way. Hundreds of Jews had been forced from their homes during the night. They were counted, their names were placed on lists, and they were locked up. On that particular morning, the Gestapo, the German police, the Jewish police, and the mayor stood guard and watched the spectacle. Shimshon Schönberg, who knew me, leaned out of the windows and shouted 'Herr Baurat, *retten sie uns!'* Herr Baurat, save us. When I walked up to a guard, I noticed that they had arrested many of the workers to whom I had issued work permits. Someone had crossed their names off my list and substituted different names. When I protested that they had locked up my people, the guard hissed, 'Do you want to go to Auschwitz, too?' That's when I made a hell of a row ... Later, the Jews informed me that the head of the Jewish police, had been responsible for the switch. He had amassed a fortune in gold from bribes and had collaborated with the Nazis all along, hoping, in vain, that the Nazis would spare his life. I persuaded the head of the Gestapo that I couldn't complete my projects without the workers who had been assigned to me. The guard had to release the prisoners after their names were reinstated. And after the prisoners descended the broad staircase, those on my list crowded around me. One of them called out, 'Herr Baurat, when we see your big hat, we know that we'll be saved.' The hat they spoke of was my broad-brimmed architect's hat, which I called my *Spucknapf*, my spittoon. It was on that day that a mother and a daughter descended the stairs of the old school for the selection. The mother, who was on my list, quickly pushed her daughter toward me and joined the group that went to Auschwitz"

My father wept, "You cannot imagine what they did to the Jews."

*　　*　　*

"Frau Laabs, you are an attractive woman and shouldn't spend so much time alone. You should enjoy life," said Herr Latz one day when he came to call. Herr Latz, a man of slight build and darting eyes, was dressed in a long black leather coat and hat. Strange, I thought, why does this man come around when Papa is not at home? What is he doing talking to Mutti about how pretty she is? It wasn't any of his business. Everyone thought of my mother as lovely. Nevertheless, it made me uncomfortable to have this strange man take notice of her in such a familiar way.

Mutti held Dagmar in her arms and Frank's hand in hers when Herr Latz arrived. Sven and I watched as she tilted her head to one side. On her lips was the odd smile she reserved for people she didn't like. Her eyes seemed to turn a shade darker blue, and in a polite but decidedly cold voice, she answered, "*Nein, danke, Herr Latz.*" She added, "Do I look lonely?"

Acting as though he hadn't heard her, he tipped his hat and replied, "I am ready to train the dog," and he walked toward the kennel of our champion Giant Schnauzer, Karlo.

That night, I made it my business to tell Papa that Herr Latz had been around and had poked his nose into everything. I said he had asked Mutti all kinds of questions and had acted too friendly toward her. Papa did not seem surprised. He lifted his right index finger, and then, pointing to his eyes and ears, he whispered, "Eyes are watching, ears are listening."

The first time he had said it I hadn't asked what he meant by that, but this time I did, "What do you mean?"

Papa frowned and barked, "Never mind. Don't talk to the man. Understood?"

I understood that, for Papa, the subject was closed, but that didn't stop me from bringing it up with Sven, "You know what old Latz reminds me of?"

"What?" Sven asked. I described a small, sneaky, skinny creature that comes at night, and, after digging holes under the coop, bites into the chickens' necks. It sucks their blood and is long gone by the time one discovers the lifeless chickens. Sven looked up and laughed, "You mean a weasel?" I nodded and reminded him of the time in Vaake when we found our entire flock dead in the hen house. "It made me sick," he replied, pretending to gag.

"I don't like the way the man sneaks around," I said. "Besides, he's too friendly with Mutti," I added.

Sven didn't seem to share my worries. But I resolved that from then on I would keep my eye on Herr Latz. Meanwhile, I continued to wonder why adults sent children away when they had their conversations. The things grownups talked about were so much more interesting than what they had to say to children. I felt I was missing out on something and devised different ways to eavesdrop. I hovered around my parents and their friends like a pesky insect at a picnic. I would keep my distance, appearing to be absorbed in whatever I was doing at the time, but stayed close enough to hear what the adults were saying. Then Papa caught on to my game. "We'd better be careful," he joked. "Eycke can hear the fleas cough."

"Just like her father," Mutti replied. "She is so much like you, even looks like you." Mutti flashed him one of her brilliant smiles. I hated it when people said that I looked like Papa. Everyone thought that he was handsome, and I agreed, but I was a girl, and I desperately wanted to look like Mutti and her sisters. I wanted to be round in places and soft.

My appetite for tasty morsels of grown-up talk remained insatiable, and I was puzzled why my parents tried so hard to keep things from me. I could tell from the expressions on their faces and the tone of their voices that the matters they discussed were serious. They lowered their voices or ceased talking altogether as soon as they became aware that I was listening. Some of the sensitive subjects they didn't want me to know about included trouble between Mutti and Papa, bad things the Nazis were doing to Jews and Poles, war rumors, death and destruction from air raids back home, and Papa's mounting troubles with his Nazi bosses.

I was unaware that Papa and Mutti argued with each other about how much they should tell me. Mutti was adamant that they should try to do everything in their power to keep from their children some of the gruesome details of the war and the atrocities committed by the Nazis. Papa believed that in order to protect us he had to keep his most dangerous activities hidden from his children, and, in some cases, even from his wife. He reasoned that if we didn't know, we would not be able to pass information on to the Gestapo in case we were questioned. On the other hand, Papa did feel that it might be wise to share some of the facts with me. Even at my age, he thought that recognizing danger and understanding some of what was happening around us would prepare me to cope with adversity later on in life. Occasionally, with reluctance and, I suspected, against their better judgment, my parents would answer a question after I had pestered them. I never felt that they told the whole truth. I wondered why they expected me to do my chores like a grown-up, but then treated me like a child by keeping me in the dark. What they said most of the time when I questioned them was, "*Nicht für Kinder*," not for children. The more they tried to hide things from me, the more curious and worried I became. What I wanted desperately, was for someone to help me unravel the mysteries that surrounded us like an impenetrable fog.

There was that time, right after we moved to Auschwitzer Strasse, when I saw Herr Latz walking toward the house. My brothers heeded Papa's order to stay out of his way. Mutti received Herr Latz at the porch door. I continued weeding my flower bed nearby. "*Heil Hitler*, Frau Baurat." Herr Latz doffed his hat and announced jovially that he had come to put Karlo through his paces.

"Good day, Herr Latz. You know where Karlo is," my mother replied. "But, first I would like to ask you about some rumors."

"Rumors? What kind of rumors?"

"What do the Jews mean when they say, 'We are being taken'?"

"Ah, that," Herr Latz straightened up as the tone of his voice changed ever so slightly. He enunciated each word carefully, the way teachers did when they spoke to their pupils. "Our mission is to resettle the Jews and put them to work for the war effort. Anything else is just rumor."

"That's it, then?"

"Yes, indeed. We all have to work, don't we?"

"We do, indeed, and that reminds me, good day, Herr Latz." I watched him make his way around the house, unlock Karlo's pen, pick up a stick, and walk into the meadow, where he commanded the dog to run, jump and fetch. A few times, Herr Latz had brought a man along, who donned a heavily padded suit.

The suit prevented Karlo's sharp teeth from tearing into the man's arms and legs when Latz commanded the dog to attack.

Mutti must not have been satisfied with the answer Herr Latz had given, because a few weeks later she questioned Fanny, who shook her head, wrung her hands, and lamented, "Frau Baurat. I'd rather not tell."

"Please, Fanny."

I eavesdropped while I cut and bundled flowers.

"They continue to come in the night. They pound on doors. They break them down, and then they take us away." Fanny covered her face with her hands.

Mutti asked Fanny to sit beside her under the birch tree. "You see, my husband … I believe he knows more than he has been telling me. And my small son … he keeps having nightmares about an old Oma getting shot up on Auschwitzer Strasse." That's when Mutti noticed me. "Eycke," she said sharply, "Go and check on your sister."

Since I got paid to supply the hotel dining room with flowers from my garden plot, I argued, "I have to get an order ready for Frau Seif."

"Now!" Mutti commanded. I obeyed, relieved for once to be sent away. What I had heard had scared me.

Then I remembered that time—it must have been the end of April and shortly after we moved into Auschwitzer Strasse—when Mutti asked me to take a letter to Herr Latz's apartment. I had noticed that Mutti had avoided going into town ever since she and I had a run-in with an SS man. He had yelled at Mutti for stepping off the sidewalk to make room for an old couple wearing yellow stars. "You there, Frau," the burly man swaggering in his black uniform had shouted at us, his face red with anger, "*Heil Hitler.* Germans don't step aside for dirty Jews."

Mutti had looked shocked and bewildered and muttered under her breath, "We were taught to honor our elders," as we fled the scene. I felt sorry for the old couple and for my mother. As a child, I was used to being humiliated and getting yelled at, but this was the first time I had seen it done to grownups.

Pleased about being trusted to run an errand, I took the letter, wondering if it had anything to do with the visit from a man who had called on Mutti the day before, but I thought I'd better not ask, not now. Mutti would probably sigh and repeat for the hundredth time, "*Kind,* you ask too many questions." So, I decided to wait for the right moment.

I skipped down our driveway, turned left on Auschwitzer Strasse, and dodged trucks and horse-drawn wagons while crossing over to Sonnen Strasse. Sonnen Strasse was a street lined with chestnut trees, beautiful villas, and attractive apartment buildings. This was the elegant side of town, where prosperous Jews and

Poles had lived until Nazi officials requisitioned their homes. Mutti had explained to me some time ago that our family was supposed to have moved into one of those places. In 1941, she had traveled to Poland carrying baby Dagmar. When she arrived in Krenau, the wife of the County Commissioner had escorted her around town and urged her to pick one of the houses on Sonnen Strasse. My parents, however, would have none of it. "Move into homes from which the Jewish and Polish occupants had been evicted and where the beds were still warm?" Mutti raged, recalling the incident. "We couldn't bring ourselves to do that. Your father kept talking about how important it was to live on the outskirts of town, so we decided instead on renting the old tarpaper-covered cottage with the option of buying it from the Christofoskis and remodeling it." My father kept to himself the other reason why the property appealed to him.

I had no trouble finding Sonnen Strasse 14. I rang a bell under the nameplate LATZ, waited for the buzzer to sound, pushed open the heavy door and bounded up two flights of stairs. As I arrived breathlessly on the second floor, a door opened slowly. There stood a most beautiful young woman. How lovely she is, I thought, with her black wavy hair, dark eyes, and porcelain pale skin. She reminded me of an orchid I had seen blooming inside the glass pavilion at the Wilhelmshöher Schloss in Kassel.

"Yes?" She asked softly, her eyes cast down.

"*Guten Tag,*" I said, as I curtsied and stared.

"Please, come in," she replied with a slight accent.

She invited me into a living room crammed with ornately carved furniture. The windows were framed with heavy drapes, and the sun filtered through lace curtains, illuminating a richly patterned oriental rug, and making the crystal in the glass cabinet sparkle in rainbow colors.

"What can I do for you?" she asked, as she looked right through me with expressionless eyes.

I remembered what I had come for and stammered, "A letter from my mother for Herr Latz." I handed her the envelope.

"Thank you," she answered in a flat voice, as she reached for the letter.

I wanted to tell her that she looked like a princess in a fairytale, to ask her why she was so sad, but all I could do was whisper, "*Auf Wiedersehen.*"

*   *   *

It was years later that Papa revealed that the young woman I had met that day was Jewish. Herr Latz had made her his mistress. Before his wife arrived from

Germany, he sent his mistress to Auschwitz where she perished. Shimshon Schönberg knew her and about her tragic fate, confirming Papa's story. After the war, Latz and one of his assistants were apprehended and returned to Poland. There they were tried, found guilty and sentenced to death by hanging.

*   *   *

After I returned home, I boasted to Sven, "I ran an errand to old Latz's house today.

Sven seemed impressed. "You know, he's Gestapo," he replied casually, showing off that he knew something I didn't.

"Who told you?"

"Papa, who else?" My curiosity about why Mutti had written a letter to Latz plagued me, and I decided to find a casual way to question her next chance I got. The chance presented itself sooner than I had hoped, when Mutti thanked me for running the errand and asked what had happened. When I told her about the sad young woman, Mutti once again got that far away look, the same look I had noticed after Ute died.

"Can't you tell me what was in that letter?" I asked.

Mutti shook her head. "Not for children." She looked out of the window where the wind gently swayed the branches of the white birch trees, and muttered to herself as was her habit when she was troubled. "How can I explain?" She turned to face me, "I have tried to protect you and your siblings."

"I know."

"Promise not to tell. The man who came to the house yesterday ordered us to attend tomorrow's public hanging. He said it was the duty of the entire German citizenry to watch justice being done to the enemies of the State. I was so shocked, that I didn't know what to say at first. Then I told him that the hangings themselves and what he was asking of me was barbarous. I said that I had four young children and that the baby was sick, and I reminded him that mothers and children were supposed to be protected by the State."

"Why didn't you show off your *Mutterkreuz*?" I asked. The *Mutterkreuz* was a small bronze medal she had received after she gave birth to her fourth child. Years later, Mutti explained to me that by encouraging women to give birth to many children Hitler ensured a steady supply of canon fodder for his wars.

"The man was not impressed," Mutti continued. "He threatened me with dire consequences unless I complied. I didn't know what to do, except to get an affidavit from our doctor excusing us from attendance due to illness in the family. That was the letter you delivered."

The following day, while my friend Waltraud and I were playing near the music school, a boy wearing a Hitler Youth uniform came running down the street and stopped, "Come on, there's going to be some fun downtown."

"What kind of fun?" I asked.

"They're going to hang some Jews."

We stopped jumping. "What did you say?"

"Are you deaf? I said they're going to hang some Jews." He motioned for us to follow. "Hurry, or you'll miss the fun."

I ran home and burst into the living room where my mother was having her "quiet time." When I told her what the boy had said, she let me drink from her teacup and stroked my hair. She sighed as her eyes filled with tears, "You did the right thing by not following him."

*   *   *

On that dark spring day in 1942, seven Jews were hanged for committing minor infractions of Nazi rules. According to Fanny, a baker and his son were accused of making a fire in their oven and were denounced by a Polish chimney sweep. The other victims were hanged for being in the possession of forbidden foodstuffs. Their hangings were intended to intimidate the Jewish community, whose members, along with the German and Polish populations, were coerced into attending the executions.

The Wandervogel

The first of May was one of Papa's favorite celebrations of the year. It was our custom to march outside and to sing the song he composed for the occasion:

Heut' ist der erste Mai …	Today's the first of May …
Guten Tag, guten Tag,	Good day, good day,
Mein lieber Freund.	To you my friend.
Wir werden noch einmal vereint	We shall be reunited
Im schönen Wesertal …	In the beautiful Weser Valley …

There we listened for the first call of the cuckoo, after which Papa ceremoniously cut the first slice of the salt-encrusted smoked ham that hung in our pantry.

Mutti sang all day while she cooked, gardened, and tended to her babies. Papa liked to sing with family and friends gathered around him. I loved listening to Papa's clear tenor and Mutti's warm alto as much as I loved hearing Papa play his violin and Mutti her guitar. Our parents knew the verses and melodies to hundreds of old folk songs. Over the years, they taught them to us, as we sat late into the night, until the embers of the hearth were but a glimmer. When I asked my parents how come they knew all those songs, they answered in one voice, "*Im Wandervogel.*" When I heard the word *Wandervogel* for the first time, I took it literally. I wondered why they decided to call themselves the migrating birds. Papa explained that they likened themselves to the birds in the sky that are free, and who view the world from a different perspective. "We wanted to enjoy God's creation, see the world, and get away from stuffy men in black frocks and high collars, and from our mean teachers, of course." Papa gave Sven a wink.

When my parents talked to my siblings and me about the *Wandervogel,* they frequently used the word "idealism," which was something they said they shared with their friends. Although I did not understand what "idealism" meant, I could tell by the light in my parents' eyes and by the excitement in their voices that it was something special they shared with each other. I could also tell that my parents would rather talk about the years they spent in the *Wandervogel* than any other subject in the world.

In the *Wandervogel* separate groups of boys and girls, led by one of their own age, packed their knapsacks, and donned their slouch hats, boots, and loden capes. They strapped on their guitars and took off for the woods, hills, and valleys. They cooked their meals over open fires and spent the night in barns or under the stars. In the process, they formed a mystical and spiritual relationship to nature. Like the protagonist in Hermann Hesse's novel, *Peter Camenzind,* they strove "to listen to the heartbeat of the earth ... keeping in mind that we are neither gods nor self-made, but children and part of the world as a cosmic whole."

Our parents sang to us about the rising moon, "*Der Mond ist aufgegangen.*" I liked the last verse, "*Gott, lass uns ruhig schlafen und uns'ren kranken Nachbarn auch,*" God, grant us and our ailing neighbor a peaceful night. Together by the fire, our mother and father opened our ears to stories, the song of the nightingale, and the old melodies. They opened our eyes to the mysteries of nature: God's creatures, the forest, the sun, the moon and the stars.

Mutti expressed herself in a poem she wrote during the *Wandervogel* period:

Wenn in der warmen Sommernacht	When during warm summer nights
Die lichten Sterne funkelten,	the stars shone brightly,
Der Ruch von Wind und Korn	When the scent of wind and wheat
ins Blut uns drang,	merged with our blood,
Wenn aus des hohen Himmels weiten Fernen	When from the heavens above
Tönt wundersamer Sphären Klang,	wondrous spherical music blessed us,
Dann fühlten wir, wir waren EINS.	We felt that we were ONE.
Wir waren selber Korn und Wind.	We were the wheat and wind.
Wir waren Glieder dieses grossen SEINS.	We were parts of this great BEING.

Mutti told us that her grandmothers, mother, and aunts were trapped in tight corsets, which they wore under the finery that covered them down to their ankles. They adorned themselves with enormous chapeaus and wore high-heeled laced-up boots. Mutti had scandalized everyone when she had gone skiing wearing trousers. She, along with the other young women in the *Wandervogel,* decided that they need not imprison nor be ashamed of their bodies, and so dressed in loose-fitting linen and cotton garments, and sandals.

Papa began each story by taking off his glasses. He carefully polished them with his handkerchief. When he was finished, he curled first the left and then the right temple piece around each ear. Then, he described in great detail how at the age of eight he followed his brother Otto into the *Wandervogel,* joined later by his sisters Irmgard and Toni. Mutti joined the *Wandervogel* when she was older. Her sister Lonie, and brother Fritz, followed her. My mother explained that she and Papa grew up in different towns—Papa in Münden and Göttingen, and Mutti in Kassel—and that they did not meet until years later. She pointed out, "Your father is much older than I am." This surprised me, since I hadn't really noticed the difference in their ages.

Sven asked, "How much older?"

"Almost nine years." Papa sounded as if he was bragging.

Frank's face lit up with an impish grin. "Is that why you get to boss Mutti and everybody around us?" Papa and Mutti looked at each other. He grinned, and she burst out laughing, but neither one chose to answer. Our parents went on to describe a beautiful valley, with the Castle Ludwigstein, built at the beginning of the fifteenth century, crowning a wooded hill high above the Werra River. They promised that some day they would take us there.

Sven asked what happened during World War I. Papa told us that in August, 1914, he volunteered and followed his brother Otto, by joining the "Green Corps" of the 234th Reserve Regiment in Belgium. On May 24, 1915, the day after Pentecost, Papa stood to the left of his brother, against the wall of their trench, as they came under fire from a British artillery barrage. When a gas grenade exploded directly on top of them, Otto was hit in the head by a piece of shrapnel, which killed him instantly. He slumped over the edge of the trench. This fulfilled Otto's premonition that he would die standing up. Papa was not injured, but spattered with his brother's blood and brains. Four comrades were wounded, others buried alive. They wrapped Otto's body in a tarp and placed him in the shade of a hedgerow. That night, under cover of darkness, they laid his body to rest near a Flemish farm. Papa wrote his parents, "God received our beloved Otto into his kingdom, the kingdom of heroes, fast and without pain. We buried him under a blooming apple tree in Flanders' soil which has, and will continue to soak up so much German blood."

My father taught us the song sung by the *Wandervogel* volunteers, written by Walter Flex, one of their members:

Wildgänse rauschen durch die Nacht	Wild geese are flying through the night
Mit schrillem Schrei nach Norden.	With eerie cries toward the northern skies.
Unstete Fahrt, habt acht, habt acht,	A dangerous journey; beware, beware,
Die Welt ist voller Morden.	This world is full of murder.
Wir sind wie ein graues Heer	We are like a gray army
Und fahr'n in Kaisers Namen.	Who marches for the emperor.
Und fahr'n wir ohne Wiederkehr,	We're marching never to return,
Rauscht uns im Herbst ein Amen!	Autumn will murmur Amen!

Fifty-thousand members of the *Wandervogel* died during the war. On two separate occasions, Papa was rescued, after being buried alive when trench fortifications collapsed on him. In June, 1918, he was wounded during a battle in northern France and spent the remainder of the war in a military hospital. On August 1, he returned home. He was twenty-one years old. He was scarred by the horrors he and his comrades had suffered and was devastated by the memory of his beloved brother Otto, dying next to him. Papa talked about the "black blood" he waded through, but he remained silent about what happened between him and his mother. It was his sister Toni, who confided in Mutti that she heard their mother ask Papa upon his return, "Karl, why did you come back, and not your brother Otto?" For the rest of his life, Papa felt guilty for having survived a brother, whom he considered to be a more brilliant and better man than he could ever hope to be. We children could tell how much Papa mourned his brother's death, and why a song he taught us moved him so deeply:

Ich hatt' einen Kameraden,	I once had a comrade,
Einen bess'ren findst Du nicht.	A better one you could not find.
Eine Kugel kam geflogen,	A bullet came a flying,
Gilt es mir, oder gilt es dir?	Is it meant for you or me?

In 1942, after years of estrangement, and after his father died, my father's mother—we called her Grossmutter—accepted an invitation to visit us. I was nine years old when I saw her for the first time, and I wondered why she had changed her mind about getting to know my mother and us children after all. Every time I looked at my grandmother, I felt like asking her why she had been so heartless to Papa when he returned home after four years of fighting in the trenches of France and Belgium. I asked Mutti what could cause a mother to say such thing. She shrugged her shoulders and shook her head. What she told me was that Papa's mother had been reared like a princess in a prosperous and devout Lutheran family, who lived in a half-timbered house on Lange Strasse in Münden. At the age of sixteen, she became pregnant by a stern and hardhearted man, who was ten years her senior. She married him and by the age of twenty-one was the mother of four children.

I had to admit that at times we were a rather rowdy bunch, but it distressed me that Grossmutter did not have a kind word for Frank, Dagmar and me, even when we were well-behaved. She liked Sven, though, and presented him with a set of toy soldiers. "These are special." Her voice and facial expression softened as she lovingly unpacked and stroked each small figure. Her demeanor changed when, in a grave voice, she solemnly informed him that they had belonged to his Onkel Otto and that he had better take good care of them. Sven whispered in my ear that he felt creepy when she patted him on the head and told him how he reminded her of her "dear Otto." In a rather snippy tone, I replied that he was lucky, because she didn't tell him every time he opened his mouth that "Children are to be seen, not heard."

Dandelions for Dessert

When Papa announced that he planned to buy some rabbits and that he expected Sven, Frank, and me to care for them, Sven asked, "How?"

Frank asked, "Why?"

And I, always ready to please Papa—even if I wasn't quite sure how I was going to do it—volunteered, "You can count on me."

Papa made a face, smacked his lips, and had us imagine the delights of feasting on *Hasenpfeffer*, a peppery rabbit stew braised in red wine and flavored with sour cream. He promised each one of us a pet rabbit if we agreed to feed the rest of the rabbits and clean out their hutches as well. Sven grumbled behind Papa's back that nobody was going to eat his pet, and I agreed with him. Papa set up shop in the barn to construct a dozen hutches out of old boards. When our father worked on a project, he had to have someone to do the fetching and holding and, most importantly, someone to yell at. Sven and I took turns holding the boards, while he measured, sawed, and hammered. Papa kept up a running comment about what he was doing. He used chicken wire for the doors, old shoe leather for hinges, fashioned the latches out of wire loops, and taught Sven how to whittle wooden dowels.

One day, Papa brought home a box with two rabbits. We stroked their soft gray fur and long ears, lined their hutch with hay, and placed them inside. When Frank reminded Papa that he had promised each one of us a rabbit, he boasted, "We'll have dozens by Easter."

"How come?"

"You'll see." Papa made us laugh by lowering his head, sucking in his cheeks and imitating the way rabbits moved their lips. He wiggled his hands over his head and pretended that they were rabbit ears. "Now, listen up," Papa continued in staccato tempo, which discouraged anybody from interrupting him. "You'll feed the rabbits cabbage leaves, potato peelings, and carrot and turnip greens. When the fields green up, you'll go out into the meadow to cut grass and collect dandelions for their dessert. Understood?"

Sven suggested that, in his opinion, dandelions tasted terrible. Papa answered that they were the rabbits' favorite food. He continued, "Every few days you will clean their cages and line them with fresh hay. Understood?"

Sven and I nodded. Frank paid no attention and concentrated on making rabbit faces instead. When Papa announced that he would make a work schedule, I was relieved that I wasn't going to get stuck with all the work. Nevertheless, I was sorry that I had been in such a hurry to agree. I asked myself how I was going to have time to play if I had to care for rabbits, weed the garden, and do my homework. After Papa went into the house I forgot all about schedules while Anita's Maria, my brothers, and I practiced making rabbit faces. We laughed each time we looked at each other. Egging each other on was our favorite pastime, and Frank could think of more ways to get us to laugh than anyone.

Our playroom was a large, L-shaped room with an adjoining bathroom. The morning sun streamed through four curtainless windows, which faced east towards the meadow. A wood stove kept the room warm during the long and bitterly cold winter months. Built-in shelves for toys and books lined the space under the windows, and along the north wall as well. Papa had attached a blackboard to one of the walls. An antique rocking horse, that had belonged to Mutti's brother Willi, sat next to a castle and village made of wood. During our frequent squabbles, Sven and I converted the blocks into flying missiles, while Frank, Maria, and Dagmar hid under the table. Mutti scolded us when she caught us fighting. We slunk off to our respective rooms, hissing insults at each other and vowing to get even.

At other times, it was Frank who stirred things up. He had turned from a sickly baby into a pug-nosed, apple-cheeked, tow-headed rascal. However, his frequent asthma attacks were frightening for him and for our whole family. With no medications available, and in desperation, my parents would hold him out of a window every time he started wheezing. Sven and I may or may not have done Frank wrong when we accused him of trying to get out of doing chores by lifting his shoulders and wheezing once or twice.

Frank had reserved one of his finest rascally performances for a special holiday dinner. In the dining room, the adults were enjoying their food and quiet conversation. The sliding doors between the two rooms stood open. Frank was sitting at the children's table, with his back toward the dining room. After shoving his food around from one end of the plate to another, he lifted his eyebrows and dazzled us with one of his most endearing smiles. Oh, oh, I thought, here he goes. He warmed up by pulling on both his ears and sticking out his tongue. Sven and I tried to ignore him and continued savoring our food.

I was looking forward to our dessert of vanilla pudding, when Frank pulled at the sides of his mouth and the corners of his eyes. Sven and I looked at each other and bit our lips. Maria managed to ignore Frank, afraid what her mother would do to her if she misbehaved. Dagmar's giggles encouraged Frank to squash his nose with his flattened hand and twirl his hand around and around until his nose turned a bright red. As hard as we tried, Sven and I couldn't ignore Frank any longer when he screwed up his face, sucked in his cheeks, squeezed his lips together and made the perfect rabbit face. The harder we tried to control ourselves, the more raucous our laughter got each time we looked at each other. Then in a flash Frank's demeanor changed. He picked up his spoon and continued eating his dinner with the most innocent look on his face. Papa scowled at Sven and me when he first noticed the disturbance. When we lost control, he got up from the table, launched himself in our direction, and closed the sliding doors behind him. Without a word, he took Sven and me by the scruff of our necks and escorted us out the door into the hallway. "Off to your rooms," he ordered under his breath.

"It was Frank's fault," I dared complain.

"No excuse. To your rooms without dessert." I turned around to see Frank with a mischievous smile on his lips.

Cattle Trains

A month after Papa had brought the rabbits, I was cleaning their cage when I noticed a nest lined with wisps of soft white fur. The following day, Sven and I sneaked into the barn before school and discovered tiny pink creatures in the nest. We could not tell how many. We shouted for Mutti to come and see. She reproached us for being late for school. When we opened our mouths, she raised her hand indicating that she was in no mood for excuses. Disappointed, we trotted off. That afternoon, we headed straight for the barn yard, where we delighted in watching the newborn rabbits squirm in their nest. Within a couple of months, they were big enough for Madam Chicowa to separate them. After a while, Sven, Maria, and I agreed to take turns collecting bushel baskets of grass and fresh dandelion leaves for our growing rabbit population. Dragging a large basket behind me, armed with a sharp knife and grumbling, I trudged into the meadow, stuck the knife into the ground, twisted it, and popped each plant into the basket.

The boys each picked a rabbit from the litter for a pet, but I begged Papa for an angora rabbit. One day he surprised me with the gift of a rabbit, which had white, silky hair, and shiny red eyes. "Here," Papa handed me a brush. "You have to groom it at least once a week."

"And when will I have enough for a sweater?"

"Maybe in a year, depends on how well you do your job."

I thought of the soft white sweater I would own one day, and I reserved the most tender dandelion leaves for my pet and brushed her long silken coat.

Railroad engines fascinated Sven, especially since he found out that Papa's father had been a railroad engineer. He had personally received a golden coin from Kaiser Wilhelm II many years ago, after pulling his sovereign's coach through Germany.

When it was Sven's turn to collect a basket of greens for the rabbits, he chose the meadow near the railroad tracks, hoping to catch a glimpse of a train from there. He did not have to wait long before he saw an engine pulling a long line of railroad cars. As the train came closer, Sven noticed that this was no ordinary train. The cars were painted a dark red, and, instead of regular windows, they had small openings near the top of the roof. Sven ran toward the train to get a better look at the puffing engine, as it slowed and stopped on the tracks. As he stood panting, he noticed hands waving from the openings. Moving closer, he heard voices, moans, and cries. These scared him so, that he ran back home to tell Mutti what he had seen. Instead of listening to him, she scolded him for roaming far from home.

"But, Mutti, I was collecting dandelions."

"There are plenty of dandelions closer to the house."

"But, Mutti, what about that train?"

Shaking her head, she muttered, "How can I tell a child?"

Aloud, she said, "Papa will talk to you about it." In a sterner tone, "Go, and feed the rabbits." She turned to the rest of us and admonished us never, ever to go near the railroad tracks again.

*   *   *

Papa waited until after the war to explain to Sven that the cattle train he had seen that day was packed with human cargo, most of them Jews, who were destined for the extermination camp, Auschwitz, eleven miles to the southeast. What Mutti had kept from us was another appalling and surreal scene, which she had witnessed earlier that year when she traveled from Krenau to Kattowitz. At the Trzerbinia train station, in freezing weather, she saw barefooted people, wearing bathing suits and beach wear, jump off cattle cars, and run across the tracks, while being chased by gun-toting soldiers and snarling dogs. She closed her eyes to dispel the nightmarish apparition. When she reopened them, most of the prisoners and their guards had vanished. That evening, Mordecai asked and received from Mutti food and clothing for "his people," who had been rounded up on the beaches of the French Riviera and transported all the way to Poland, without proper clothing, food, or water.

Chasing Dagmar

Dagmar's hair was the color of ripe wheat, her eyes a deep violet blue, her complexion pink, and her cheeks rosy. Every part of her body was well rounded and delicate. My mother called her *Zuckerpuppe* and Papa his *Maiglöckchen*. Anita loved taking her for walks in town. People stopped in the street to admire her. She went to anyone who reached for her, even after our mother gently explained, "Dear, you must not sit on the lap of strangers. To be friendly, you curtsey and smile instead." Dagmar looked at Mutti with her eyes wide, trying to understand who was a stranger and who wasn't. But she could tell that her mother was being serious, so she smiled, and nodded. After she hopped off Mutti's lap, she quickly forgot all about the warning. As a result, it was Dagmar who caught lice most often and then shared them with the rest of us. We itched and scratched. Our scalps became sore and infected. The treatment consisted of a rinse and vigorous scrubbing of the scalp and hair with an evil-smelling, chemical solution. Since it was too strong for Dagmar, Mutti used a special comb and carefully picked each louse and nit from her daughter's hair.

"Like monkeys," Sven joked, as he hooted and scratched himself. Mutti was not amused. Neither was I, when I discovered that I had to keep a towel wrapped around my chemical-soaked head for hours to kill the lice.

From the time Dagmar started to walk, she began exploring the house, the barns, the garden, and beyond. As a result, Mutti gave strict orders that she be watched at all times. Whenever we discovered Dagmar's shoes, neatly placed side by side somewhere in the garden, we knew she had gone on one of her adventures. Our flock of geese had fascinated Dagmar ever since Papa taught her to sing:

Suse, liebe Suse,	Suse, dear Suse,
Was raschelt im Stroh?	What is rustling in the straw?
Die Gänschen laufen barfuss.	The goslings are barefoot.
Sie haben keine Schuh.	They do not have shoes.

When nobody was looking, Dagmar crawled through a hole in the fence and followed the flock into the meadow. For us children, looking for Dagmar was a game of hide and seek. For the adults, the search was fraught with anxiety. Many times, Mutti, panic in her voice, could be heard shouting, "Find Dagmar!"

As soon as Papa cut off one of her escape routes, she would find another one. One time we discovered her in the meadow, kneeling at the edge of the creek, which was filled with succulent watercress. Tiny snails floated on its surface. She gently tapped each snail with her index finger and waited for it to rise up again; then she gingerly hopped back and forth across the creek until we dragged her back into the compound. Papa had to attach a heavy weight to the gate in order to keep her from opening it.

Later that summer, Gitta, a recent high school graduate, took over Dagmar's care as part of her *Pflichtjahr* duties. She arrived each morning dressed in her "uniform"—a red dirndl skirt, a starched white blouse, black velvet bodice, and green apron. She played with Dagmar the way I played with my dolls, by dressing her in beautiful outfits and strolling up and down Deutsche Strasse. On a cold day in the fall—it must have been Gitta's day off—Dagmar got away once again and tumbled into one of the ponds. When she popped up, she flailed about with arms and legs, remaining afloat on her back. Herr Bornstein, a Jew Papa was protecting, jumped into the water fully dressed to retrieve her. She coughed and sputtered when he carried her to the house, where Mutti took her daughter from his arms and thanked him profusely. Mutti quickly undressed the shivering child, rubbed her down with warm towels, and fussed over her until she stopped crying and fell asleep.

*   *   *

Years later, my father recalled a question Herr Bornstein had asked him, "You Germans are a cultured people. Why do you persecute and annihilate us Jews? You read Goethe and Schiller, you listen to Bach and Mozart, yet you act with such brutality." Papa couldn't explain. He did, however, tell Herr Bornstein not to expect any mercy from the Nazis, and he suggested that the Americans were their only hope. Papa was shocked when Herr Bornstein, who had owned a prosperous wholesale business of prized Polish geese before the Nazis confiscated it, shrugged his shoulders and answered, "I don't think the Americans are going to help us. We're their ignorant cousins," and he added, "Could be, they are ashamed of us."

When I asked what happened to Herr Bornstein, Papa replied that the affidavit for saving Dagmar's life, along with the work permit he had issued him, protected him during a number of roundups. In the end, he was denounced by his own people, deported, and murdered at Auschwitz.

I wondered how Herr Bornstein's people could do such a thing. Papa answered, "because of personal enmities." Then he reminded me what had happened to Mutti's friend and Dagmar's godmother, Li Rosenkranz. Neighbors had accused her, her partner, and his son, all of them Gentiles, of listening to BBC radio. They were executed and buried in a mass grave at Bergen Belsen Concentration Camp in the spring of 1945, one month before the end of the war. Papa explained that those were times when Germans, Jews, and Poles betrayed each other, and when children informed on their own parents.

Winter of 1942-43

Polish winters struck suddenly and fiercely, and they lasted for six months. Overnight, the water froze and trapped our flock of geese in the middle of the pond. We cracked the ice with poles and set the geese free. They thanked us with a chorus of honking, and they awkwardly slipped and slid across the ice to gobble up the maize kernels that Madam Chicowa scattered for them. "Stupid geese," Frank jeered, as he pointed to the geese, then to me, and grinned. He knew that Papa sometimes called me a "stupid goose" and how much it upset me. What he didn't know was that I had vowed to show everyone, but especially Papa, that I was smart. Sometimes I succeeded and sometimes I didn't, but I never stopped trying to prove him wrong. One day I read that geese are especially smart and loyal birds, that they take turns in leading their flocks across oceans and continents, and that pairs bond for life and remain with an injured mate. I decided then that Papa didn't know everything.

Once the ice became thick enough to support us, we cut holes into its surface and stuffed sheaves of straw into them. "So that the fish can breathe and survive the winter," Madam Chicowa explained. We lashed skates made of wood, metal clamps and rusty iron blades to our boots and ventured onto the pond. I had dreamed of dancing, jumping, and twirling across the ice in a beautiful white outfit, as I had seen Sonja Henie do in the movies. But I was frustrated when all I could do was stagger across the pond to the mocking cheers of my brothers. I stretched out my tongue at them, and every time I fell, picked myself up and brushed myself off. Slowly my staggers turned into glides—rhythmically, left foot, right foot, left foot, right foot. Then I was flying across the ice, as in my dreams, even though I had to crash into a snow bank in order to stop. It wasn't until Mutti tempted us with a treat of hot *Ersatzkakao* that we agreed to come inside.

Every day after we finished our homework, Mutti would call out, "Time to get some fresh air." She had us put on our warm clothes, helped us retrieve our sleds and skis from the barn, and sent us into the meadow in front of the house, where Sven and I raced each other down a small hill. We helped Frank and Dagmar build a snowman. We played our old games: we threw snowballs at each other, stretched out on our backs to catch snowflakes on our tongues, and flailed our arms to create angels in the snow until we were covered with snow burrs and were numb with cold.

Papa told us that Eskimos hunt polar bears, seals, walruses, and whales, and that they wear furs. While he talked, he showed us how to build an igloo. First, he measured the size of the snow blocks, and then he demonstrated how to cut them, pull them into position on an old potato sack, and stack them up. Sven and Frank decided that the structure was a fort. They acted out one of their favorite scenes from Karl May's Wild West novels by stomping out an Indian dance, while they whooped and pretended to drum. When the igloo was finished, I crawled through the entrance, and I lay on my back. I marveled at the blue light that filtered through the snow. When I asked Papa how the Eskimos kept warm, he answered with a grin, "They eat whale blubber for their supper."

I was not surprised when Papa announced, on December 6, that Saint Nicholas was arriving by plane that evening. My siblings and I believed that all the weird and wonderful people, as well as the creatures that Papa conjured, were real. He had persuaded us that animals talk to each other, and that there were human beings who understood their language. Our mother taught us that the world was full of wonder, especially at Christmas time. "There is more between heaven and earth than …," and she let us imagine the rest.

When the sun disappeared behind the tailings of the abandoned coalmine, and dusk settled over the land, we gathered in the living room. The only sound was the fire crackling in the big tile stove. We sat and listened. We did not have to wait long before we heard the hum of a motor, followed by someone pounding on the door. Papa winked at us and asked, "Shall we let him in?" Without waiting for an answer, he opened the front door. "Greetings, Saint Nicholas. Come in, come in," he boomed. We heard muttering, shuffling, and the sound of heavy boots. A swirl of cold air made the candles on the Advent wreath flicker, as Papa ushered in a gigantic, bearded Saint, wrapped in a gray, hooded cloak, covered with a fine dusting of snow. With each step, he pounded the floor with his shepherd's staff. Over his shoulder, he carried a sack from which a bundle of birch switches protruded. In a deep voice he recited:

> From out of the deep forest I come to you.
> I tell you it feels like Christmas out there.
> Tree branches are covered with golden lights,
> And who do think I saw at the heavenly gates?
> It was the *Christkind*, who looked at me with large eyes.
> "Are you ready, old Nicholas?" he asked, and I answered,

"I am, indeed. I'm on my way to visit the children,
To tell them that Christmas is nigh."
The *Christkind* replied, "Go then, hurry, faithful old servant,
But remember to ask wherever you go,
Do good, or naughty, children abide within?"

Saint Nicholas rummaged in his sack, pulled out a book, opened it, beckoned me to approach and addressed me solemnly, "Eycke, it says here that you've been talking back to your mother, dawdling after school, fighting with your siblings, snitching cookies from the cupboard, and—what's that?" He lowered his voice, "Been telling fibs, have you now?" I was stunned that Saint Nicholas knew just about everything I had done wrong during the past year.

My voice quavering, I answered, "I'm sorry."

"*Tsk, tsk, tsk,*" he shook his head, picked up his switches and commanded me to turn around. Out of the corner of my eye, I saw Dagmar hide behind Mutti. Sven and Frank looked on with open mouths as the Saint administered three swats to my behind and asked me to be a good girl in the future. Chastised and humiliated, I bit my lips as tears spilled from my eyes.

After Saint Nicholas finished reading the misdeeds of my brothers, he gave them each a few swats and a warning. Dagmar refused to come from behind Mutti's chair. Papa invited the Saint to sit, and he gave the signal to proceed with the program. Frank sang, *Ihr Kinderlein kommet,* an invitation for children, and the shepherds to adore the *Christkind* in the manger. He made the Saint smile when he called the shepherds *eklich,* nasty, instead of *redlich,* virtuous. Sven scratched out a melody on the violin, and I played a piece on the recorder.

"Well done," the Saint praised us. He shook our hands, tied up his sack, and got up to leave. Before he reached the door, he turned around and emptied the entire content of his sack. Apples, nuts, and small favors rolled around the floor. "Yay!" we shouted and scrambled to pick up the treasures. Saint Nicholas departed into the snowy night as noisily as he had come.

I had reason to be especially grateful that evening. There was one misdeed, which Saint Nicholas did not make public. I believed that my most serious transgression was not recorded in the Saint's book, because of Mutti. For a few weeks during the past summer, I had shared my room with a new maid. On the windowsill, she kept a glass jar filled with small change. From time to time, I had taken some of the coins, thinking that she would not notice, but notice she did. She told my mother, and when Mutti asked me if I had taken the money, I confessed. Mutti sent me to my room to reflect. Later that day, she had me sit on her lap and asked, "Do you know what you did was wrong?" I nodded. "Why was it wrong?"

"I'm not supposed to take what belongs to somebody else without asking."

Mutti nodded. "You wouldn't want anybody to take the things that belong to you, would you?" I shook my head, as tears stung my eyes.

"I'm so sorry. I won't do it again," I sobbed.

When my mother put her arms around me, the shame and fear of losing her love began to drain out of me, like water from a leaky pail.

At bedtime, from then on until the day before Christmas, we carefully placed our houseshoes under our beds. Upon awakening, we would find either a small trinket or a lump of coal in our shoes. I tried extra hard that Christmas season to be obedient and helpful, to earn treats instead of lumps of coal.

During Christmas vacation, Papa took us back to Germany, where we visited Marianne in Kassel and the Blankenburgs in Vaake. In Kassel, we spent much of our time huddled in the basement, while enemy planes droned overhead, and bombs exploded around us. I refused to use the pail behind the blanket in the corner and begged my parents to let me go upstairs. On the way, I opened the front door to take a breath of fresh air and got a lung full of smoke and a mouth full of dust instead. The sky was ablaze with searchlights, probing the dome of the night sky. The lights looked like a web that had been woven by a demented spider. The droning of the planes resonated in my chest, as anti-aircraft fire filled the air. Luminous clusters of light, called "Christmas trees," gently floated down to earth. Papa had explained that they helped light up the targets for the bombers. When Papa shouted for me to come down, I knew better than to dawdle any longer and closed the door quietly. Shortly after re-entering the shelter, I heard the whistling and counted, one, two, three, four … followed by the shaking and heaving of the ground beneath us. The next day, we left for Vaake. From the safety of the Blankenburg's courtyard, we watched the sky above the Reinhardswald glow crimson from a firestorm over Kassel and chased charred paper that floated on air currents.

It was during our visit to Germany that I learned what had happened during the air raids on Hamburg, the city that Addie and her family called home. At the end of July, Addie and Uwe were caught in one of the most horrific firestorms of the war. It destroyed the city and left thousands dead. My aunt and her son Uwe, wrapped in wet blankets, escaped with their lives. They ran along streets littered with the bodies of people burned beyond recognition from the effects of phosphorus devices.

Upon our return to Krenau, we emerged from a warm train compartment into the bitter cold. A white cloud of steam from the train's engine enveloped and warmed us, before a gust of a bone-chilling wind took my breath away and threatened to topple me over. With our battered leather cases piled around us, Papa bent down to adjust Frank's cap. "Are we there, Papa?" Frank asked weakly. Frank had been unusually quiet during the trip. When Mutti put her hand to his forehead, she discovered that he was running a fever. Papa took off his long scarf and draped it around his son's neck, head, and face, so that only his eyes were exposed. Frank lifted up his arms, and Papa picked him up. Porters appeared out of nowhere and carried our luggage to the front of the railroad station, where a row of horse-drawn sleighs waited to take passengers to town. Teams of horses stood covered with heavy blankets and munched on hay from pouches suspended around their necks. "To Auschwitzer Strasse 36b, please," Papa told a driver.

"Yes, Sir. Please, Sir, me help," bowed the man, who looked like a bear, dressed in felt boots, a fur hat, and coat. His breath had turned to ice crystals on his enormous mustache. The driver took Frank from Papa's arms, and placed him on the back seat of his sleigh. "What's that?" Frank asked, as he pointed to plaited straw shoes fastened to the floor of the sleigh.

"Keep feet warm," answered the driver, as he helped Mutti, Dagmar, Sven, and me into the cab, where he tucked us under layers of furs and blankets. Then he saw to it that the luggage was stowed away properly. He stashed the hay pouches in a box under the driver's seat, and lit the two lanterns attached to the sides of the sleigh.

Papa climbed up next to the driver, turned around, and asked, "Everybody warm enough?" We nodded sleepily. The driver unwound the reins from the brakes, released them, whistled sharply through his teeth, and artfully flicked his long whip over the heads of his team. He clicked his tongue, lifted up the reins, and moved them up and down, once or twice. The horses shook their heads, making the bells on their halters jingle, exhaled puffs of white air, and off we went. The smooth ride took us past small cottages half hidden under roofs laden with snow. The fleeting rays of the setting sun illuminated their tiny windows and turned them into golden mirrors. A few German army vehicles honked as they passed us. When we got home, Frank and Dagmar were asleep between the warm covers. Gela and Madam Chicowa had heated up the tile stoves throughout the house. They had placed earthen bottles filled with hot water in our beds. I crawled under my featherbed and imagined gliding across the ice in a white dress trimmed with fur.

Sometime in February, rumors concerning German losses on the Russian front began to spread. Under brutal, arctic conditions, and after more than five months of bitter fighting for the Russian City of Stalingrad, only a remnant of German troops survived. At the end of January, 1943, they were exhausted. They had run out of ammunition and food, and were outnumbered by Russian troops. Against Hitler's orders, Field Marshall von Paulus surrendered what was left of the sixth German Army. Papa understood that this was the turning point of the war. He told Mutti that Germany would lose the war. No one knew at the time that the Battle of Stalingrad, with more than one million lives lost, would become known as the bloodiest of World War II.

What Happened to Herr Helms?

My brother Sven and I had been attending the *Volksschule* for Germans and ethnic Germans since Easter, 1942. Sven went into the second grade, and I into third. Each morning, we left home, carrying our leather satchels with school supplies on our backs, and our midmorning snacks in pouches around our necks. Sven, who didn't want to be seen with me, ran ahead. I entered a *Feldweg*, a narrow and dusty dirt path that led through rye fields past Madam Chicowa's hut. I could hear the racket her geese made, as Sven passed her rickety stick fence. They were still in an uproar, honking and hissing, when I arrived. Madam Chicowa peeked out from behind the ragged sack that hung over the entrance to her doorway, gave me a toothless smile, waved and called out, "God's blessing on you."

I waved back and hurried on. Before I crossed Auschwitzer Strasse to enter Schul Strasse, I remembered Papa's orders, to look both ways before crossing the street. I continued another two blocks before I arrived at school, a large two-story stucco building. The students waited in the courtyard until the principal and the teachers descended the stairs. They then sorted and lined us up by grades. We faced the flagpole in the middle of the schoolyard. Two boys in Hitler Youth uniforms stood smartly at attention next to the pole. One of them played a trumpet, while the other pulled the flag up the pole. The principal and the teachers raised their right arms, and the student body followed suit, as we shouted in unison, "*Heil Hitler.*" Only then did we enter the school in orderly columns.

Although I was apprehensive about going to a new school, I adjusted quickly and breezed through the lessons. It soon became apparent that academically I was ahead of the class. When the teacher and the principal suggested that I skip the third grade altogether, my parents agreed. To my chagrin, they transferred me into the fourth grade. I did good work in all fourth grade subjects, except for arithmetic, where my grades plummeted. I didn't ask for extra help, and nobody offered. I barely got by with "threes" and lost confidence. Fortunately, I quickly made friends. There was Waltraud, a big, kind, gentle girl, with a round face and short hair; Helga, a lively, diminutive, blonde, with the smile of a pixy; and sweet, dark-haired Renate. My special friend was Jürgen Helms, the first boy I liked. He was a skinny kid, with bright red hair, a shy smile, and lots of freckles across his nose and cheeks.

Our teacher, Fräulein Rost, looked so much like my first and second grade teacher, Fräulein Alles, that they could have been sisters. She, too, wore her graying hair combed back into a bun. She, too, dressed in gray garments. She, too, was an old maid. The difference between them was that Fräulein Rost was even stricter than Fräulein Alles. On one occasion, during a theatrical rehearsal of *Schneewittchen*, Snow White, in which I played one of the dwarfs, Fräulein Rost caught me talking backstage and slapped me hard across the face. "Quiet," she hissed. Tears spilled from my eyes and my cheek burned. I felt humiliated in front of the other children. I had received an occasional slap on my backside from my parents, which hurt my feelings more than my bottom. When an adult spoke to me harshly, particularly when it was my father, I felt a surge of pain through my body into my hands. The pain was followed by a torrent of tears. Most of the time, all it took was a stern look or a sharp, "Eycke," for me to mind.

I had been spanked only once before by a stranger. It happened when I was eight years old. As usual, Mutti had been busy with her chores and with the new baby all morning. Each time I tried to get her attention, her answer had been, "Don't bother me now. Can't you see I am busy?" That was when I decided to sit in the middle of the highway that passed in front of our house. It didn't take long before a car approached. I heard the squealing of brakes and saw a lady driver get out of the car and walk toward me. She pulled me up. Without saying a word, she gave me three hard, well-placed slaps on my backside. The shock caused me to wet my pants. I was mortified when she walked me through the front gate and complained to Mutti about my behavior. I had to apologize, was banished to my room, and there decided I would have to figure out a better way to get attention.

My friend Jürgen's father, Herr Direktor Helms, was the headmaster of the Krenau Elementary School. He and his family lived in an apartment above the school. Herr Helms, a short, bald, portly man, had a friendly smile for teachers and students alike. He regularly observed our class and showed particular interest in listening to our recitations. I was a little worried when he called me into his office, but was flattered when he announced that he had chosen me to recite a poem for the Christmas program. I blushed, curtsied, and stuttered, "Thank you, Herr Direktor."

I returned home, bursting into the living room without so much as a knock. I told my mother the news and asked her to help me. My mother was only too happy to coach me, even though, all the while, she grumbled about the inferior quality of contemporary poetry. She loved telling us that she had been a champion poetry reciter throughout her school years. Since she was tiny, they had to put her on a pedestal. "From the moment I got on that podium, I knew that was where I belonged," she said. My mother delighted in reciting poetry. It amazed me that she could remember every verse she learned years ago.

In spite of the news that the war on the eastern front was not going well, Herr Helms decided that the Christmas program would go on as planned. The night of the program, our grade sang *Oh Tannenbaum* on a stage decorated with the ever-present Nazi flag. My heart beat fast as I stepped forward. Herr Helms stood on the right side of the hall and signaled me to start. When my first line was not loud enough, Herr Helms moved his hand up a notch. I took a deep breath, picked up the volume, and was surprised to hear my voice project loudly and clearly. With my eyes fastened on the beaming face of Herr Helms, who set the pace like a conductor, I finished with the last stanza:

Hohe Nacht der klaren Sterne	Holy night of crystal stars
Die wie weite Brücken steh'n.	Like bridges in the sky.
Über eine tiefe Ferne	Over great distances
Drüber unsre Herzen gehn.	Our hearts extend.
Brücken bilden heut' die Herzen	Forming bridges
Über Tag und Zeit und Raum	Across the ages.
Und im Glanz der Weihnachts-	Illuminated by Christmas
kerzen	candles
Strahlt der deutsche Wunderbaum.	Glows the German wonder tree.

Not long after Christmas, Herr Helms disappeared. When I asked Papa to explain, he gave Mutti the look, which said, do you think we should tell her?

"Arrested," my father responded, after a pause.

"Arrested?" I asked.

"Trouble with the Gestapo."

"What's going to happen?" I anxiously searched Papa's face for an answer. All he would say was that at a hearing, Herr Helms had been accused of disloyalty. The fact that he was an "old Nazi" hadn't helped him. When I pointed out that Herr Helms wasn't old, Papa explained that an "old Nazi" was somebody who had been a party member for a long time. Herr Helms was one of these old-timers who openly opposed the brutal treatment of the Jewish and Polish population. Papa swore, "I told those Nazi *Arschlöcher* ...," those Nazi assholes.

Mutti interjected, "Karl, please."

Papa waved her off and continued, "that they were making a mistake, that Helms was doing a good job, and I mentioned for good measure that his two eldest sons were risking their lives as fighter pilots." He pulled one of my braids and smiled wanly, "Let's hope it helped."

"And if it doesn't?" I asked.

Papa paused for a moment. "They'll send him ..." He stopped in mid-sentence, leaving me to wonder if Herr Helms' trouble had anything to do with the poster I had seen in town:

Proclamation

Subject: Housing of Jews in Flight
In accordance with the third directive of residential requirements
in the *General Gouvernement* [occupied Poland] dated October 15,
1941, Jews who leave the Jewish quarter will be punished by death.
In accordance with this order, persons who knowingly house, feed
or sell food to them will also be punished by death.
The non-Jewish population is therefore urgently warned not to:
1. Hide Jews.
2. Provide Jews with food.
3. Sell Jews food.

The following week, Herr Helms was back in school. Instead of spending recess on the schoolhouse steps being sad, Jürgen came to join us on the playground for "break the chain," a game in which one child attempts to break through a chain of children linking arms.

I pounced on Papa when he came home. "Herr Helms is back," I rejoiced.

Papa replied, "I warned him."

"About what?"

Papa hesitated, lowered his voice, and went on, "To keep his mouth shut."

At the risk of being too brazen, I pointed out, "You don't keep your mouth shut."

I expected Papa to yell at me, but instead, he tried to reassure me. "I'm careful," he said. "What did you call me when you were just a slip of a girl?"

"*Alter Fuchs.*"

"And what are old foxes?"

"Wily, sneaky, and they hunt mostly at night," I replied, proud for remembering.

Papa nodded and held his index finger up to his mouth. "Right you are. Now go and help your mother."

A few weeks later, Herr Helms, dressed in his Wehrmacht uniform, called the teachers and students to the assembly hall, "Dear faculty, dear children. It has been my privilege and honor to serve as principal, and it saddens me to leave you." A collective groan came from the audience. He continued, "My message to you is: Remain true to your convictions and your conscience." Herr Helms then lowered his voice and added, "whatever the cost."

"Herr Helms is going to war," I cried out to Papa when I met him at the gate that evening.

"Nothing I could do."

"Is he getting punished?"

Papa nodded. "He is a courageous man, but there are other ways." I was going to ask him to explain, when he lifted his hand, his signal for me to stop pestering him. I felt I had no choice but to obey.

I wondered what Papa meant by "other ways." Then I thought of the song he and Mutti had taught us:

Die Gedanken sind frei!	My thoughts are free!
Wer kann sie erraten?	Who can guess them?
Sie fliegen vorbei wie nächtliche	They fly like night
Schatten.	shadows.
Kein Mensch kann sie wissen,	No man can know them,
Kein Jäger erschiessen,	No hunter can shoot them,
Mit Pulver und Blei.	with powder and lead.
Die Gedanken sind frei!	My thoughts are free!

And the last stanza:

Und sperrt man mich ein	And if they imprison me
Im finsteren Kerker,	in the darkest dungeon,
Das alles sind nur vergebliche	no matter—it'll be,
Werke,	
Denn meine Gedanken zerreissen	My thoughts will tear down
die Schranken und Mauern entzwei.	the walls of the dungeon.
Es bleibet dabei	Forever it shall be
Die Gedanken sind frei!	My thoughts are free!

Ten days after Herr Helms departed, news arrived that he had been killed at the Russian front, where German troops were in retreat. There were tears in the eyes of faculty and students alike. When I told Mutti, "Herr Helms is dead," she did not seem surprised and whispered, "Child, we live in terrible times."

When Papa didn't come home that evening, I asked Mutti with a lump in my throat, "Has Papa been arrested, too?"

Mutti shook her head. "No, dear. He has things to do."

I prayed that night that the Gestapo wouldn't come for Papa and send him off to die. Then I cried myself to sleep. When Jürgen returned to school a few days later, he wore a black armband, like the one Mutti and Papa had worn after Ute died. At recess, he sat on the schoolhouse steps by himself, refusing to play. When I joined him, he burst out, "The telegram said that my father 'fell on the field of honor for *Führer, Volk und Vaterland,*' but my mother said it was his comrades who killed him."

"How come?"

"By forcing him into a *Himmelsfahrtkommando.*"

"A what?"

"A suicide mission." My friend sniffed and wiped his nose on his sleeve. "My father told my mother that he wouldn't be coming back."

"I'm sorry." I reached out but stopped short before touching him. Girls and boys our age didn't do that sort of thing, didn't even talk the way we had been talking. We mostly fought, played, pushed, and teased each other.

Not long after Herr Helms was killed, Fräulein Rost asked me to run an errand. I found myself at the bottom of a wide staircase leading to the Helms' apartment on the top floor of the school. I noticed a telegram messenger mount the two flights of stairs and ring the doorbell. I had the feeling that something bad must be happening. My feet were riveted to the floor. When Frau Helms opened the door, the messenger saluted, "*Heil Hitler,*" and said something in a low voice before he handed her an envelope. I watched the blood drain from her face. The messenger raised his arm, saluted once again, "*Heil Hitler,*" and quickly descended the stairs. Frau Helms stood in her doorway, tore open the envelope with trembling hands, and read the telegram. She dropped the envelope on the floor and crumpled up its content with her left hand. With her right hand, she tried to muffle a cry that escaped her mouth. "*Nein, nein,*" she moaned, as she turned, and closed the door behind her.

I ran back to class, having forgotten all about the errand, and whispered to Fräulein Rost, "Frau Helms has received bad news." Fräulein Rost gave us a reading assignment and asked Jürgen to accompany her. When Fräulein Rost returned, she announced that the plane of the oldest Helms boy had been shot down. Later that year, Frau Helms received a third telegram notifying her that her middle son had been killed in a plane crash as well.

Frau Doktor Pieczenko

Sometime in February, 1943, Sven was suffering from another one of his severe earaches. Mutti announced that Frau Doktor Pieczenko was coming to take a look at him and join her for tea afterwards. I commented on the doctor's strange name. Mutti explained that Frau Doktor was a "White Russian," who had fled the Ukraine and opened a practice in town.

I watched Mutti prepare the tea and asked, "Do Russians come in different colors?"

She laughed and answered that the "White Russians" supported the ruling Tsar in a fight against the "Reds" or Bolsheviks, during the revolution. "That is the reason the current communist government of 'Reds' don't like the 'Whites'." I asked Mutti why people had to flee from the Russians when the radio announcer claimed that our troops were victorious. Mutti whispered back not to believe everything I heard, because it was mostly propaganda. The word "propaganda" intrigued me, because I had heard it spoken only in hushed tones. I also noticed the frightened look on Mutti's face when Papa declared, after the defeat at Stalingrad, that this was the beginning of the end. From all these things, I had gotten the sense that talking about politics, and especially any mention of losing the war, was not safe.

I asked, "Can Frau Doktor make Sven's ear better?"

Mutti replied, "She is going to try." I slipped the tea cozy on the teapot, pushed the teacart into the living room, and helped set the table.

The living-dining room was a warm and inviting refuge, with a sofa, a round coffee table, easy chairs on one side of the room, and an oval dining table and chairs on the other. A bookcase and a sideboard took up one wall, a seascape and a painting of wild geese in flight dominated another, and a charcoal drawing of a female nude by the artist, Georg Kolbe, the third. Each afternoon Mutti closed the door to the room and had her "quiet time." This was the hour when she stretched out on her lounge chair close to the green tile stove. She listened to music, and read and drank her tea laced with milk from a glass cup.

I watched Frau Doktor arrive on her bicycle. I opened the gate, curtsied, and told her that my mother was expecting her. Frau Doktor, older than Mutti, was tall and slender and had dark eyes and heavy eyebrows. A luxurious fur cap covered most of her graying hair. Mutti greeted Frau Doktor, helped with her coat and hat, and then handed them to me. The coat was heavy, made of finely woven brown cloth, lined with exquisite sable fur. I gently stroked and blew on the fur and held the coat up to my cheek to feel its softness before I hung it up in the entrance hall. After Frau Doktor examined Sven, Mutti asked me to get a prescription at the apothecary in town. Mutti's raised eyebrows confirmed that I was being too bold, when I begged Frau Doktor to lend me her bicycle. Frau Doktor graciously consented, but told me to hurry back. Worried that Mutti might object, or Frau Doktor would change her mind, I grabbed the bicycle, wobbled and wove down our rutted and rocky driveway. Mostly I peddled standing up, but had to rest and coast ever so often. I walked the bike across busy Auschwitzer Strasse and so reached the apothecary in record time. A shrill bell rang as I entered. *"Guten Tag,"* I wheezed out of breath. The lady behind the counter glared at me.

"Don't you know any better?" she asked sharply.

Red-faced, I quickly added, *"Heil Hitler,"* and handed her the prescription. With pinched lips and a sour face, she measured a white powder into an envelope, made a notation, handed it to me, and demanded one Mark. I paid her, put the envelope in my pocket, and was just about to say, *"Auf Wiedersehen,"* when I remembered, *"Heil Hitler."* I rushed out the door, eagerly anticipating the ride back home. Legs pumping fast, hair flying, dodging cars and carriages, I peddled toward home. I got as far as the wooden barrier at the entrance to our driveway, when I noticed that the front tire was flat. I sat in the ditch and muttered to myself the way Mutti did when she was troubled. What was I going to do? Maybe I could sneak in and hide in the barn loft, or, better yet, under the linden tree where nobody could find me. What worried me most was how embarrassed Mutti would be on my account. Realizing that procrastinating wasn't going to help, I got out of the ditch and pushed the bicycle home while dragging my feet.

My mother and Frau Doktor had finished drinking their tea and were waiting for my return. "There you are," Frau Doktor said, and arose from her chair.

With a flushed face and a stutter, I said it fast, my voice barely audible. "I'm sorry. I broke your bicycle."

"Pardon?" said Mutti and Frau Doktor simultaneously.

"I broke the bicycle. I'm sorry," I blurted out.

"How could you have been so careless? Didn't I tell you that I needed the bicycle to visit my patients?" Frau Doktor scolded. A deep furrow knitted her eyebrows together, as she loomed tall and intimidating above me. I wanted to melt into a puddle and disappear between the cracks of the floorboards. "Oh, dear," Frau Doktor lamented, "Where am I going to find someone to repair it this late in the day?"

Helplessly, Mutti wrung her hands. "I am sorry, Frau Doktor."

As I watched Frau Doktor push her bicycle down the driveway, I hoped that I would never see her and her cursed bicycle again. Mutti scolded me for being brazen as well as careless. She sent me to my room, where I spent the rest of the day ashamed and humiliated. From that day on, whenever Frau Doktor came to visit, I stayed out of her way.

A few months after the bicycle incident, Sven and I came down with earaches at the same time. Mutti dripped warm oil into our ears and plugged them with cotton. When we didn't get better, she decided to take us to Frau Doktor. I would have done almost anything if I could have avoided the visit. I pleaded in vain with Mutti. I even told her that I didn't hurt too badly any more. Mutti looked at me and shook her head, "You know I can tell when you are lying. It's written up there," she pointed to my forehead. I turned around and wiped the lie off my forehead.

Frau Doktor lived and practiced in an apartment building on the street, which ran parallel to Auschwitzer Strasse. I felt queasy as we mounted the dark staircase to the apartment. Mutti rang the bell. A nurse opened the door and, instead of leading us into the waiting room, invited us to make ourselves comfortable in Frau Doktor's living room. A grand piano took up a large part of the room. Above it, hung a stark white mask. "What's that?" I asked Mutti, pointing.

"It's a death mask of Ludwig van Beethoven."

"Oh," I said, pretending to know who Beethoven was. Frau Doktor invited Mutti and Sven into the office, leaving me behind to stare at the mask. It seemed like an eternity before Sven, his eyes red in his pale face, returned to the living room with a bandage wrapped around his head.

"What happened?" I asked. Before he could answer, the doctor's assistant motioned me to follow her. Mutti and Frau Doktor were waiting for me in the office, which reeked of a disinfectant. Frau Doktor wore a white coat. A band encircling her head had a small silver mirror attached to it. I curtsied and took her outstretched hand, while I kept my eyes on the floor. She invited me to sit and flipped the mirror over her left eye. With a tiny funnel, she peered into my ears and pressed the bones behind them. She lifted a white towel from a tray at her side, picked up a gleaming lancet, and leaned closer.

My mother stood behind the chair, both her hands on my shoulders. "Be brave," she said. Without warning, an indescribable pain exploded inside my head and spread throughout my body. A scream escaped my lips, and tears rolled down my cheeks. Frau Doktor stepped back. My mother stroked the top of my head. Enraged, I shook off her hand. When I tried to get out of the chair, Frau Doktor, her face expressionless, shook her head. I looked at Mutti, pleading with my eyes for help and protection. "It's almost over," Mutti said in an attempt to soothe me. Shaking, I gripped the sides of the chair and leaned back. Frau Doktor stuffed a plug of cotton into my ear and wrapped a bandage around my head. She stepped back and motioned for me to get up. I jumped up, scorned her outstretched hand, and left the room without looking back.

To Sven I blurted out: "That witch hurt me because I broke her bicycle. I hate her."

Sven, calm and reasonable beyond his years, replied, "She's done it to me before, although I never gave her bicycle a flat." I refused to accept his explanation and remained convinced that Frau Doktor had seized this opportunity to take her revenge. I don't remember walking home that day. All I recall is a consuming anger and the sense that my mother had betrayed me. I fumed for days and intended never to forgive Frau Doktor. However, I couldn't stay angry with Mutti for very long.

Several months had passed when Frau Doktor brought a gentleman to our house, whom she introduced as Herr Doktor Markin. He explained in whispers that he, along with the Charkow Opera Company and their dependents, had fled to Krenau to avoid capture by the Russians. I assumed that the reason Herr Doktor spoke only in whispers was because of an ailment, but Mutti explained that he had been whispering ever since living under the threat of Bolshevik informants. Doktor Markin became a regular guest at our house. In gratitude to the town for having given them refuge, the Opera Company gave a magnificent concert.

Papa is in Trouble

I don't believe that Marianne expected my mother to answer her when she asked for the umpteenth time, "Tutti, how do you put up with that man? The way he spends money and lends money to anybody who asks. He takes too many risks, and there is his eye for the ladies and theirs for him. Remember, in Kassel, they even called him their white dream?"

I loved my aunt dearly, but I couldn't understand why she picked on Papa every chance she got, and I didn't always understand what she meant, not exactly. What about Papa's eye for the ladies and a white dream? When Marianne brought it up, Mutti shrugged her shoulders and fed Dagmar another spoon of oatmeal. "*Ach*, Marianne, what can I say? He's a handsome man. He doesn't drink, he doesn't smoke, he doesn't gamble, and he loves me and the children."

I do not recall when I first realized that Papa stood out in a crowd. With his slender, wiry build, he appeared taller than he was. His features were sharply defined, his hair prematurely white. His pale blue eyes shimmered behind his immaculately polished, rimless glasses. He cut a dashing figure, in his cream-colored jacket and knickerbockers, fashioned of hand-loomed wool. In his broad-brimmed architect's hat and with the tails of his white duster floating behind him, he looked more like the artist-pilot he was, than the staid German *Beamter*, he was supposed to be.

Early on, I became aware that Papa had a taste for living dangerously. In 1935, when we still lived in Wilhelmshausen, he nearly killed himself when he lost a wheel, driving his sports car around a sharp curve down Hemelberg. Years later, he showed us the scarring on the tree into which he crashed. Every time he climbed into a glider and soared into the skies, he took a risk. I knew that, but I sensed that he was in even more danger after we moved to Poland.

More than once Papa got annoyed when I listened to an adult conversation. One day, he returned from work looking upset. Mutti asked him what had happened. Papa mentioned a surprise visitor. "A man dressed in civilian clothes sauntered into my office and threw two passes on my desk. I knew right away that he was from the Gestapo. He pointed to my signatures and demanded to know if they were mine, I shot back, 'I sign hundreds of these, what of it?'" When I made a noise, Papa discovered me standing in the hallway, waved me off with the back of his hand, and growled, *"verschwinde."*

*   *   *

Years later, Papa cast a net into the past. "The documents belonged to two Jewish women, who escaped from Poland. A Swiss border patrol caught them and turned them over to the Nazis." Papa put up his hand. "Don't ask me why." He continued, "When I saw the documents, I realized that this was a trap. I took a deep breath and shouted, 'Who do you think you are? Coming into my office questioning me. I have approved lists and am authorized to give out hundreds of work permits and passes. This is my jurisdiction. I say what goes, and unless you are prepared to prove beyond a shadow of a doubt any wrongdoing on my part, I suggest that you leave my office immediately.'" Papa chuckled. "You should have seen the look on the man's face. His eyes were this big, he wiped his forehead with a handkerchief, stammered something, then quickly and quietly left my office. I don't mind telling you that after he left, I broke into a cold sweat." I asked Papa what made him use that kind of tone with the agent. He answered, "Early on I learned how to deal with certain individuals: act like you have authority, even if you don't. Shout, roar and bellow, and do it with conviction."

I had no trouble believing him, because I had seen him use those tactics on any number of occasions. I asked, "Papa, did you know the women who tried to escape?" My father nodded, averted his eyes, and waved me off.

*   *   *

In March of 1943, when the snow began to melt into a dirty slush during the day and refroze during the nights, Papa appeared more restless than usual. His temper flared easily, and he flew in and out of the house, leaving me wondering what the trouble was this time. Then one day, Papa announced that he would be going away soon. "Why?" I asked.

"Can't talk about it."

"Where?" Sven asked.

"Don't know yet. Won't be working for the county any more," he replied. I was just about to open my mouth and ask him another question, when I thought better of it. I simply added it to all the unanswered questions I carried around with me like a heavy rucksack.

*   *   *

My father's professional abilities were sterling. In 1942, he had been rewarded with a promotion to *"Beamter,"* tenured civil servant. His relationship with the authorities, especially the Nazi county commissioner, was quite another matter. Papa had little regard for rules and regulations with which he disagreed. He could be arrogant, and, above all, he lacked diplomatic skills.

In 2002, the German historian Dr. Reinhold Lütgemeier-Davin, wrote about my father in *Luftwaffen-Feldwebel und Baurat Karl Laabs: Ein Jugendbewegter als Judenretter im polnischen Krenau.* "He was prepared to publicly oppose political authorities, without regard to whether or not that could harm him socially or professionally … [he] was not inclined to seek social status through the enhancement of reputation, power, influence and money."

On the other hand, my father was not a foolhardy man. As my mother observed, "When he sensed danger, he kept his thoughts to himself and eeled his way through. He was a master of disguise and deception. He made use of his uncanny ability for role-playing and for lying. He could make the Nazis believe that he agreed with them, and promptly go behind their backs and do what he thought was right. There were times when he found it expedient to howl with the wolves, but he refused to run with them." She added, "I believed what your father was doing was right, but I did warn him to be careful … I was petrified that he would be found out, and I was constantly torn between my concern for the Jews and my worries about the safety of you children."

My mother watched, as the man she loved risked his life over and over again. She sensed that he was keeping some of his most daring rescues from her. I can't imagine how difficult this must have been for her.

On March 3, 1943, my father received a letter from the Krenau County Commissioner, notifying him of a *"Strafverfahren,"* a criminal proceeding against him. This was shortly after he had rescued over one hundred young Jews from transport to Auschwitz. It was also shortly after the Nazis had rounded up the remaining Jews including the three Hartmann girls. There was nothing Papa could do to save them. In the end, the Nazis achieved their goal to make the town and county *Judenrein.*

The concluding paragraph of the letter read, "Due to unprofessional conduct in his profession and in private life, the civil servant, Karl Laabs, is hereby sentenced to a *Strafversetzung,* a penalty transfer." What was mysterious is that the letter did not mention any of Papa's "illegal" activities on behalf of Jews and Poles.

Papa responded by pleading "not guilty." His suspicion was that the transfer order was part of a plan to send him to Auschwitz. This was confirmed, when an informant warned him of his impending arrest. Immediately he set in motion a number of complicated maneuvers, with the intent to outwit the Gestapo. Papa traveled to Kattowitz to confer with his friend Sassmannshausen, an old glider buddy from the twenties. Flight Commander Sassmannshausen was in charge of the Luftgaukommando VIII of the Luftwaffe. He persuaded his superior, in charge of the Wehrbezirkskommando Kattowitz, to issue Papa backdated induction papers. After Papa's return to Krenau, he took sick leave and waited for the Gestapo to make their move.

A few days later, two men in civilian clothes knocked on our door and asked to see Papa. Gela led them into the study, where Papa joined them. Sven, who picked up on things I paid little attention to, sidled up to me, nudged me in the ribs, and whispered, "Gestapo." Mutti fled into the garden, where she paced up and down until the men left. She then ran into the house, where she fell into Papa's arms. Papa put his arm around her, led her into the living room, and closed the door. At that time, I had no idea how perilously close Papa had come to being sent to the concentration camp at Auschwitz.

Twenty-nine years later, Papa reminisced: "This is what happened. As expected, one morning in March, two Gestapo agents arrived with a warrant for my arrest. I knew the men and greeted them politely. I invited them to take a seat and poured each one of us a glass of schnapps. After one of them read the warrant, I handed them two copies of my induction papers, proving that I had been a member of the Luftwaffe for some time. Everybody breathed a sigh of relief. The agents politely apologized and departed. On a Friday, I traveled to Krakau, where I had myself fitted for a uniform. After a short furlough, I called on the county commissioner, who was one of the instigators of the arrest." Papa chuckled, "Imagine the surprise on his face when I appeared before him dressed in my Luftwaffen uniform, with my World War I decorations pinned to my chest."

*   *   *

Soon after the visit by the Gestapo agents, Papa sent for Sven and me and announced that he was now a soldier in the Luftwaffe. "I want you to do your homework, do your chores, practice your music and above all, mind your mother. Can I count on you?" Both Sven and I nodded.

"Are you going to be sent to the Russian front?" I asked, with my heart racing.

"Don't think so." He pulled one of my braids when he noticed my worried face.

When Anita found out what had happened, she decided that it was time to leave Poland and make her way back to Spain. Maria, who had become especially attached to Papa, didn't want to go. At the railroad station, she wrapped her arms around Papa, clung to him, and cried bitterly. That was the last time we heard Anita threaten to bash Maria's head in.

Shortly after Anita and Maria left, Papa went away too. When I asked Mutti why he hadn't said goodbye, she answered, "Before he left early this morning, he looked in on each one of you and told me that he would try to get home soon."

"You're sure they're not going to send him to the Russian front to get killed like Herr Helms?" I asked.

She shook her head and replied, "Let's thank God that he hasn't been assigned to the front; not yet, anyway. We have to pray that he'll be all right."

Sven and Frank were all excited that Papa was a soldier. My brothers crawled on their bellies, threw dummy hand grenades and yelled, *"Deckung,* bam, bam, you're dead." I thought it was all a silly game. My brothers loved it, but they seldom saw eye to eye about whose turn it was to play dead. Shouts of "You're dead," followed, "No, you are dead." Once they had worked out these disagreements, they competed with each other about who could die in the most dramatic manner. Over and over, they rehearsed death scenes they had watched in the movies. After being hit by imaginary bullets, they grabbed their chests, fell to the ground, where they jerked, writhed, twisted, trembled, twitched, and groaned.

For weeks after Papa left, I found myself looking out the window, expecting him to walk down the driveway. I didn't miss his shouting and bossing. What I longed for was his gentle touch and the times he sat at my bedside putting cold compresses on my feverish forehead. I missed the times when he sang to me and told me stories. Even Tante Marianne, who rarely had anything good to say about Papa, admitted, "I've never seen a man who could sooth a sick baby the way your father did. He held and walked you children all night, singing lullabies."

Papa did come home on furlough for a few days in April. He came home for one day in June, and for two weeks in August, ostensibly to help with the harvest, but instead, took us to visit relatives and friends in Germany. It made me sad that he and I never again went for a ride in a horse and buggy. Whenever I missed him, I thought of the times he took me along on one of his inspection tours. Papa was forever in a hurry. I loved walking at his side, even if it meant having to take two or three steps for every one of his. I watched as workmen pounded the first stakes into the ground and strung lines to mark the corners of a future building. I watched masons place brick upon brick, fling trowels full of mortar onto each one, and tap the bricks down. I watched them deftly scoop up oozing mortar from between the bricks before they added another trowel full, and then put the next brick into place. With pleasure I inhaled the odor of raw timber as I walked through unfinished buildings. I looked for signs of future doors, windows, stairwells, and walls. I imagined what everything would look like when it was completed and how I would arrange the furniture.

The most important part of Papa's job was the planning and supervision of the construction and remodeling of public facilities throughout the county of Krenau. He apprenticed as a stonemason before he studied architecture, and he was familiar with every facet of the building trade. He got along well with his foremen and workers, who were ethnic Germans, Poles, and Jews. He asked about their health and their families and helped them when they were in trouble. He addressed each foreman formally with *"Herr Meister."* But when it was time to talk about matters concerning construction, he gave orders in his terse, no-nonsense, concise, clipped way of speaking.

On our Own

In Papa's absence, Mutti took on the responsibility of raising us children by herself. She ran the household, and she supervised the cultivation of the land and the care of the animals. She didn't need the orders Papa had tacked on the wall to remind us of what needed to be done, but every once in a while, when we neglected to do our chores, all she had to do is point to his list. The job Sven and I loathed most was our weekly trip across town to the slaughterhouse, where we picked up a vat filled with putrid organ meats for Karlo. We did a lot of complaining as we pulled the heavy handwagon over the cobblestone streets to our house, where we boiled the stinking scraps over an open fire in the barnyard until yellow globs of fat collected on the surface of the broth.

I much preferred working in the garden. The late summer and fall were the times for harvesting what we had planted and whatever we could forage in the fields and woods. We dug for horseradish roots along the edges of fields and meadows. First, we bared the roots with a spade. Then we pulled as hard as we could, often landing on our behinds in the process. Mutti scrubbed the horseradish and cried tears while she grated it, to spice up dishes and sauces. Enormous boletus mushrooms grew abundantly under the pines beyond the hills made of tailings from an abandoned coal mine. The maids knew where to find the mushrooms, and they carried them home in washtubs. They chattered around the kitchen table while cleaning, slicing, and stringing them up for drying in the attic. The remainder Mutti turned into tasty soups, or sautéed with herbs, served them over pasta or potatoes.

When Papa supervised a job, he had a habit of ordering us around. He bellowed, cajoled, and criticized, all of it at the top of his voice. With a lighter touch, Mutti tried to keep everything running smoothly, but, she, too, could lose her composure. She shouted at us for misbehaving. She chided the younger, less experienced maids for loafing and neglecting to follow instructions. However, I noticed that Mutti never lost patience with Gela, the young, ethnic German woman, who worked for us between 1942 and 1944. She was pleasant with a round face, short brown hair, and large hands. Gela spoke German with a slight accent and introduced us to the dishes of her people.

When the green cabbage heads turned solid and fat in the rear of the garden, we whacked off their heads. The first batch Gela turned into a soup. She called it borscht. I watched as she shredded cabbage, red beets, carrots, chopped onions, and whole heads of garlic, to which she added water and vinegar. The piquant odor spread through the kitchen, as the soup simmered at the back of the stove, making my mouth water. Gela topped off the dark red soup with sour cream and served it with her crusty rye bread. We smacked our lips and asked for seconds and thirds, until our stomachs could hold no more. When no one was looking, we licked our plates.

Among the things Gela had learned from her mother and grandmother was how to turn the cabbages into sauerkraut. First, we dragged wagons full of cabbages and stacked them up in a pile near the kitchen door. Then we made them bob, by dunking them in a tub filled with water. For the rest of the day, the girls took turns shredding the heads by sliding them across a metal grater. The next morning, they soaked and scrubbed their feet in sudsy water. Afterwards, they took turns stomping the shredded cabbage with their bare feet, while they gossiped, joked, laughed, and sang. Mutti added salt and spices and divided the mass into large gray earthen crocks. She covered the crocks with linen cloths and wooden lids, weighted the lids with heavy rocks, and stored the crocks in the cellar.

During the following weeks, I sneaked down the dark stairs, lifted a rock and lid, stuck my finger into the juice, and tasted it to find out if the cabbage had turned sour. I can't remember how many weeks went by, but I do recall that one day it tasted just right. I scooped up the sauerkraut, ate it raw by the handful, and shook myself with the pleasure of it.

To feed a woodstove properly was tricky. In order to adjust the amount of heat during the preparation of different dishes, each one of the six cooking spaces was made up of three removable concentric rings and a sphere. To start a soup boiling, Mutti used a hook to take one or two rings off, put a large Dutch oven directly over the flame, and after the mixture started bubbling, she pulled the pot aside, replaced the rings and the pot over the closed fire station. This slowed down the cooking, and after about thirty minutes, she moved the pot to the back, where the soup bubbled gently until dinnertime. The rear of the stove was reserved for the simmering of stocks and the braising of meats. On the far right, water warmed in a large, oval copper reservoir. A ladle hung from a hook to the right of the stove. The firebox into which wood was fed at regular intervals, was located below the cook top and the ash box below that. When the ashes threatened to overflow, Mutti gathered them in a bucket and sent us to spread them on the compost.

My favorite place to stand and watch Mutti and the maids was next to the stove on the wood bin, until, that is, the day I helped stir a pot filled to the brim with glistening apple jelly. I lost my balance and seriously burned my arm with a ladle full of sticky liquid. Mutti quickly led me to the sink and pumped icy cold well water over the burn. She dried me off and expertly wrapped a gauze bandage from my wrist all the way up to my elbow. To immobilize the arm, she put it in a sling. With four children, Mutti had ample occasion to keep up her nursing skills. I was banned from the kitchen for a while, but after a week, I wheedled my way back in and avoided teetering on the coal bin.

Unlike most women, Mutti preferred to wear a starched white nurse's smock instead of an apron. Nor did Mutti use written recipes. She didn't talk much while she cooked; she preferred to sing instead. As I watched her chop, sauté, season, and stir, roast, knead, bake, and serve with such energy and enthusiasm, my mother passed her passion and love for cooking on to me.

Vegetables and potatoes made up the greatest part of our diet. There were times when the rich odor of onions browning in butter or diced fatback lured me out of the playroom into the kitchen. As long as I kept quiet and out of the way, my mother and the maids tolerated my presence. I watched Mutti make a roux by tossing a dollop of butter into a pot on the stove until it melted. Using a wooden spoon, she blended in some flour and for a minute or two stirred the mixture over low heat until it bubbled. At this point, she quickly pulled the pot to the side of the stove and added hot liquid all at once. Whipping rapidly, she allowed the sauce to boil for another minute, and then she flavored it with salt and a grating of nutmeg. This made a perfect sauce, to be served over cauliflower or Brussels sprouts.

For a simple but nourishing soup, she browned diced onions, to which she added potatoes, beans, peas, cabbage, or beets—whatever was in season or stored in the root cellar. Depending on how many hungry mouths she had to feed that day, she poured a good bit of broth into a pot. She tied up some celery root, a few sprigs of parsley, thyme, lovage, a leek, and a carrot, and added it to the soup for flavoring. She let the soup come to a boil, then moved it to the back of the stove, where it simmered until all the flavors were blended. Before serving, she added a pinch of salt and some freshly chopped parsley for garnish. For a holiday dinner, she might roast chicken, duck, or goose, prepare a rabbit stew, or a flavorful goulash with lots of onions and paprika. Over the years, she perfected her wild game dishes for special occasions. Her specialty was a well-seasoned and larded rack of venison, roasted on a bed of aromatic vegetables and flavored with juniper berries and herbs. She deglazed with a savory stock and added a dollop of sour cream to the sauce. To her grateful family and guests, she served the tender, medium-rare venison with braised sweet-and-sour red cabbage, curly kale, and potato dumplings.

I was especially intrigued with the method Mutti used to boil potatoes. After she washed and peeled them, so that long curls fell into the bowl in her lap, she quartered them lengthwise and dropped them into lightly salted water. After fifteen minutes, she tested them for doneness with a sharp three-prong tine, and when they were done to her satisfaction, she pulled back the lid ever so slightly and poured the liquid into a bowl, to be reserved for later use in a soup or sauce. She removed the lid and placed the pot on the back of the stove, where the potatoes "steamed off" moisture. From time to time, she replaced the lid, picked up the pot with both hands and gently bounced the potatoes exactly three times. She replaced the lid with a clean dishtowel to absorb any remaining moisture, while keeping the potataoes hot. Before serving, she sprinkled a handful of freshly chopped parsley on top, announced *"c'est parfait,"* put her thumb and forefinger to her lips and mouthed a kiss.

The Thousand-Year Reich

In 1943, the week before Easter vacation, I entered a building that I would revisit in my nightmares for years to come. At the age of nine, I had completed fourth grade, and, along with my report card, my parents received the news that after only three years in elementary school, I was to take the qualifying examination for entrance into the *Gymnasium*, the German high school.

The morning of the examination was the third time I had walked, trembling at my mother's side, on the way to a new school. The first time was in the spring of 1940, back in Germany, when I entered first grade at the age of six and made a spectacle of myself. The second time was after we arrived in Poland, when I started third grade at the Krenauer *Volksschule*. After an initial period of adjustment, I made friends there, soaked up every subject with enthusiasm, and did well academically. But nothing prepared me for the next hurdle. My mother and I made our way across Auschwitzer Strasse. As we continued down the main street, Deutsche Strasse, I tugged at my mother's hand. "Mutti, why can't I stay at the *Volksschule* for another year?"

"Because your teacher says that you're ready for the *Gymnasium*," was Mutti's terse answer, the same answer she had given every time I asked. Mutti's voice was tight, and she looked straight ahead while she spoke. Her pace was fast and resolute. I felt her grip on my hand tighten, as I vainly attempted to make eye contact.

The *Gymnasium*, a three-story, red brick building the color of dried blood, loomed before us. We entered through large wooden doors and walked the long and dark corridor, leading to the school office. A musty odor mixed with fresh floor polish hung in the air. I shivered when Mutti knocked on the door of the school office. We heard a flat *"Herein,"* and exchanged the required *"Heil Hitler"* with an elderly secretary. The woman glanced at me with dead fish eyes and immediately began questioning my mother. I stood silently by and stared at my freshly shined shoes. In a monotone voice, she rattled off, "Last name, first name, middle name, date and place of birth, religious affiliation, parents' names, father's occupation and your address?" The woman entered the information into a ledger and stretched out her hand. "Your *Ahnenpass*, please. We have to make sure that all of our pupils are of Aryan blood." After carefully examining the small booklet, the secretary made a notation, returned the document to Mutti, and exclaimed, *"in Ordnung."* She asked us to wait in the hallway until the start of the examination at 9 a.m., dismissing us with another hearty *"Heil Hitler."* I sneaked my hand into Mutti's, while we waited in the hallway. More mothers arrived with their boys and girls, registered, and joined us.

"What was that about Aryan blood?" I whispered in Mutti's ear. She squeezed my hand, moved her right index finger to her lips, and whispered, "Later."

The sound of a shrill bell startled me. The secretary emerged from her office and announced that it was time for mothers to leave the building. Mutti gave me a peck on the cheek, walked down the long corridor, and disappeared from my view. At that moment, a tall, heavyset man appeared and ushered us into a classroom. Naked light bulbs hung from the high cracked ceiling, and only a trace of natural light stole its way through the tall, dirty windows. The man assigned each one of us a seat at individual wooden desks. I did not see one familiar face, but I noticed that I was the smallest of the group. The man lifted his right arm and shouted, *"Heil Hitler."*

"Heil Hitler, Herr Lehrer," we answered dutifully.

"My name is Herr Burkhardt, and I shall assume that all of you understand why you are here. We expect that you will do your best." Herr Burkhardt handed each one of us a sharpened pencil and two black notebooks. I noticed that he neglected to give us an eraser. "We are first going to have a dictation, followed by the writing of a theme, followed by a math test. You will be graded on spelling and handwriting. Open your notebooks, now." Paper rustled as we turned to the first blank page. Herr Burkhardt took his gold watch from his vest pocket, checked the time, and tucked it back in. He was bloated with importance and authority, as he began to read, "The title of the dictation is, 'Why I am Proud to be a German Citizen.'" The knot in my stomach tightened, as I listened and concentrated on spelling each word correctly. I remember little of the story, except that we had the honor to be born German and as such we were obligated to love the fatherland, and to obey and honor our Führer. I breathed a sigh of relief when the dictation was over. "Next, you will write an essay describing your *Heimat.* You have an hour to complete it, starting now." He looked at his pocket watch. His voice popped *"Los!"* like a pistol shot, signaling the start of a race.

I had no trouble conjuring up images of home: a red-tiled, high-gabled house surrounded by a big garden, and the wind waves on golden grain fields. I wrote about the smell of freshly plowed fields, the dusty footpaths lined with brilliant poppies and bachelor buttons, and the luminescent buttercups and pale, delicate foam flowers, growing in the moist places along the Lange Ahle Creek. I described the creaking of the water wheel at Wallbach's grist mill, and the Weser River as it winds on its way to the North Sea, like a ribbon of molten silver, through a valley of lush meadows, before it passes through undulating hills covered with deep, green forests.

My cheeks burned as I drew word pictures of a river meandering past small villages with crooked, two-hundred-year-old half-timbered houses, ancient churches, and monasteries. I wrote that long before a road was built, the river served as the main route for large and small boats, barges, and wooden rafts. This I had learned from Fräulein Alles in *Heimatkunde*. I wrote of watching fishermen move their long, flat, narrow skiffs upstream by poling against the current, of them casting their nets and setting their traps for the fat eels that teemed in its waters, and of how, after their work was done, they allowed the river to carry them back home. I wasn't finished when Herr Burkhardt snapped his pocket watch shut and ordered us to stop writing.

Next came the math examination. I struggled with half of the ten problems. I was convinced—and secretly hoped—that I had failed the examination. Herr Burkhardt collected the notebooks and dismissed us with *"Heil Hitler."* A week later, to my surprise and dismay, the school notified my mother that I had passed the examination and was to report after Easter vacation. I complained to Mutti that all the boys and girls were older, and I asked her once again to let me go back to the elementary school. She answered that, since I passed the exam, it was proof that I was eligible, and that the matter was settled.

I asked Mutti again to explain to me why it was so important to have Aryan blood. She shook her head and replied that it was an insane Nazi ideology, which holds that only those people with a pure Aryan family tree deserve to have rights. It meant that Aryans and Jews are not allowed to marry, and that anybody who has a Jewish ancestor—as far back as grandparents and great grandparents—is considered undesirable. She added, "and what's worse ..." but stopped before finishing the sentence.

Glad that I had Mutti's undivided attention, I continued questioning her. "What I still don't understand is why the Nazis hate the Jews and why they took all of the Hartmanns away."

Her eyes brimmed with tears, and she shook her head. "I don't know, dear, I don't know. It is a terrible, terrible thing. But please do not talk about this with anybody outside the family. Not even the maids. Will you promise me?"

"I promise," I replied meekly.

When classes started after Easter vacation, I was apprehensive, and disappointed that the class had been divided and that none of the friends from elementary school were in my class. I was dismayed when I found out that Herr Burkhardt would be our *Klassenlehrer*, homeroom teacher. He was my first male teacher, and I was convinced that he had grown even taller and more overbearing. On the first day of classes, he informed us that his greatest wish was to serve the fatherland on the front line. "Unfortunately," he added as he pushed back his wire-rim glasses on his shiny nose, "this privilege has been denied me, and the teaching of ignoramuses gives me no pleasure. Nevertheless," he said, fingering his party insignia, "I intend to do my duty. I demand strict obedience from you. Unless, of course," he sneered, "you are prepared to deal with the consequences." Then, Herr Burkhardt rattled off: "Name, father's name, his profession, date and place of your birth and religious affiliation?" In the process, I learned that I was the youngest and only Protestant in the class. I didn't realize at the time that this fact would make my life so disagreeable.

I never really thought much about being Protestant until we came to Poland. I had been christened at home by a Lutheran pastor at a private ceremony when I was five months old. My father had grown up in a devout Lutheran family. My mother's family was Evangelical Reformed. However, we, like most Germans, did not attend church on a regular basis. But after we moved to Vaake, I occasionally accompanied my friend, Brigitte, to the ancient church on the Weser River. We sat in her family pew, listened to her father preach and to the villagers sing out of tune and pray with monotonous voices. What I liked best about going to church was being allowed to climb into the church bell tower and help pump the huge leather bellows, while we listened to the organist play Bach chorales.

None of my limited church experience of the past prepared me for religious expression in Poland. I remember the day when I walked past the Catholic Church with our maid Lucie. I pleaded with Lucie to hurry because a crucifix next to the entrance of the church frightened me. It was a larger than life-size alabaster Jesus clad in a loincloth, wearing a crown of thorns on his bowed head, bright red blood flowing down his face and from wounds in his side, feet, and hands. Lucie stared at me, shook her head, and wrinkled her nose as though she smelled something unpleasant, which made her appear downright ugly. She covered her head with a kerchief, crossed herself and hissed something about "going to hell for sure," and dragged me into the cool, damp church, which was filled with a sweet scent. Hundreds of votive candles illuminated the darkness. I saw pictures of Saints and statues of the Virgin Mary in glittering robes, cradling the infant Jesus. I watched as Lucie dipped her fingers into a stone bowl filled with water. Then she crossed herself, plunked a coin into a metal box, curtsied toward the altar, lit a candle and prayed on her knees. On our way home, Lucie told me that the nuns had taught her that the reason people's teeth have to be pulled after they die is so that they cannot bite off their tongues in purgatory. But what frightened me the most was when she told me that Protestants go straight to hell.

"Why would the girl fill your head with such horrid lies?" my mother fumed when I told her what had happened.

I shrugged my shoulders. "Are we going to hell just because we are Protestants? Are we?"

"Of course not. Don't worry, *Schätzchen*." Mutti promised that she would have a serious talk with Lucie.

I continued to feel trapped in Herr Burkhardt's classroom. Much of what happened there remains hidden or lost somewhere inside my head. What I remember is that I tried to do my work diligently. Sometimes I succeeded. When I failed, especially in math, he made me stay after school. Herr Burkhardt never praised me for work I did well. Instead, he belittled my efforts every chance he had. When I made a mistake, instead of talking to me, he explained to the class, "She's Protestant, you know." Every question I asked seemed to irritate him. "In this classroom," he bellowed, "the teacher asks the questions."

I came to despise him, and I carried the weight of white-hot loathing and fear in my satchel to and from school every day. My wrath strengthened me and diffused my feelings of helplessness and vulnerability. Eventually, I began to lose some of my enthusiasm and love of learning. At a conference, Herr Burkhardt reported to Mutti that I was a daydreamer, with unacceptable ideas, and that some of my schoolwork was unsatisfactory. Afterwards, Mutti started helping me with arithmetic and with my English vocabulary. She urged me to try harder. When I feigned a sore throat or a headache, and I begged her to allow me to stay home, her answer remained the same—"All children have to go to school." I started having nightmares about being ridiculed for not knowing the correct answer. In one dream, I was unable to write a single word on a blank sheet of paper. All of this left me with a sense of failure and shame.

Some of my classmates began imitating Herr Burkhardt. They pointed at me, wagged their heads, and whispered—while making sure that I heard—"She's Protestant, you know." I wrapped myself into an imaginary mantle to keep from hurting. Once I made the mistake of referring to the area we lived in as "Poland." In response, Herr Burkhardt raged, "Poland? You stupid girl, what do you mean?" His face turned the shade of our rooster's comb as he urged the class, "Tell her, where do we live?" Herr Burkhardt called on a boy dressed in the uniform of a *Pimpf,* the lowest ranking member of the ten to fourteen-year-old boys who belonged to the *Hitler Jugend.*

The boy jumped up and shouted, "We live in East-Upper-Silesia, *Herr Lehrer,*" as he pointed to the insignia on his sleeve. He clicked his heels and shouted enthusiastically, *"Heil Hitler."* The girls seated behind me giggled.

Herr Burkhardt nodded his approval. "East-Upper-Silesia. Right you are, my boy." He patted the boy on the shoulder, then turned to the class and asked, "And is that in Poland?"

Another boy raised his hand. "This is German soil, *Herr Lehrer.*"

"And don't you ever forget it!" Herr Burkhardt pulled down a large map and made the pointer dance. "This is *Grossdeutschland.* We are here, a few kilometers west of what has been known since the Napoleonic wars as the *General Gouvernement* or *Kongress Polen.* East Upper Silesia is where the empires of Austria, Russia, and Prussia once intersected. It was known as the *Dreikaiserecke,*" the three emperors' corner. He added that "the majority of the population in this area decided in a plebiscite—that's a vote—that they preferred to be governed by Germany." He circled lands west of Krakow on the map. "They voted in favor of being part of Germany. Always remember," he looked in my direction, poking the map with the pointer, "that it is holy German ground." He paused, then continued, with his voice rising, "After the *Endsieg,* when our enemies are defeated, and the Jews are dead and gone, all of this,"—he encircled on the map northern and southern Europe, the Balkans, parts of the Soviet Union, and parts of Africa—"will be one glorious German Reich. The Führer has promised that it will last for one thousand years." At that point, the bell rang. Herr *Lehrer* raised his arm, shouted a triumphant *"Heil Hitler,"* and the class followed his example.

I wonder what Herr Burkhardt thought, in the late fall of 1944, when he closed the classroom windows to keep out the sounds of artillery fire, carried on the wind from the east?

Luckily, I had four classes that provided relief from Herr Burkhardt. One was the botany class which met in a sunny room at the end of the hall, where a woman teacher—I do not remember her name—showed us how to collect, classify, dry, and press flowers and plants between heavy books. Back home *Kräuterlieschen's* teachings had awakened in me a passion for plants. In botany class, I learned the Latin names of plants, which we mounted between waxed paper and displayed on the walls in the school's hallway. When a medicinal herb collection office opened in Krenau, I ventured forth with two large split-oak baskets, which I filled with horsetail, yarrow, plantain, willow leaves, linden tree blossoms, comfrey, goldenrod and blackberry leaves. I received points for each basket I turned in and the promise that at some time in the future, I would receive the tidy sum of fifty pfennig for each basket of herbs. I planned to add the money to the two hundred Reichsmark in my savings account and dreamed that, together with the income I earned by selling flowers I raised for the tables of the big hotel in town, I would be rich someday.

The second class was English, which consisted of everybody taking turns reading short paragraphs from stories, and then translating them into German. The language exercises included the endless declination of verbs as well as vocabulary drills during which the teacher called on us to identify between fifteen and twenty new words each day. The third class, physical education, was fun. I was good in gymnastics, and I could out-sprint and out-jump most of the students in my class, although I was the shortest and the youngest. Dressed in black satin shorts and white shirts emblazoned with a swastika, we gathered once a week to practice after school on the athletic field. Once a month I competed with girls my own age and regularly won the 100 meter-dash and the broad jump. When I led our relay team to victory, nobody seemed to care that I was a Protestant.

The fourth class, in which Herr Zelter had us read Nordic mythology, I found exciting. We learned about the god Wotan, who had magic and power and his son Thor, who rode through the sky, throwing thunderbolts in every direction. After we finished the required lessons, Herr Zelter put on his glasses, made himself comfortable behind his desk, and read to us from the *Iliad* and the *Odyssey*. He lamented, "How I wish that you could read these in the original."

Mutti didn't like it when I listened to Adolf Hitler's speeches on the radio. I couldn't understand most of what he was shouting about anyway. It was always the same: about our enemies, foreign and domestic, about honor, bravery, blood and sacrifice for our great fatherland, and about victory, of course. Some of what he said I had already heard from Herr Burkhardt. But I shivered, and my heart pounded in my ears when I heard the roar of thousands cheering, *"Sieg Heil, Sieg Heil! Sieg Heil!"*

I asked why the Führer spoke with such a strange accent. For once, my father did not hesitate to answer, "He's not a German."

"Not German?"

"No, Austrian by birth." As an aside, Papa added, "Your mother and I saw him in the late twenties getting off an airplane at a small airfield. We didn't think much about it at the time."

"Herr Burkhardt said that he was born in Braunau, on the Inn River."

"That's in Austria. It was annexed in 1938." He added, "What's important is that you don't believe everything your teachers say, and don't repeat what you overhear at home."

Although I recalled what he and Mutti had said in the past, I wanted to see if he had changed his mind, so, I asked, "Why?"

It didn't surprise me when he replied in a brusque tone, "Because it's dangerous."

Angel in a Pond

Small circular ponds shimmered in the grazing land behind our house like burnished coins when the sun shone, but on cloudy days, they turned into ugly pockmarks. In previous years, workers from a nearby tile factory had dug out the buff colored clay and left the pits to fill with ground water. Now, cows quenched their thirst and waded in ponds to cool themselves. Children from the surrounding area joined the cows to frolic in the milky waters. On a hot summer afternoon in 1943, Sven and I decided to explore. "I don't think Mutti would mind if we looked around a bit, do you?" Sven asked.

I wasn't as sure as my brother and replied, "We should have told her where we were going."

"Let's hurry, and maybe nobody will miss us," Sven answered. We were drawn to a big pond, full of children bathing under the watchful eyes of women, who sat on blankets in the grass, surrounded by babies and toddlers and picnic baskets.

The water was refreshing after our run, and we splashed each other, happy to be out from under adult supervision. I played my favorite game of pretending to swim but suddenly lost the ground from under me. "Uh, oh, a hole," I thought, "Maybe if I let myself sink down, I'll be able to push back up to the surface." In seconds, I realized that the pond was too deep for me to reach the bottom. I held my breath, and with my eyes closed, propelled myself to the surface. When I thrust my head out of the water, I found myself in the middle of the pond. I tried to stay afloat, swallowed water, choked, coughed, and went under. When I opened my eyes, I saw that the diffused rays of the sun had turned the water into liquid gold. Looking up, I had a vision of an angel with enormous white wings floating above me. An angel? What was an angel doing in a pond? Then someone grabbed me by my hair and pulled my head out of the water. I saw a girl no older than I floating on two wings made of pillowcases filled with air. She spoke to me in Polish, a language I did not understand and pulled me to the edge of the pond. My eyes filled with tears as I coughed and coughed. Sven pounded my back. When I looked up, the girl had disappeared.

"Did you see her?" I asked my brother. He nodded.

"I wish I could have thanked her," I croaked. Neither one of us spoke, as we made our way back home and crawled unnoticed through a loose board in the fence at the back of the garden.

A few weeks later, I fell ill. I felt a sharp pain under my ribs, and it hurt every time I took a breath. Mutti put her cool hand on my forehead, took my temperature, and called the doctor. I was enthroned in my parent's bedroom when Doktor Shrenovski and his wife arrived. He listened with a stethoscope, knocked on my chest, and poked and prodded my body, while Mutti and the doctor's wife watched and talked in whispers. The doctor looked into my eyes, stuck a depressor on my tongue, and made me say, "*Aaaaah.*" He gave me a tablespoon of an ill-tasting black liquid from a purple bottle, a short pat on the head, and mumbled, "This'll make the pain go away. I'll be back tomorrow." He packed up the medication and his instruments and headed for the door, followed by his wife and Mutti. I heard him say, "Collapse," and "we'll have to see what develops," before he left the room.

I began to shiver uncontrollably. A minute later, I pulled the covers off, because I was too hot. Then I began to shake again. When Mutti returned, I asked her between chattering teeth, "What did the doctor say?"

"He said that your body is trying to fight off an infection."

"Am I going to die?"

"No, of course not, dear." She gave me a drink of water, reached over to stroke my tangled hair, tried to wipe the worried look from my forehead, and added, "We're going to have to move you back to your room."

"Why?"

"I'm sorry, dear, but until we're sure what's causing your illness, we're going to have to isolate you."

"Because I might infect everybody?"

Mutti nodded, wrapped me in a blanket, and helped me across the hallway into my own bed. I felt the cool linen absorb the heat of my body and dozed off. I dreamt I was swathed in a bed sheet and lifted by invisible strings above my bed. When I awakened, I was alone and the room smelled of disinfectant.

The next day, I was too weak to make my way to the bathroom, and when I found a chamber pot under my bed, I was grateful that Mutti had anticipated my need. When I was finished, I noticed that something was wrong. My legs buckled. I held on to the side of the bed for support and called out, "Mutti, come quickly." She must have been nearby and was at my side in seconds. "Look." I pointed to the contents of the chamber pot, "It's white."

Mutti didn't answer right away. She tucked me back in bed, checked my eyes, and made me wash my hands in a bowl of water laced with disinfectant. "I think I know what's wrong," she said quietly. "We'll see what the doctor says, but I believe you may have to stay in bed for a while."

I was feeling so weak and addled I didn't reply. For days—Mutti later told me that it was more like two weeks—I hardly budged. I slept most of the time. Every time Mutti entered the room, she took her white nurse's smock from a hook, put it on, washed her hands in a bowl of disinfectant, took my temperature, checked my pulse, and entered the numbers on a chart. She continued to urge me to swallow some vile tea and eat a few spoonfuls of a bland oat mush that looked like snot. Upon leaving my room, she took off her smock and washed her hands in disinfectant. I vaguely remember the doctor's visiting every day. He checked my chart, listened to my heart, poked and prodded my belly, but didn't say a word until he and Mutti entered the hallway, where they talked in whispers.

One day, Mutti stood at the entrance to my room, with Dagmar sitting on the crook of her arm. My sister had a bouquet of daisies in her outstretched hand. "For Eycke." She stuck her nose into the flowers, gave a fake sneeze, and flashed a smile.

"Not now, dear. Your sister is sick, and you'll have to wait until she gets better."

The sweet scent from the flowering jasmine bush near the gate drifted through the open window. The voices of my brothers and sister at play—even their quarrelling—sounded exciting. Karlo's barking, hens clucking, and geese honking made me feel even lonelier. I whined to my mother, "It's vacation time, and I was so looking forward to playing and swimming. I need to tend my flower beds and supply the hotel with fresh flowers. Besides, my eyes hurt from all that reading, and I don't like being alone so much."

"Try to be patient, dear. We have no medicine that'll cure you. Your body has to heal itself." My mother promised to bring me some of her art books, and new colored pencils and paper. But I wasn't ready to let Mutti leave. I asked, "What did the doctor say I have, anyway?"

"He said that you have paratyphoid and that your liver has been affected."

"Is that why my skin is yellow?"

"Yes, and your eyes."

"My eyes are no longer blue?"

Yes, they are. It's the whites of your eyes that have turned yellow."

"It's a good thing Sven and Frank haven't seen me. I would never hear the end of it. What is it I have? Para? How come I'm the only one who is sick?"

"It's called paratyphoid. We'll never know for sure why you are the only one who caught it. Maybe you swallowed some bad water. But I'll tell you what. Tomorrow, we'll help you practice walking, and then you can watch from the window what's going on outside."

"And when may I have some tasty food?"

"We'll ask the doctor. Perhaps you can start on a normal diet soon. But you won't be able to eat anything with butter, fat, or sugar for a while."

The most wonderful thing that happened was that Papa came on a weekend furlough. He breezed into the room, wearing his uniform, and gave me a big hug and a kiss. He brought with him the smell of fresh air and sunshine. "How are you, *mein Schatz?*" he asked, and without waiting for an answer, he continued, "I hear you're feeling better and can't wait to get out of bed." He encircled my wrist with his sunburned hand and commented, "Oh, dear, you've lost a lot of weight. Haven't they been feeding you?"

"The doctor put me on a diet of bland, slimy oatmeal gruel and bitter tea. But Mutti said that she'd ask the doctor if I could have some regular food soon. Please remind her."

"What would you say if I told you that I'm going bird hunting tomorrow? And, if I am lucky, I'll shoot a couple of squabs. Mutti will roast them especially for you. Wouldn't that be a treat?"

With the biggest smile I could muster, I answered, "That would be wonderful, but why do you say, 'If I am lucky?' You are the best shot in the world." I smacked my lips. "I can already taste those birds, brown and crispy and delicious."

"Then, you shall have your roasted squabs, and I'll talk to the doctor myself." He gave me another hug and was gone.

Papa's visit left me feeling all happy inside.

For the next two days, I could hear Papa's voice in and around the house. He peppered the boys and the maids with commands. He shouted, and he scolded when the work wasn't done well or fast enough to suit him. I had visions of the whole household running around like crazy to please him. "Come on, Sven and Frank, let's get some work done. Rabbits need fresh dandelions, and Mutti needs kindling and firewood. Dagmar, you are big enough to check the chicken nests for fresh eggs. Here is a basket." On and on he went, causing me to secretly admit, that, at least for today, I didn't mind at all staying in bed.

Papa kept his promise. For Sunday dinner, he and Mutti came to my room. Mutti carried a tray with mashed potatoes, peas and carrots, and two squabs, roasted to perfection. They watched me lift the plate to my nose and smell the food, before I gobbled up every single morsel. I even sucked on the tiny bones. I was tempted to lick my plate, but I decided to mind my manners. "Thank you. I feel so much better," I beamed. My parents looked at each other and back at me and smiled.

"Good," they said in one voice.

"And tomorrow, we'll try to get you back on your legs," Mutti promised before they left the room.

Since I had been bedridden for over a month, my legs were too weak to support my body. Mutti and one of our maids had to hold me up while I practiced walking. The first day it seemed as if they had to drag me across the room. "My legs don't mind me any more," I complained. But I got stronger day by day, and after a week or so, I wobbled across the room by myself to wave and shout out the window, "Hey there, boys. I'm getting better, and before long I'll be able to boss you around again."

My brothers waved and hooted. Sven yelled back, "We'll see about that."

Frank grinned, made a few coltish jumps, and echoed, "Yeah, we'll see about that."

No matter how hard our mother and the maids tried, they were unable to keep track of my siblings and me. We roamed around the garden and the meadow outside the fence. Our biggest attractions were the three ponds on our property. One day, Frank asked Dagmar to join him on an egg hunt. When she refused, he called her a baby and jumped onto the planks leading to the ducks' nesting coop in the middle of the round pond. He crawled inside the house and emerged carrying two eggs. With his pocketknife, he punched a hole in each egg and sucked out the contents, grinned, rubbed his stomach in an exaggerated fashion, and waved. On his return trip, he teetered on the narrow boards, leapt off, and ran past us in the direction of the swimming pond, where Sven was busy hammering the last nails into a wooden raft. "What have you been up to?" Sven asked.

"Sucking eggs."

"Just as I thought. A good thing Mutti didn't catch you."

Frank shrugged his shoulders and stuck out his tongue.

"Yep, you do get away with all kinds of stuff," Sven commented dryly, as he tightened a rope on his raft and boasted, "Nice job, if I say so myself."

"Show-off," Frank responded. "It's going to sink."

"We'll see," Sven countered confidently. Dagmar pleaded for Sven to give her a ride on his raft. Instead, he got her to help him look for a beanpole in the garden, to be used to test the depth of the pond. He pulled the pole out of the water, set it next to his sister, pointed to the wet mark, and patiently explained that the water was too deep for her. Disappointed, she watched Sven jump onto his raft and pole along the edge of the pond.

Meanwhile, Frank crept Indian-style along the shore. With his shirt in his right hand, he was poised to throw it on a frog as soon as he spied one. When two frogs splashed into the water in front of him, Frank decided to go after them. Paying no attention to our warning to stay out of the water, he stripped off his pants and entered the pond. He managed to entice Dagmar into the water by promising her a piggyback ride, and before anyone could interfere, Dagmar followed him into the water. She climbed on his back and held on to his neck. Frank choked and went under. Dagmar swallowed water, coughed, let go, and sank. Sven poled over to where they had disappeared. I rushed over in time to watch Frank's head pop out of the water. He held on to a tree root while Dagmar floated face up, eyes wide open, just under the surface. Sven grabbed her by the hair and pulled her onto the raft, where she coughed up water. He maneuvered the raft back to the dock, helped her get off, and smacked her on the back the way he had seen Mutti do when we swallowed something the wrong way. He yelled at Frank that he was an idiot and to get his naked butt out of the water.

Frank shouted back, "You can't make me," and "It's her fault. She choked me and then let go." I ran into the house to get Mutti.

Dagmar was still coughing and crying, when Mutti appeared and demanded to know what was going on. "Frank and I went under. Sven pulled me out," Dagmar blurted out between sobs. Mutti ordered Frank out of the water and Sven off the raft. She then took Dagmar's hand and yelled at them for playing in the water without adult supervision, scolded me for not watching out for them, and threatened to tell Papa what had happened.

Ivan and his Cow

I believe it was the early summer of 1943. It seemed that German troops were fighting all over the world and, after some setbacks, winning battles in North Africa and the Ukraine. Papa was home on furlough when Sven waved to us to come and have a look. "Papa, there's an old man coming up the driveway, leading a cow," Sven shouted.

Papa, giving Dagmar a piggyback ride, shouted back, "Don't just stand there, boy. Open up the gate. Let's find out what he wants."

Papa, Sven, Dagmar, and I watched, as the man slowly walked toward us on feet wrapped in dirty and torn rags, stopping at the gate. Sven and I rushed up to the gate to watch him lean his walking stick against the fence, put down a sack securely tied with a rope, straighten, and rub his lower back. While he tied his cow to the gate post, we heard him talking to her, "What you thinking, Ruschka? Barn looks good. This good place for you give birth to calf?"

Ruschka looked with her big brown eyes at the old man and, as if in agreement, replied with a sonorous, *"Moooooooo."*

"You like? I go ask then." He gently patted her rump, took off his grimy cap, wiped his forehead with his right arm, spit into his hands, slicked back his graying hair, and replaced his cap. He smiled at us and entered the compound, where Papa waited to greet him. "Good afternoon, dear sir," the visitor said, took off his cap and bowed low. "God's blessings on you and your family." He bowed once again.

Papa introduced himself and put Dagmar down, so that she could chase a duck and her clutch of ducklings, which had escaped from their pen. "Welcome." He pointed to the man's feet, "Been walking a long time? Come, rest." They walked toward the table and benches under the beech tree. Papa sent Sven to the kitchen for food and drink while he and the old man took a seat. Turning to our visitor, Papa asked, "What's your name? Where are you from, and where are you going?"

In broken German and with a peculiar accent, rolling his R's, the old man answered, as he pointed toward the southeast, "My name Ivan. Cow and I walk from home, Ukraine."

146

"All the way? You have a family?"

"Yes," he bowed. "Grandfather come from Germany in Czar's time." He paused, wiping beads of perspiration from his forehead with a dirty rag. "Czar, grandfather, father—all dead now." He crossed himself. "I hear fighting. Leave wife, take Ruschka." He pointed toward his cow. "We walk long time. Ruschka, she big," he made a circle with both arms. "Soon have calf. Need place to stay. You have big barn. Ruschka have calf. You, me have milk," he offered, as he rasped his enormous, calloused hands against each other.

Sven sidled up to Ivan and asked, "You left your wife behind?"

With a grin, Ivan answered, "Wife, she talk too much. She no want to walk. Cow walk. No trouble. No argue with Ivan."

"I understand," Papa chortled.

Sven and I hung around, gaped at our visitor, and listened to every word. When Sven heard Ivan's explanation about leaving his wife behind, he gave me a nudge. "Did you hear that? No wonder he took his cow," he whispered in my ear and winked. I made a face and stuck out my tongue.

Genia, who joined us after Gela moved away, brought a beaker of water, which Ivan gulped, causing his Adam's apple to bob up and down. We watched him wolf down the slices of dark rye bread with homemade strawberry jam. He wiped his moustache on his sleeve when he was finished.

"We might be able to work something out," Papa said, rubbing the stubble on his chin. "There's plenty of room in the barn for your cow. We could use an extra hand. We have many mouths to feed, and we grow most of our own food. My wife would love to have fresh milk."

"God's blessing on you and your family, dear sir." The old man put his hands together and bowed. Ivan had taken off his coat, which had hung from his short sturdy frame like discarded garments on a scarecrow. He folded it neatly and placed it on the bench beside him. When the coat was new, it may have been black or brown, but years of rain, wind, sun and dirt had turned it an eggplant purple, accentuated with shiny brown patches down the front and around the pockets. Ivan wore a frayed, collarless shirt, a heavy long-sleeved undershirt, and a pair of tattered pants. The bottoms of his pants were tucked into the rags wrapped around his feet all the way up to his ankles. Because of the many layers of rags, his feet looked bulbous and enormous, like those of an elephant.

"We'll have to find a pair of boots for you," Papa suggested.

"No have work boots." Ivan looked at his feet and shook his head. "Good boots for Sunday in bundle." He suddenly remembered his cow and pointed to the gate. He got up, put on his cap, and asked, "With kind permission, sir. Me take care of Ruschka." He bowed and hurriedly walked toward the gate. Papa followed.

"You may let her drink from the creek, and tie her up to graze. I'll have a bed made up for you next to the kitchen," Papa offered.

"Please, sir, with kind permission. Me prefer sleep in barn next to Ruschka," Ivan said, as he lifted his cap and scratched his short, cropped hair.

"Goodness," I thought, "He's got lice. Our mother is not going to like that, especially since she just finished giving Dagmar and me one of those stinking delousing treatments."

"Agreed," Papa replied as he shook hands with Ivan. "When you've taken care of your cow, come meet my wife, and I'll show you around the barn."

"I think that Papa was mighty pleased about Ivan showing up," I told Sven.

"Why wouldn't he be?" he answered. "Ivan has a cow. Besides, Papa is always inviting people to come stay with us. I already know what Mutti is going to say when Papa brings home another mouth to feed 'It's all right, Karl. We'll put a little more water in the soup.'"

Ivan settled down in the livestock barn with Ruschka. Every chance she got, Dagmar sneaked through a hole in the fence into the meadow and waited patiently for Ruschka to lift her tail and deposit dark green mounds. When Ruschka's calf arrived, Ivan named it Nuschka. I begged him to teach me how to milk Ruschka. Ivan smiled kindly, but shook his head and wouldn't even let me touch her. He brought pails of creamy milk into the kitchen. Mutti strained it through cheesecloth and poured herself a glass. "I like it rich and still warm," she said as she drank, relishing every last drop. We scooped up the rich cream, which had risen to the top of the pail, and Genia churned it into butter. I liked my cream whipped and heaped on top of fresh strawberries from the garden. Papa's favorite evening meal was a bowl of sour milk, sprinkled with sugar and cinnamon and served with a slice of dark rye bread.

Every day at lunchtime, Ivan came in from the barn, took off his ratty cap, hung it on a hook, spit in his hands, and slicked down his hair. He pumped some water into a bowl, washed and dried his hands and sat down at the kitchen table by the window. Mutti placed an enormous bowl with steaming potatoes and vegetables in front of him. He bowed his head, folded his hands, mumbled a prayer, and crossed himself. He hunched over, encircled the bowl with his left arm, and began shoveling the food into his mouth. Sven, Frank, and I watched with amazement as he chewed and swallowed every morsel. I wondered if he were going to eat the bowl next.

"Ivan, would you like some more?" Mutti asked him. He nodded and polished off another serving.

"Amazing," Sven whispered to Frank. "Even I could never, ever eat that much. Could you?"

"Sure I could," Frank bragged.

"Let's see you try, then," Sven challenged his brother.

"I could if I wanted to, but I don't want to," Frank answered in a snippy tone.

"Yeah, just what I thought," Sven replied.

On Sunday mornings, Ivan came into the kitchen, carrying a chipped enamel bowl. He asked for warm water, which he carried back to the pump in the barnyard. After he slowly lathered up with a cake of soap, he scrubbed his face, neck, and hands and squinted into the shard of a mirror tacked up next to a long leather strap he used for sharpening his knife. He grimaced as he shaved the stubble from his chin up to his high cheekbones and dried himself off with a towel.

The creases on his leathery, sun-dried face, neck, and hands were so deep that the dirt between them never disappeared no matter how hard he scrubbed. We never did see him take off his shirt, and we figured that must have been the reason why a pungent odor followed him around. After he finished shaving, he wet his hair, and parted and combed it. Then he moved his head from right to left and smiled, exposing the few teeth he had left, his tiny eyes twinkling at his image in the mirror. Satisfied, he disappeared into the barn. A short time later, he emerged wearing a hat, his Sunday boots, and a black suit. The suit was a bit worn, but in spite of the wisps of hay clinging to it here and there, it looked quite respectable. Under his right arm, Ivan carried his well-worn Bible. "My German grandfather's," he explained to us with pride. With his left hand, Ivan led Ruschka by a rope. Her calf followed close behind. They walked slowly and solemnly—as if on their way to an important occasion—through the front gate and into the meadow where Ivan tied up Ruschka and sat down in the shade of the big birch tree. Sven and I followed them and sat down at a distance. Ivan took no notice of us. He removed his hat, pulled his Bible from under his arm, crossed himself, licked his thumb and right index finger, and, with his calloused hand, leafed through the good book until he found the text he was looking for. Pointing at the lines with the finger he had just moistened, he read to Ruschka in a loud and grave voice. From time to time, he pointed to the sky and gesticulated as if to make an important point, and then he would ask Ruschka, "You hear that? God loves *all* creatures who walk this earth: you, little Nuschka, me and Laabs family."

Music Lessons

Sven and I stood side-by-side, facing Herr Professor Tarkovski. A tall man with a mane of white hair and a patrician demeanor, he was dressed in a black suit and an impeccable white shirt and black bow tie. We were gathered in my room for our weekly violin lessons. He sat on a chair next to the old, out-of-tune harpsichord. The Professor began each lesson by inquiring in lilting German, "Eycke, would you permit me to tune your violin?" He gently took the violin from my hand and put it under his chin, as if it were a precious instrument. With his ear close to the instrument, he plucked the strings and turned the pegs until he was satisfied before he started tuning Sven's violin.

After we had scratched out our scales, the Professor asked us to play a simple piece from Mozart's *Magic Flute*. "Stand up straight and control your bow. You mustn't let it dance all over the place," he reminded us. "Up and down, up and down," he added, "and watch where you place your fingers. I would like to hear pure tones, only pure tones, if you please."

At the end of each lesson, Herr Professor politely asked for my violin, removed a neatly folded handkerchief from his pocket, placed it on the neckpiece and, with a flourish, gently put the child-sized instrument under his chin. The old gentleman stood with his eyes closed as he elicited the most exquisite sounds from my ordinary violin. I let the magic of his music carry me to a place, a source of beauty and light that gave me a fleeting sense of oneness with something sublime.

My brother was less impressed by those performances. He took advantage of the fact that the Professor played with his eyes closed, and with exaggerated motions, mimicked him behind his back. When the Professor finished, he placed the violin into my hands and thanked me. Referring to the composer of the piece he had played, he said, "Remember the great Paganini, Maestro unequaled."

It was the spring of 1944. Professor Tarkovski had been teaching Sven and me for a year and a half when an official called on my mother. He clicked his heels, saluted *"Heil Hitler,"* and informed her that it had come to the attention of the authorities that a certain Tarkovski had been giving lessons to her son and daughter. He added that Polish nationals were prohibited from teaching German children.

I watched my mother's face turn crimson. "You can't be serious," she said. In a mocking tone she continued, "Are you afraid that the old gentleman is going to shoot somebody with his bow?" Her wrath swelling, she added, "Herr Professor Tarkovski was first violinist of the Berlin Philharmonic. He is a renowned musician, now forced to give lessons to children. First, you robbed him of his precious instrument. I wonder if the fact that it was a Stradivarius had anything to do with it? Now, you're taking away his livelihood? Is there no end to this chicanery?" She shook her head. "It is unbelievable."

In a voice low, calm, and haughty, the man enunciated each word carefully. "If you do not comply … steps will be taken. The lessons are to be discontinued immediately, and your children must enroll in the *Musikschule* run by the Hitler Youth." He looked at me, paused for a moment, and then raised his voice a notch. "Furthermore, your daughter should have been enrolled in the *Jungmädel* last November when she turned ten. We expect her to appear at the health department for a physical examination tomorrow." He clicked his heels, saluted "*Heil Hitler*," turned around and left.

My mother remained agitated, but she finally decided that Sven and I would have to start attending music school once a week. At the same time, she brazenly requested that Professor Tarkovski be allowed to supervise our practice sessions. My mother got her way, because, first, she was considered *kinderreich*, being the mother of four children and therefore due special consideration; second, she explained that she was too busy nursing a sick child and tending to the rest of her offspring to supervise our violin practice; and third, because she was not easily intimidated.

The arrangement for the so-called practice sessions suited Sven and me just fine, because the Professor had so much more patience than our mother. Once after Sven missed a note repeatedly, Mutti shouted, "This noise is anything but music. You are hopeless," and bopped him on the head with his bow. To her and his utter surprise, the bow broke in half. She looked at the broken bow in her hand, then at Sven and back at the bow. She dropped it on the floor, stroked his head as if to reassure herself that she had done no serious harm, or perhaps to let him know that she was sorry, and fled the room.

Mutti's surprised look puzzled and amused me. After all, I thought, what did she expect? Bows are not made for hitting children over the head. They are intended for making music. On the other hand, I had to admit, who would call what we were making, music?

Sven rubbed his head and broke into a devilish grin. He picked up the bow and followed our mother out the door, proudly bearing it like a trophy before him. I heard him brag to Frank, "Now, do you believe me? Didn't I tell you that I have a hard head?"

The following Wednesday, I set out for the music school with my violin and my recorder. Sven followed reluctantly, several steps behind, griping. We had only to walk up our driveway, turn left, and walk another two blocks along Auchwitzer Strasse to Sonnen Strasse. There on the corner stood an old stucco villa painted a dirty yellow. Fräulein Bensch, the woman director, was young and pretty. She wore the uniform of the *Bund Deutscher Mädchen*. She smiled, welcomed us, and showed us around the school. She introduced us to the other children and began teaching us the violin and recorder in groups of ten. We played simple pieces by Mozart and Haydn. I was disappointed that Fräulein Bensch never performed for us the way Professor Tarkovski did. Instead, after each lesson, she taught us rousing marching songs:

Unsere Fahne flattert uns voran.	Our flag flutters in the wind.
Und die Fahne ist mehr als der Tod.	Our flag is greater than death.

Another song glorified Horst Wessel, a Storm Trooper martyr:

Die Fahne hoch,	High flies the flag,
Die Reihen fest geschlossen,	We march in closed ranks,
SA marschiert …	SA is marching …

Followed by *Deutschland, Deutschland über Alles,* which I had learned to sing in first grade.

A large portrait of Adolf Hitler, glowering at us with piercing black eyes, hung on the wall above our heads. Fräulein Bensch told us about our Führer and his struggle to lead Germany into a great future. She said, "The Führer loves all children and wants you to be healthy in body and excel in every endeavor for the fatherland. He wants you to discipline yourselves, to become as swift as greyhounds and as strong as Krupp steel." "Above all," she added, "You must be prepared to shed your last drop of blood in defense of our fatherland and for the Führer." At the end of the first class, Fräulein Bensch gave each of us a photograph of a smiling Führer accepting a bouquet of wild flowers from a small blond girl. I put the picture in my pocket. On my way home, I thought about what Fräulein Bensch had said about this man with the burning eyes and the black mustache. He's the one I blamed for Papa leaving us for years at a time. In the photograph Fräulein Bensch had given us, he beamed and looked as if he liked children. But how could this be? He couldn't possibly love all children. Nobody did. It all sounded quite puzzling, and I wished I had had the courage to ask what our bodies, fast dogs, steel and spilled blood had to do with music.

It did make me think of what had happened a year ago in the early spring of 1943, before Papa got into trouble, was fired from his job, and was drafted into the Luftwaffe. I had taken a different way to school and was passing a large red brick building, an old school, when I heard wailing and crying from inside. What was going on? Who were these weeping people, and what were the uniformed guards doing in front of the doors? I stopped and looked through the iron fence into the courtyard. It was as if I had come upon a dark place, where unexplained and diabolical events were taking place, the kind of things one is afraid to look at. I tried to imagine what was going on behind the walls, when a soldier noticed me and without saying a word, motioned with his rifle for me to move on. With the sound of crying in my ear, I paid little attention in school that day. When I returned home that afternoon, I told my parents what I had seen. My father explained, "Bad things are happening." He looked at my mother who shook her head. Papa paused. It seemed that he was thinking about what to tell me before he continued: "The voices you heard were those of Jewish families." He took a handkerchief from his pocket, took off his glasses, turned around to blow his nose, and gave me his wave, which meant, "I don't want to talk about it any more."

I reasoned that if bad things could happen to Jewish children, they could just as easily happen to my brothers, my sister, and me. I imagined myself in their place. I had sensed for a time that our family was in some kind of danger. Why did the Gestapo agent, Latz, keep snooping and sniffing around? I asked my mother that day, "When are they going to come for us? What shall I pack?" Then I remembered the linden tree. Yes. There I would be safe, secluded under its branches and near the pond, where white water lilies floated on black water and iridescent dragonflies darted back and forth. There I would hide and breathe in the fragrance of its blossoms.

My father stayed home from work the next day. He appeared to be sick, vomiting and looking pale. I had the feeling that he knew a lot more than he had told me.

*   *   *

Thirty-five years later, my father recalled how enraged and powerless he had felt about what he had witnessed that day. With his list, he had arrived at a large, grassy fenced-in field where Jews from the town and the surrounding areas were routinely rounded up before a selection. As had happened in the past, he expected that he would be able to obtain the release of the men and women on the list he carried in his pocket. What Papa saw, instead, were dozens of infants in carriages surrounded by a group of older children. Watching over them were town elders and the Jewish Police. Their parents were nowhere in sight. An SS officer in charge of a *Sonderkommando,* dressed in a black uniform and shiny, black boots, paced back and forth, in front of his troops. "Gentlemen," proclaimed the officer arrogantly. "You see those children? Shortly a pile of gold will be placed at my feet." He turned to the Jews. "I'll give you pigs a chance to save your children. If you bring me your treasures, I shall let them go."

My father described what happened next, "The Jewish elders did as the SS officer commanded, but the officer refused to keep his word. Instead, he pointed to the children with his riding crop and sneered, 'I want those children more than you do.' He faced his soldiers and ordered, 'Take them to Auschwitz.'

"He [the officer] looked like an ordinary sort of man. Except that he, like all the others, was driven by a lust to dominate, to brutalize, to exterminate. They are still looking for him. One day they'll find him. If I could have, I would have killed the bastard that morning, but I couldn't." He paused to wipe away his tears. "I will never forget those children."

The Lair of the Fox

After school and during summer vacation, we spent most of the day outside, doing chores or playing in and around our ponds.

The black surface of the swimming pond reflected the tall poplars and birch trees, until my brothers and I broke the spell. We shouted, "*Auf die Plätze, fertig, los!*" Get set, ready, go, and jumped through the mirror—naked as usual—scaring dozens of frogs that plopped into the water behind us. The water, warmed by the sun, enveloped me, and I shivered with delight and revulsion at the thick, velvety muck on the bottom of the pond, squishing between my toes. Sven climbed on his rickety raft and paddled around the pond, hunting tiny bugs, which skated on spidery legs across the surface of the water. Frank, who was too short to reach the bottom, pulled himself along the steel cable stretched across the pond. I pretended to swim, doing breaststrokes, splashing the water with one leg, and hopping along on the other. "Mutti, watch me. I can swim," I boasted. Mutti smiled and shook her head. "Be careful," she warned.

Most days, Mutti was busy cooking and gardening or telling the maids, my siblings, and me what to do. But, she had not been well lately, and that day she seemed lost in thought as she sat quietly on her bench under the pine tree, dressed in a billowy, blue and white garment. Dagmar played at her feet near the edge of the pond. Sven teetered precariously on his raft. He imitated my movement by standing on one leg and extending the other one behind him. He wiggled his foot and moved both arms in semicircles in front of him. He laughed raucously and nearly upset the raft as he mocked, "Mutti, look at me, I can swim, I can swim."

I didn't appreciate my brother's performance and shot back, "Go drown yourself, you ugly toad." That, of course, spurred him on to more grotesque pantomimes until he tipped over the raft and came up sputtering but still laughing.

All the shouting and splashing had gotten Mutti's attention. "I have to go into the house for a minute," she called out. "While I am gone, I want you to get out of the water and watch Dagmar." We obeyed reluctantly. Sven and Frank played one of their favorite games. With sticks they stirred the grass around the pond, which started the frogs hopping. Dagmar continued dressing and undressing her doll. I sat on the steps leading to the pond and let the sun warm me. That is when I heard the faint sound of a plane in the distance. The boys stopped bothering the frogs and listened too. We looked up and saw the plane. From a distance it looked like a toy. We had experienced air raids when we visited Germany, but it was unusual to hear or see planes in our part of Poland. We watched as the plane began to circle with the sunrays glinting off its silvery wings. A high whistling sound followed by a succession of explosions made us jump. Dagmar began to cry. When I grabbed her hand, I noticed that both of us were shaking.

"Air raid! Duck!" Sven yelled, but instead of ducking, we craned to watch a plume of black smoke grow in the clear northeastern sky over the poppy field.

"Let's hide," I shouted.

"Hide where?" Sven shouted back.

"In the barn, hurry." I pulled Dagmar behind me and motioned Sven and Frank to follow.

"I want to see," Frank begged.

"You wanna die? Move your naked ass," Sven yelled at his brother and grabbed his hand. Running, shouting and wailing, we crossed the hundred yards to the hay barn and scrambled through the open trap into the cool, dank cellar.

Next to the linden tree, the hay barn was my favorite hiding place. I used to climb high up into the rafters, spread my arms, and abandon myself to the thrill of flying into the hay below. There I would lie on the mounds of sweet hay that we had harvested during the summer, watch dust motes dance in rays of sunshine, and dream of rescuing a downed enemy flyer and hiding him in the barn. I had explored every nook and cranny of that hundred-year-old barn, except for the root cellar. The rectangular space, dug into the soil below the floor, struck me as too dark and scary. But that is where we found refuge on that sunny afternoon.

"I'm cold," Dagmar cried out.

"I know, dear. So am I," I answered.

"Me, too," added Sven and Frank. Too scared to move any further into the darkness, we huddled next to each other near the entrance, where a shaft of light fell through the trap door. From time to time, I peered over my shoulders into the shadows.

"I think we had better stay here until somebody comes to get us," I whispered. My siblings responded with chattering teeth and by nodding their heads. It seemed like an eternity until we heard Mutti's panicky voice, "Genia, I left them at the pond. Check the barn."

When Sven suggested, "Let's get out of here," we didn't waste time. We scampered up the steps behind him. Mutti met us near the trap door and gathered us into her arms. I noticed that her cheeks were wet.

"Let's get you warmed up," she suggested, her voice trembling. She and Genia wrapped us in blankets and made us take a warm bath before they pampered us with hot apple cider.

The plane, which had long disappeared from the sky, had blown up the oil refinery near Trzebinia, about three miles to the northeast of our location. The date was September 9, 1944. It "rained" oil for three days, staining the white sheets on the clothesline and covering the ponds and every leaf with a glistening, iridescent film.

*　　　　*　　　　*

What I did not know was that between 1941 and February, 1943, the house and property at Auschwitzer Strasse 36b became the temporary hiding place for many Jews. Papa revealed to Mutti the atrocities he witnessed, but, to protect us, he did not confide in her the details of all his rescue activities, although he had shared with Mutti most of his efforts on behalf of the Hartmann family.

Mutti had become acquainted with Mother Hartmann and her children in 1942. She and Papa were their guests for a Sabbath celebration behind locked doors and closed curtains. In time, Mutti became especially close to two of the Hartmann children, Fanny and Mordecai. Mother Hartmann was fifty-one years old and sickly. Papa was concerned about what would happen if she were to be caught by the Nazis during an *Aktion.* Fanny recalled Papa's advice, "Go tell your mother to hide, do not allow her to go to the *Sammelplatz,*" the place where the Nazis rounded up and separated those destined for labor camps from those who were destined for the death camps. But Mother Hartmann ignored Papa's warning and her children's pleas and accompanied them to the *Sammelplatz.* There, the Nazis tore her from Fanny's arms and dragged her away to be sent to Auschwitz. Papa remembered that Fanny arrived at his office minutes later, out of breath, distraught, and screaming hysterically, "Herr Baurat, Herr Baurat. Come quickly. Save my mother." It was too late. Papa was angry with Fanny, first, because she had not heeded his advice to keep her mother hidden, and, second, because she didn't think about the trouble she might cause for him and herself by making a scene in public. He recalled how profoundly powerless he felt for not being able to save Mother Hartmann. In the end, he vowed to redouble his efforts and save as many as he could from a similar fate.

One night in February, 1943, more than one hundred young Jews in small groups had arrived at our house after dark. They quietly slipped through the open gate, where Papa directed them to hide in the loft of the hay barn, in the root cellar, and, in other secret places on our property. He shared food, clothing, and money with those who were in need, and promised that he would try to take them to safety during the night.

An elder of the Jewish community had informed Papa that a large roundup or *Aktion* was planned the following day. During that roundup, the Police, the Gestapo and the SS would scour the town and arrest the remaining Jewish population for deportation. The elder asked Papa to find a way to transport some of their young people to Mislowitz. With the help of Sassmannshausen, who by that time had become an officer in the Nationalsozialistischer Fliegerkorps, the National Socialist Aviation Corps, Papa borrowed two military trucks. Sassmannshausen and Papa had become friends before 1933, when both were glider pilots and members of the Akademische Fliegerkorps, the Academic Aviators' Corps. Without asking questions, Sassmannshausen made the arrangement. It was planned that the trucks, whose drivers were bribed, would arrive during the night and wait at a designated place in town for Papa and the contingent of young Jews.

At three a.m., the young people crawled out of their hiding places. These hiding places were arranged like the lair of a fox and had a myriad of back entries and exits. Those who knew Papa, crowded around him and one called out, "You are our father, Herr Baurat. When we see your big hat, we know we'll be saved." He warned his charges of the danger ahead and, in his gruff but well-meaning manner, told them to "line up and keep your mouths shut."

Papa wore his aviator's uniform and an armband on his sleeve. He was armed with a machine pistol, carried a lantern in one hand, and led our watchdog with the other. As they marched toward town, auxiliary police stopped them, and demanded to know where Papa was taking the prisoners. Papa hurled their question back at them, "Where do you think I'm taking them? To Auschwitz, of course, where else? And, I don't have time to stand around talking to the likes of you." Apparently intimidated by his bravado, the police allowed the marchers to pass into town, where everybody climbed onto the trucks. Papa had them pile up their luggage in the rear of the trucks so that it would look as though the trucks carried cargo instead of people. Off they went to Mislowitz. Although no place in those years was one hundred percent secure for Jews, Papa had been assured that they would be in relative safety, at least for the time being. To make sure that they were all right, he visited them a week later. They welcomed him and invited him to share a meal.

When I asked Papa what happened to the Hartmanns, he shook his head and replied, "The boys were safe for the time being, but the girls were taken in the last big *Aktion* in front of my eyes. There was nothing I could do."

After the war, some of the women and men who owed their lives to my father began to search for him. Among these survivors, who had suffered unimaginably during their years in work and concentration camps, were the four Hartmann siblings—Fanny, her sisters Ester and Hava, and their brother Mordecai, the only brother who survived the Holocaust. After their liberation from the camps, in 1945, Fanny and Hava returned to Poland to look for family. They received a hostile reception from their Polish neighbors. They discovered that the rich and vibrant Jewish culture of their hometown had been totally annihilated by the Nazis. Not a single Jew survived in Chrzanow. Deeply distressed, the two sisters returned to Germany, where they were notified that their brother Sam perished on a death march somewhere in Germany during the last months of the war. They also received confirmation that their mother and their youngest brother, David, were murdered in Auschwitz. They never learned the fate of their oldest brother, Shmuel, who escaped to Russia before Papa met the family.

In the spring of 1948, my father received a telegram from Hava. A letter followed:

> Dear Herr Laabs,
> My letter will surprise you. After a long search, I was finally able to
> find out where you live. I am writing to you without delay. More than
> anything, I want to tell you who I am. My name is Hava Hartmann. Do you
> remember the town of Krenau in Eastern Silesia? During 1942, I worked
> at the reception desk, in the same building where the county development
> department was located. My brother worked in the zoning department as
> a stoker and in the summer in your garden. I have suffered much in the con-
> centration camps, but I shall remember you forever with the deepest
> gratitude. I shall never forget how you so often stood by us in those—for
> us—terrible times; how you even saved our lives and exposed yourself to
> danger. I have been looking for you for a long time. I would like to know
> how you, your dear-hearted wife, and your children are. Perhaps, I thought,
> I could repay you some way. Believe me, Herr Laabs, I would do anything
> in my power for you and your family. Even then, my gratitude would never
> be enough to repay for what you did for us. Please write back immediately.

I would be happy to hear from all of you. I shall tell you more in my next
letter. My address is Hava Hartmann, Passau/Bavaria, Maria-Hilfgasse 4.
I await with great anticipation your prompt answer. Meanwhile, I send you
and your family my best regards.
Yours forever-in-gratitude,
Hava Hartmann

A month later, we had a tearful reunion with Hava's sister Fanny, during a
surprise visit she and a friend paid us. They came bearing gifts of food, ration
stamps, and clothing, and told of the horrors they had lived through.

When the Hartmanns heard that my father, like all adult Germans, was being
subjected to a denazification proceeding, they and other former residents of
Krenau banded together. They wrote letters and gave evidence that my father had
risked his life by helping them escape death at the hands of the Nazis. Six former
residents of Krenau testified:

> We, the undersigned, Jews from Krenau, Poland, swear under oath that the
> architect, Karl Laabs, during the years 1941–1945, saved our lives from the
> terror and danger of the Gestapo. By doing so, he endangered his own life
> many times. Because of his work as a supervisor of building projects, he suc-
> ceeded in employing hundreds of Jews, thus saving them from certain
> death. When necessary, he found hiding places for many Jews. He saw
> to it that we would be fed, and he supplied us with documents enabling
> us to move about. He kept many Jews hidden at his own home. All of
> them were Jews destined for Auschwitz, who could find no other refuge.
> Mr. Laabs did all this, even though he knew that he was under continuous
> surveillance by the Gestapo.
> Signed: Salomon Maringer, Moses Limmer, Abraham Maringer, Sara
> Zimmer, Hania Bodnen, and Ezriel Rabinowicz

With the help of these and other testimonies, my father was cleared and once
again permitted to teach at a professional school and to resume his work as an
architect. The above letters are among many documents, which are on deposit at
Yad Vashem, in Jerusalem.

In May, 1983, Shimshon Schönberg, who had settled in Haifa, Israel, revealed
to me that my father had saved him and some of his colleagues three times from
transport to Auschwitz. Shimshon had been officially assigned to a municipal
work detail in a nearby town during the week. He had received a special permit
for that purpose from my father. However, instead of working, Shimshon was

able to stay home, or travel, or take care of his business, as long as he showed up at work for the official count every Friday before returning to his home for Shabbat. He recounted that on one occasion, my father had warned him of an impending roundup and directed him to an underground hiding place at the county gardening center, down the street from our home. There, Shimshon, his wife, their six-year-old daughter, and some friends hid out for two weeks, only surfacing once to obtain food.

Fanny, Hava, Ester, and Mordecai eventually married and applied for visas to Israel and the United States. Ester found a home in Israel. Fanny and Hava immigrated to Denver, Colorado, where I visited them in the 1980s. Mordecai raised his family in Indiana. With energy, courage and resilience, they all raised wonderful children and grandchildren.

In 1995, the Shoah Visual History Foundation, founded by Steven Spielberg, interviewed Hava. She recounted the horrors her family had endured, giving tribute to my father. She said, "… I would like to thank the Baurat for what he did for us, that he saved so many lives … this is such an unusual story. And I know that Baurat Laabs would be glad … he would see those people … alive and successful because of what he did … this man is one in a million … saving human lives and putting himself in the biggest danger possible."

Before Fanny passed away, she, too, gave an interview. She, too, told her family's story. She recalled that my father helped "maybe one hundred to one hundred and fifty boys to survive." She remembered that my father saved her "three times from the road to Auschwitz," and that "he helped my mother twice from going to Auschwitz," until the day he could no longer protect her. Fanny's most heart-rending account was of her mother being torn from her side and sent to Auschwitz. Fanny is now dead, and at peace. Hava still lives in Denver. She recently celebrated her eightieth birthday, is a proud mother and grandmother, revered, and loved by her family and friends.

The Warning

Around the end of August, Madam Chicowa began to warn Mutti, "Frau Baurat, tonight lock all doors and windows. Take dog, children in bedroom. Turn off light. Not move."

Mutti was startled, "But, Madam Chicowa, why?"

"Partisans."

"How do you know?"

"From my daughter. She hates Germans. You good people. I tell you. The Baurat, he save Polish workmen from hanging."

"Thank you. I'll do as you say." Mutti decided to bring Karlo inside.

He bit me," Frank protested.

I told him, "You can only hope that he has forgotten how mean you were to him."

Sven reminded Frank, "Karlo wouldn't have bitten you if you hadn't poked him with a stick."

"See here? I still have the scars." Frank showed us four scars from puncture wounds. Frank's screams had brought the entire household running. He was very frightened and cried for a long time, but afterward, proudly showed off his heavily bandaged arm.

"Served you right," said Sven. "If you are smart, you'll leave him alone."

"I am going to hide under the covers," Frank pulled an imaginary blanket over his head.

"Karlo will smell your dirty feet," Sven teased.

We were delighted when Mutti announced that she would let us spend the night with her. After supper, we dressed in our nightclothes and gathered in our parents' bedroom. In spite of our promises to be good, we did a bit of shoving and squabbling. Karlo, who had received a good scrubbing, made himself comfortable in front of Mutti's bed. He kept one eye open under a bushy eyebrow, waved his shaggy tail, and rested his head on his extended paws. Our parents' bedroom was a large, sunny room on the second floor, with a view of the meadow. It was furnished with two beds pushed together, nightstands, an easy chair, a table, a bookcase, and a wardrobe with a mirror. A thick, white wool rug covered the floor between the beds and the wardrobe, where Dagmar practiced her summersaults.

For a nighttime story, Dagmar asked for "Little Red Riding Hood." Frank cheered when the hunter cut open the wolf's belly, and little Red Riding Hood and her grandmother jumped out. Sven got to take the part of the wolf and ask, "What's rumbling and bumping in my belly?" At the end of the story, we celebrated the wolf's demise and sang, *"Der Wolf ist tot, der Wolf ist tot, der Wiwa, Wiwa Wolf ist tot."*

"The wolf got what he deserved, didn't he?" Mutti asked. "But should little Red Riding Hood have strayed from the path, instead of going straight to her grandmother's house?"

"Noooo," Dagmar replied, wagging a finger. It seemed that no matter how many times we heard the fairytales by the Brothers Grimm and Hans Christian Anderson, we never tired of them. There were times when I lived in them.

Dagmar pleaded with Mutti to sing to us. In a voice low and soothing, she sang the song Papa had written for us, his forest children:

Nun hört ihr Kinder hört,
Der Hirsch im Walde röhrt,
Er seine Schmaltier Frau nicht fand,

Sie ist ihm weggerannt.

Listen children, listen,
Father deer roars in the forest,
He searches around for his dear mate.
She must have run away.

Schliesst schnell die Äugelein.
Im Wald das wilde Schwein,
Es rufet seine Kinderlein,
Husch, husch in's Bett hinein.

Quickly close your little eyes.
The wild boar grunts in the forest,
He calls out to his little ones,
Hush, hush, it's time for bed.

Macht zu die Äugelein fest,
Eichhörnchen sitzt im Nest,
Auf seinem hohen Tannenbaum,
Wiegt es sich in den Traum.

Close your little eyes tightly,
The squirrel sits in his nest,
High in the branches of a tree,
It rocks itself and dreams.

Nun schliesst die Äugelein schnell,	Close your little eyes quickly,
Der Fuchs im Walde bellt,	The fox barks in the forest,
Die Häslein die nicht schlafen ein,	The little hares, who do not fall asleep,
Die beisst der Fuchs in's Bein.	He will nip in the leg.
Jetzt schliesst die Augen zu,	Now, close your little eyes,
Der Waldkauz ruft "uhu,"	The owl calls out "who-who,"
Er ruft "uhu" die ganze Nacht,	He calls "who-who" the long night through,
Bis dass die Sonn' erwacht.	Until the sun awakens.

One after another, we fell asleep under our featherbeds. During the night, a distant explosion awakened me. I pulled the covers over my head, snuggled up to the soft, warm body of my sister, and prayed, *"Lieber Gott mach mich fromm, dass ich in den Himmel komm,"* Dear God, help me to become virtuous, so that I may enter heaven," and, "Please, God. Don't let the Russians get us, and please send Papa home. Amen."

A short time later, I heard gunfire close to the house. Faint moonlight illuminated my mother—big with her sixth child—as she stood at the window. Karlo, at her side, growled. She patted the dog and whispered, *"Shshsh.* Good dog. I wish to God your master were here." The gunfire subsided. I had not heard any rattling of cans. That meant that the tripwires strung around the house had not been disturbed. As Mutti turned away from the window, I noticed a black object in her right hand. Before she returned to her bed, she lifted the mattress and hid it underneath.

I awoke to the ordinary sounds and smells of our household the next morning. My mother greeted Madam Chicowa and the girls, who came to help with the day's work.

There was the clattering of pots and pans, and the smell of *Ersatzkaffee* and oatmeal bubbling on the stove.

"Eycke," asked Sven. "Did you hear the explosion and the gun fire last night?"

"Yes. You heard it too?"

"Yep, and did you see Mutti's pistol?"

I nodded, "Scary, huh?"

"Must have been partisans. Papa showed Frank and me their hideout."

"You saw where they live?"

"Back in the woods, toward the west near the mine tailings," he answered.

"Did you see them?"

"No. All we saw is where they hole up. Papa said that the partisans have radios and all. They shoot people, blow up rails, and power and telephone lines."

"Is that what they did last night?"

Sven shrugged his shoulders, "I bet the *Mädchen* know what happened." Then he continued, "We got pretty close to where they live. Papa, Frank, and I pretended we were soldiers and crawled on our bellies to take a closer look at their earthen dugouts, hidden among the trees. We saw smoke curling into the air from a rusty pipe sticking out of the sod."

"You are making this up, right?"

"No. I'm telling you the truth. Next to their dugouts, were ponds. Above the water were strange wooden racks supported by poles. On these racks lay stinking, rotting carcasses—we couldn't tell what kind of animal they were from. Papa said that as the flesh rotted, it dropped into the ponds below and provided nourishment for the fish."

"Disgusting. But weren't you scared?"

"Naw, Papa was there. But he did warn Frank and me never to go near that place again."

"You'd better not."

"I'm not. What do you think I am, an idiot?"

Sven and I talked about how we could defend ourselves against partisans and the Russians should they attack. Papa had supervised our shooting at targets with a .22-caliber rifle the year before; and he had taught us how to throw dummy handgranades at imaginary targets. To demonstrate his marksmanship, he had shot a dragonfly in flight. Mutti had reluctantly taken potshots at leaves on a tree near the hay barn. The boys and I hadn't done too badly either. It had been kind of exciting making all that noise.

I did think, at the time, that Papa was making too much of a fuss about being prepared. But in light of what happened during the night of explosions and gunfire, I thought that Papa might have been right after all. Then again, neither Sven nor I had any idea where Papa kept the .22, nor did we believe that the dummy hand grenades stashed in the hay barn were going to do us any good. I decided that thinking about it was too confusing and too scary and tried to put it out of my mind.

A few weeks after Madam Chicowa had warned us about the partisans, we found Karlo dead in his kennel. Nobody knew for sure what had happened, but the explanation we chose to believe is that someone had poisoned him. With tears running down our cheeks, we buried Karlo in the garden. Papa brought home another watchdog, a German shepherd, whom we named Brando. He was not as big and well-trained as Karlo, but a good watchdog, nevertheless.

Mutti is Expecting

Mutti asked me to help prepare for the arrival of the baby she was expecting. We moved Dagmar's crib into a corner of the nursery, scrubbed the wicker bassinet she had outgrown, and aired out the mattress made of peat fiber. After we replaced the skirt and stretched fabric over the canopy, Mutti opened a drawer and took out a silver bell on an ivory ring. "You remember this?" she asked. "I bought it when you were born." Mutti chuckled, "You loved the sound it made when you touched it, and that's how I knew that you were awake." I rang the bell, which over the years had picked up a few dents. Mutti helped me attach it to the bassinet with a bow.

Soon after, Frau Doktor Pieczenko paid us a call. I must have forgiven her, for I no longer hid when she came for a visit. "Frau Laabs," Frau Doktor asked, "would you mind showing me your baby's layette?" I followed Mutti and Frau Doktor to the nursery, where Mutti placed the freshly laundered and neatly folded bundles of diapers, undershirts, sweaters, caps and blankets on the changing table. With babies being born almost every other year and the rest of us growing so fast, every piece of our clothing was carefully mended and passed down to the next child.

I watched Frau Doktor divide up the clothes into two neat piles, without saying a word. When she was finished, she explained that a member of the Charkow Opera Company was expecting a baby. Then she touched each pile lightly, looked at my mother, and spoke in a gentle yet firm tone, as if she expected no argument: "One for the German baby, and one for the Russian baby." Mutti appeared not to be surprised, responded with a nod, and folded half of the layette into a receiving blanket. I stared with my mouth open. Frau Doktor left with the neatly wrapped package clamped securely to the baggage rack of her bicycle. As she regally pedaled down the driveway, she lifted her right arm and waved without looking back.

A few weeks later, Mutti was resting on her rattan recliner in the shade of the birch tree. I was nearby, when Frau Doktor returned from delivering a letter she had written to the authorities. In it, she had requested that Mutti be permitted to return to Germany with her children to give birth to her sixth child. I could tell that Frau Doktor was agitated from her rapid breathing. "I am sorry to have to tell you, Frau Laabs, that those *Bonzen*,"—she took a deep breath—"those corrupt imbeciles, denied my request." Frau Doktor went on to complain about high Nazi officials and their families who were planning to scuttle to safety, along with the loot they had stolen from the Jews and Poles. She dropped into a chair next to Mutti and fanned herself.

Genia, who had been watching over Mutti ever since Gela moved away, brought a tray with two tall glasses of water laced with elderberry syrup. "You and I,"—Frau Doktor honored Genia with one of her rare smiles—"are going to have to take special care of Frau Baurat, aren't we?"

Genia nodded, "Yes, Frau Doktor."

Mutti looked wan, and her voice was unusually weak. "Genia, what would I do without you?" Beads of perspiration covered Mutti's forehead as she spoke. "Thank you, Frau Doktor, for trying." She told Frau Doktor that she didn't hold out much hope that we would get permission to leave and that she was not sure it would make much difference when the cities in Germany were being bombed night and day. That much we knew from our relatives who lived in Hamburg and Kassel. After my mother looked over her shoulder, she told Frau Doktor, "There is no place where we would be safe. Karl was right when he said we had lost the war at Stalingrad." Then she leaned close to Frau Doktor and lowered her voice, "I am worried about my husband. A few nights ago he came home for two hours. He didn't have permission to leave his post and had to ride on the bumper of a locomotive to get here. The train crept along so they could watch out for land mines. I was happy to see him, but when he left before daylight, I begged him not to take any more chances." Mutti continued, "A few weeks ago he helped a soldier desert his unit so he could look for his family missing in the rubble of his hometown." Frau Doktor sighed and crossed herself.

I remembered hearing Mutti say, "Karl, please be careful. Don't get into any more trouble."

Papa shook his head, took her into his arms, and gave her a long kiss, "Tutti, dear," he said softly. "You worry too much."

Mutti's mentioning trouble made me think of the times I heard my aunt Marianne tell Mutti, "Trouble and Karl are the best of friends." As usual, Mutti shrugged her shoulders and replied, "Marianne, aren't you exaggerating?"

"No, I'm not," my aunt shot back. "And you know it."

There were times when I had to agree with my aunt. I remembered how upset Mutti was when Papa lost his job, and the Gestapo came to our house a short while later. I didn't want Papa to be in any more trouble either. I worried about him, even though I kept these thoughts to myself.

I crawled into my refuge under the linden tree, where nobody could see me, and I tried to make sense of what I had heard. I was proud of Papa for being brave. At the same time, I agreed with Mutti that he shouldn't be taking so many chances. But I was much more worried about Mutti right now. She hadn't regained her strength since we all got sick a while back. She was no longer the strong and energetic mother I could run to with my problems. Not the mother whose eyes turned dark during an outburst of anger. Not the mother who fixed me with penetrating eyes when I was wicked, the one who could see lies written on my forehead. "You don't have to tell me, but do not lie," she admonished. Every time I lied, I vowed I wouldn't do it again, but then …

Only during the last two years had I noticed how beautiful my mother was. Her eyebrows, well-shaped and gently angled, were the color of her thick chestnut hair, which she wore swept up and rolled into large curls in the fashion of the day. She was all of five feet tall, had an athletic build and tiny feet. When she walked, her silk stockings rubbed together making a swishing sound. The hems of her linen, silk, and cotton garments fell a fashionable inch above her knees, and showed off her well-formed legs.

I sneaked into Mutti's bedroom when she was gone. I tried on her robes and the evening gowns her friend Li had given her. One gown was made of silvery gray satin on one side and a deep moss green on the other. I slipped into the dress, put on Mutti's high heels, and piled my hair high on my head with one hand. I pranced, tripped on the seam, danced in front of the long mirror, and made believe that I was beautiful. When I dressed in Mutti's black kimono adorned with large pink and red flowers, I saw before me a geisha in one of Mutti's art books. While I sat on the floor, pretending to drink tea out of a tiny bowl, I tried to be as graceful as the woman in the woodcut.

When she was well, Mutti was in constant motion, unless she was reading or nursing one of her babies. Her lips were soft when she kissed me. She drew adults and children alike into her orbit. She was happy when she hugged Papa, or one of us children, or nursed a baby. She was happy when she played her guitar and sang, or recited a poem. She was happy when she prepared a special meal, or when she had her hands in the soil. In the past, when she was expecting a baby, she seemed especially radiant.

Sometimes she was shy, but when she was the center of attention, she dazzled. She confided in Marianne that she dreamed of becoming an actress. My aunt laughed and remarked, "Tutti, you are an actress, and, from the looks of it, you are creating your private audience." Like an actress, Mutti possessed a wide range of vocal expression. Her voice was soothing and gentle as the evening breeze when she cooed a lullaby or a love song. It was shrill and strident when she scolded her children for misbehaving, or when she admonished one of our maids for filching curtain fabric to make herself a dress. Mutti's voice could be icy when she responded to Herr Latz's advances, or when she gave an arrogant Nazi official a piece of her mind. Yet, she sounded passionate, clear, and resonant when she read to us and recited the poetry she loved. I had no doubt that she would have done well on the stage.

When my mother embraced me, her breasts felt soft and warm. After a bath, she smelled of sandalwood. After a morning's strenuous work in the garden, she smelled of fresh air and pungent sweat. Her small, strong hands, at times rough and chapped, got caught in my hair when she braided it. When she sang and laughed, I, too, felt light and happy. When she was in pain, her sorrow and melancholy covered me with the paralyzing heaviness of a lingering nightmare. I could not bear seeing her so weak.

A Bear Cub in the Family

Our summer vacation ended, and I reluctantly returned to school. On September 16, a warm and sunny day and three days before her fortieth birthday, Mutti went into labor. I tried to keep busy by arranging and rearranging the furniture in the dollhouse my parents had made for me out of two old wooden file cabinets. The next day, during the last hours of Mutti's labor, Genia shooed my siblings and me outside. We tried to keep straight-faced while we played "make me laugh." We had to admit that Frank was best at making us laugh every time he meowed, howled like a banshee, or hooted like a monkey and scratched himself in strange places. After we got tired of the game, Frank built a fort in the sandbox, and Sven pushed Dagmar on the big swing. I paced back and forth, kicked up dust on the path to the swimming pond, hid under the linden tree, and prayed, "Please, *lieber Gott*, don't let Mutti die."

Although Mutti was giving birth at home, she did not lack medical attention. Two doctors, a midwife, and her friend Frau Seif went in and out of the house. Frau Seif put Brando on a leash and walked him up and down the long driveway. Papa arrived just in time to see the baby being born and announced with a big smile, "You've got a baby brother who weighs ten pounds and resembles a bear cub." My parents named their youngest son Björn, which in German means bear. My father had a Swedish ancestor, and that was the reason why my parents gave some of their children Swedish names. We nicknamed our baby brother Bärlein. In the past, Marianne and Mutti had reminded me that I didn't like sharing Mutti when Sven was born. I don't remember much of what happened when Frank was born, but I do recall the twinge of jealousy, mixed with delight when my sisters Ute and Dagmar came into the world.

Toward evening, after we bathed, and dressed in our pajamas, Papa led us into the bedroom to see Mutti and to welcome the baby. Mutti looked ashen and exhausted. I kissed her and told her that I loved her. She smiled, closed her eyes for a second and nodded, too weak to answer. The bassinet that Mutti and I had prepared with so much care stood by her bedside. The baby was asleep, his face round and smooth. I wanted to hold and cuddle him, but I tried to understand when Papa explained that the baby and Mutti needed their rest. The doctors ordered Mutti to stay in bed because of a weakened heart muscle. Every day, Frau Doktor Pieczenko lunched at Mutti's bedside. A perky young woman, Inge Biewald, arrived to take care of my siblings and me. Genia bathed, diapered, and dressed the baby. Fortunately, Mutti had enough milk to nurse the baby, because one morning we discovered that Ivan, his cow, and calf had vanished during the night and moved on—in a westerly direction, we assumed. I wondered if we would be allowed to leave before it was too late.

For Mutti's fortieth birthday, we performed for her: *"Wenn eine Mutter ihr Kindlein tut wiegen, lächelt der Mond in das Fenster hinein. Wenn eine Mutter ihr Kindlein tut wiegen, tut sich der Himmel der Erde anschmiegen."* It was a song about a mother who rocks her baby while the moon smiles upon them and the sky caresses the earth. As Sven and I scratched out the melody on our violins, Frank and Dagmar got the text all mixed up. In spite of it, we sounded better than the time we surprised Mutti with a musical offering and a quarrel on Mother's Day. Sadly, we lacked the musical aptitude to fulfill Mutti's dream to perform proper *Hauskonzerte*.

Remember Auschwitz

Later that fall, Papa's friend Sassmannshausen used his influence to get Papa, who had been promoted to non-commissioned officer—his promotion to officer had been denied on political grounds—permanently attached to a glider camp in Libiaz. Libiaz was located about ten miles southwest of Krenau. There, Papa helped train young cadets to be glider pilots. Papa had been an avid sports glider pilot since the early nineteen-thirties. I had watched him soar from the time I was little, and I had told everyone that my Papa had wings.

* * *

Papa had volunteered at the camp for a number of years. In previous years, the glider camp at Libiaz had played a significant role in the life of a Jewish survivor. In a letter dated November 20, 1972, addressed to Yad Vashem, the Memorial for the Holocaust in Jerusalem, Markus Buchbinder testified:

> In the years 1940, 1941, and the beginning of 1942, I worked on the construction of the airstrip, Libiaz, that was on the outskirts of Krenau in Poland. Karl Laabs was the supervisor on the job, and in his dealings with me and the other Jews, he was friendly and considerate. I lived in Krenau, and every day I took the train to and from work. From time to time, the Germans would take some of the people from their homes, collect them in the market place, and then select some of them for deportation to death camps. I was twice part of the group assembled in the market place, and each time Karl Laabs came to town and demanded my release. He thus saved me twice. He also did this for some of my colleagues.
> Yours faithfully,
> M. Buchbinder

*   *   *

Papa electrified the whole household whenever he rushed through the front door. One day he blew in with a radiant smile and announced at the top of his voice, "Children, I have a surprise for you."

In unison, we asked, "What?"

"Tomorrow I am going to take you to the glider camp."

"Hurrah!" we cheered.

"Will you teach me how to fly?" asked Sven.

Frank chimed in. "Me too, me too."

"What about me?" I fretted.

"Hush, children, hush." Papa said, "One at a time. The boys at the camp are older than you."

"How old?" Sven asked with his hands on his hips.

"Between fourteen and seventeen. You are still a little too young, you know. If you are good, I might let you sit in one of the trainers and you could pretend to fly. How about that?"

Sven grumbled, "Always too young to do really exciting stuff. I can't wait to grow up."

"Me, too," Frank joined in and added, "Did you bring us some *Hasenbrot?*" Four pairs of eyes looked up at Papa expectantly.

"Let me see." Papa rummaged in his huge rucksack, retrieved four sandwiches from several crumpled layers of brown paper, and, with a flourish, he presented slices of buttered bread with hard sausage to each one of us. I sniffed mine before I took my first bite and smiled back at Papa. "Thank you, Papa," we chorused as we smacked our lips and munched away. For some reason sandwiches tasted so much better after they had been aged properly in Papa's knapsack or pockets.

When we arrived at the glider camp, the sun shone and a breeze rippled the tall grass on the hill from which the gliders were being launched. Papa pronounced it to be "good flying weather."

Sven, pointing to the primitive gliders sitting on top of the hill, said disdainfully, "Funniest looking contraptions I've ever seen."

"Those trainers don't look like much, do they?" Papa answered as he sat down in the grass where we joined him. "But they do the job, a better job than many of the gliders men have constructed before. There once lived a man called Leonardo daVinci," Papa continued. "DaVinci dreamed about flying. He built a glider which one of his friends tried out. His friend crash-landed, and everybody laughed at him. But you'll see in a minute that when the air moves just right under and across the wings of a glider, it soars."

"May I tell something I learned?" I asked Papa. He nodded. "Herr Zelter read us a Greek story. He said that it was a myth, about a boy named Ikarus. In that story Ikarus and his father Daedalus, glued feathers to their bodies with wax, but Ikarus ignored his father's warnings not to get too close to the sun. He flew higher and higher until the heat from the sun melted the wax, his feathers came off, and he fell to his death into the sea below."

"Naw," interjected Sven. "Nobody would be that dumb."

"I told you it was a myth, didn't I?" I answered.

"I imagine that humans wished that they could fly when they first laid eyes on the birds in the sky," Papa interrupted our argument. "Pay attention. You see that boy sitting in the glider?"

"The one who is wearing the funny helmet that looks like a cooking pot?" jeered Sven. "He doesn't even have a cockpit."

Papa chose to ignore Sven's comment. "You see the two long ropes attached to the nose of the glider?"

We watched as two groups of cadets took hold of the long ropes, shouted in unison, "*Hau ruck, hau ruck,*" and then dashed part way downhill while pulling the glider behind them. For a minute, the ungainly contraption slid along the ground on its skids and then rose into the air. The student pilot released the bungee cords. The glider soared for a few minutes and landed safely at the bottom of the hill.

"Just a short hop," Papa said, "but it gets the boys used to the controls. Every once in a while one gets lucky and catches a thermal."

"What's a thermal?" I probed.

"It's an invisible current, like a tall column or a wave of air warmed by the sun. A thermal develops over grain fields and along ridges and can carry a pilot way up into the sky for hours on end, if he knows just how to use it by circling within it. It is a thrill to catch a thermal under your wings." Papa's face flushed with excitement every time he talked about flying.

We stood and watched as one of the older boys down below harnessed a horse to a two-wheel trailer. Two more boys, one at each wing tip, held the plane's wings off the ground. They huffed, cursed, laughed, and shouted encouragement to each other, as they slowly made their way to the top of the hill.

Papa got up, dusted himself off, and said, "Let's have a closer look at the *Zöglinge*. That's what we call these small gliders." Papa introduced us to one of his fellow instructors, a jolly fellow in a rumpled and stained uniform. The only indication that he was a real soldier was the air force insignia on his cap.

"Ready to launch one of your own fledglings?" he joked with Papa.

Papa grinned. "Maybe we'll teach them how to fly next time."

"Eycke," Papa waved me over, "You are the oldest, it's your turn first." My cheeks reddened as I became aware that everybody was watching. "Let me show you," said Papa, after I settled down on the small seat. "First, place both feet on these wooden paddles. Push one foot down and look over your shoulder. Check how the tail rudder moves to one side. Do the same thing with the other foot, if you want to go in the opposite direction. To steer this thing, put your right hand on the stick and move it either forward, backward, to the right, or to the left. It's as simple as that."

"I wish I could really fly," I whispered.

"Maybe some day you will," Papa replied.

For a minute, I imagined that I had wings, that I had caught a thermal, and that I was turning circles in the sky, feeling light and free. Papa took a photograph of me at that moment. My right hand is on the joystick. I am wearing a white blouse, a short skirt, white socks, and heavy walking shoes. My braided hair is looped over my ears, my eyes are on the horizon, and a hint of a smile is on my lips.

We watched the student pilots take off, land, and pull their gliders all afternoon until the sun was low over the horizon. It was then that Papa called out to us, "Come to the other side of the hill. I want to show you something." We followed Papa, taking two and three steps to every one of his. Papa stopped and cupped his left hand behind his ear, "Listen, can you hear the rumbling?" We nodded. "Those are Russian guns, you know, heavy artillery. You mustn't tell anybody that I said so, but I believe that it won't be long before they get here, and we'll have to leave."

"Are we going to lose the war?" Sven asked, his eyes wide.

Papa nodded and put his index finger on his lips. "It's our secret. You wouldn't want your Papa to get into trouble, would you?" We shook our heads. Then Papa pointed into the valley, where we saw rows upon rows of barracks within a high wire fence. Smoke rose from the area. Our father spoke slowly and deliberately, "Children," he said, "down there is Auschwitz. That is where they take the Jews. I want you to take a good look." Here he paused a moment. "And remember."

Watching the Old Fox

Winds from the East brought us bitter cold and snow, which piled up into high drifts around the house and barn. It was the middle of January, 1945, and with temperatures at minus thirty degrees Fahrenheit, we were experiencing what the adults called a "Siberian winter." What we didn't know is that two days before, the Russians had launched a major offensive in southern Poland and were closing in on Warsaw to the northeast of us. We could hear the distant thunder of a battle. Added to it was the sporadic gunfire in the woods to the east and west of us. "Polish partisans," Sven whispered in my ear.

The grown-ups were preoccupied and in a rush. Mutti and the maids were filling wooden crates with household goods. Dagmar cried as her toys disappeared in one of the boxes. When I asked, "Mutti, are we leaving?" she answered that we had to wait for Papa, as she stuffed another down comforter into a crate. "Sven says that the Russians are getting closer."

She nodded, then snapped, "Don't bother me now. Go to your room and pack your things."

I couldn't make any sense of what was happening around me. The night before, my teacher, Herr Zelter, had come to the house during a snowstorm. His slight frame was wrapped in a bulky overcoat, and a fur cap dwarfed his head. His glasses fogged up when he entered the house with a blast of icy wind. He carried a copy of his beloved "Tacitus" under his coat, expecting to read and lead Mutti, Fräulein Rost, Frau Doktor and Frau Seif in a literary discussion. Mutti didn't hide her astonishment as she received him amidst half empty crates and household goods strewn throughout the hallway and living room. "I am sorry, dear Herr Zelter," she said politely, "but today we are otherwise occupied." He nodded absentmindedly, and after he drank the hot cup of tea she offered him, disappeared into the howling wind and a curtain of snow.

Dagmar was upstairs in her room playing. Sven and Frank were in theirs, and they were having an argument. "Don't be stupid, Frank. You can't take your trucks," Sven said.

"All right." Frank sounded reasonable, but he insisted, "I am going to hide them in my closet, and when we get back, I'll get to play with them." I took refuge in my room and whispered to my doll Brigitte that we had to get ready for a long trip. I dressed her in her blue wool suit, matching hat, and the mittens Mutti had knitted for her. I stuffed her white lace dress and fancy patent leather shoes with the rest of her clothes into my knapsack, made sure that her head stuck out at the top and gently tied the chord around her neck.

A pattern of ice crystals covered the windowpanes. I melted a circle with my breath and peeked outside, hoping to catch a glimpse of Papa. What I saw was an old man hobbling down the driveway toward the house. He knocked on the front door, handed Genia something, and left. Minutes later, Mutti rushed into my room and explained that we had finally received permission to evacuate and to be ready in half an hour. The document the old man delivered that day read:

Citizen!

During relocation, pay attention to the following:

1. Each family is permitted to carry no more than 66 pounds of luggage, therefore take only what is absolutely essential!

2. Make absolutely sure that you have:
   Silverware
   Bowl
   Cup for drinking

3. Above all think of your baby! He needs: linens, milk bottle, baby food, if possible a featherbed.

4. Wear sturdy footwear!

5. Do not forget to take your personal identification papers and proof of your assets.

6. Carry food supplies for approximately three days.

7. Keep your relocation permit safe! It will entitle you to receive food ration cards and relocation funds for your family.

8. At your destination you must use the relocation permit to register with the authorities in charge: the N.S.V. [National Socialist Organization], with the Office for Economics and Nutrition and with the Family Support Organization (Mayor and County Commissioner).

9.   REMAIN CALM!

B/0202 1000 000 January, 1945

I reminded Mutti that we couldn't possibly leave without Papa, and I was relieved when she announced that he had just arrived. Mutti was not pleased when she looked into my knapsack and discovered only my doll and doll clothes. Her anxious expression and the manner in which she hastily threw the doll clothes on the bed, and replaced them with my own warm clothes, made me think that this wasn't the time to express my disappointment.

I was consoled when she allowed me to keep the doll and take one book, my photo album, napkin ring, christening cup and my silver bell. She laid out several pairs of woolen knee socks, warm underwear, a pair of slacks, a dress, a sweater, a coat, a hat, a scarf, mittens, and a new pair of knee high felt boots. "I'm afraid that's all you can take." I wondered if she had lost her mind when she stuck a broken toothbrush into the outside pocket of the pack, but I kept my mouth shut. As she left the room, she urged me to get dressed in a hurry and to join everyone in the hallway. "Don't forget your violin," she called out before she disappeared into the boys' room.

After I dressed in multiple layers, I struggled to put my knapsack on, picked up the violin case, and hurried down the stairs. In the entrance hall Genia, Madame Chicowa, Herr Christofoski, and Herr Bobeck, a Polish colleague of Papa's, had come to accompany us to the railroad station in the next village, Conti. Papa stood by the door wearing his uniform and looking somber. "Ready, everybody?" Each child, even four-year-old Dagmar, carried a knapsack. As for the baby, four-month-old Björn, I could hardly make out his tiny shape under the blankets and stuff piled on top of him in his carriage. I took one last look around the house. Half-empty crates still stood around the living room, Papa's study, and the entrance hall. Books, paintings, records, clothes, pillows, and bed covers were strewn about. Papa's Voigtländer camera dangled from a window latch.

Genia sobbed. "Why don't you come with us?" Mutti asked, patting her on the back.

"I wish I could, but my mother is ill." Genia sniffled and wiped her red nose with a hanky.

"We'll miss you," Mutti said, putting her arms around Genia's shoulders.

"Let's go." Papa sounded gruffer and more impatient than usual.

In a moment we were outside. The sun was brilliant, and the snow sparkling, piled into snowdrifts and crunching under our boots. I found it difficult to move with my extra clothes on. My new boots felt too tight, but my pack wasn't heavy at all, not yet. Each breath of cold air stung my lungs. The bright sun and the cold made my eyes water. Mutti told us to pull our hats down and to put our scarves over our mouths.

After I had been worrying for months, the time to leave had finally come. I felt uneasy and all mixed up. It had to be that old *Reisefieber*, the travel fever, that was making me shaky. I started thinking about returning in the early summer, with the war over, lying under the linden tree in full bloom, inhaling its sweet fragrance. The imagining made me feel warm as I stumbled along the icy path toward Conti and the railway station.

Mutti took the lead, pushing Björn in his carriage. Dagmar and Frank held onto the handle. Brando trotted at Mutti's side. Sven and I followed. Madame Chicowa and Genia walked behind us. Herr Christofoski, Herr Boback, and Papa brought up the rear. We moved at a fast pace past the crawfish ponds on the right and the abandoned factory on the left. We put down our loads several times to rest.

"Where are we going?" chirped Dagmar.

"To visit grandmother Laabs," Mutti replied.

"Is it far away?"

"Yes, it is."

"When will we get there?" Frank asked.

"I don't know. Now hush and hold onto the carriage," Mutti answered.

"Papa, carry me, my legs are tired," Dagmar pleaded. Herr Christofoski took one of Papa's suitcases, and Papa carried Dagmar in one arm. After what seemed like an hour or more, we reached the station, where we piled up our luggage on the platform. While Frank and Dagmar amused themselves on top of the bags, Mutti, who was unusually quiet, busied herself with the baby and absentmindedly patted Brando. Papa and the others stood around talking in hushed tones. Maybe if I had known what was going to happen, I would not have felt so anxious. It worried me that the adults looked like they didn't know either.

When we heard the train, the stationmaster, wrapped in a heavy coat and fur cap, stepped out of his hut. To stop the train, he held up a signal that looked like a huge spoon. We hugged and cried as the engine, puffing white smoke, came to a stop with a screech. "Grab your stuff, get ready. Tutti, you get on first," Papa ordered.

The stationmaster blew his whistle and called out *"Einsteigen!"* Mutti pushed the carriage toward the door of a car. Somebody opened it from the inside. Papa, Sven, Frank, and I were right behind her. Mutti and Papa lifted the carriage onto the train. Papa took the lead to search for a place to sit. Leaving our suitcases on the platform, we scrambled aboard and followed Mutti to the compartment Papa had located. We sat down, while Papa quickly opened the window, leaned out, and grabbed the suitcases and bundles handed to him. A number of suitcases and bags for which there was no room in the compartment remained behind on the platform. Madame Chicowa, Genia, and Herr Christofoski waved. Herr Bobeck held back a whining Brando by the collar.

It was then that Mutti screamed, "Dagmar?" Her eyes were huge and black, her mouth wide open as though she was not getting enough air.

I heard the whistle and the voice of the stationmaster announcing the departure of the train. Papa's voice boomed in my ear. "Dagmaaaar." We crowded around the window to see.

"There she is," Sven pointed. Her head popped up from behind the pile of luggage. Herr Christofoski bounded over, grabbed her, and ran alongside the train as it began to move. Running faster, he held Dagmar up to Papa and placed her into his outstretched arms. Dagmar was laughing, her eyes sparkling, her nose, and cheeks red from the cold. Papa handed her to Mutti, who hugged her tightly. Tears rolled down Mutti's cheeks. Smoke and cinder entered the compartment through the window. Papa closed it, then he stowed away our bags in the nets above our seats.

Breathing heavily, Papa asked, "All present?" He counted: "One, two, three, four, five, six, seven." We settled down. The train gathered speed.

Our flight was a journey through a long, long dark tunnel with no light at the end and no exit. I felt trapped, pushed, and pulled by a torrent, along with hundreds of people. I had no control. I could sense, taste, and smell the fear of strangers. Their bodies pressed against mine threatened to tear me away from my family. My fear of becoming separated from them was relentless and constant. I heard: "Stay close, hold on, or you'll get lost."

After traveling north, we waited all night at the station in Myslowitz for a train, which would take us west. I felt the cold enter my body through the bottom of my feet. Train after train, some of them empty, passed us by. We piled luggage around the carriage and huddled to protect the baby from the icy wind and the drifting snow. Mutti had been right in insisting that we wear several layers of clothing. "You'll see, it'll keep you warm and save us from having to carry so much." My brand new, fancy lady's boots were a bother. Made of gray felt and trimmed in black leather with a small heel, they looked pretty, but they didn't keep my feet warm.

I mumbled to Sven under my breath, "My houseshoes would have kept my feet a lot warmer than these stupid boots." With three pairs of socks, there was no room for my toes to move around to keep them from freezing. The cold clawed at me and numbed me.

Papa showed us how to get warm: "Pay attention, everybody! Together! Start! Stamp your feet, flap your arms, and hug yourself. Stamp your feet, flap your arms, and hug yourself. Stamp your feet, flap your arms, and hug yourself." Our faces and noses turned red from the cold and the exertion. My upper body felt warm, but my feet were like clumps of ice. Toward evening, Papa found us a corner inside the crowded waiting room, where we thawed out as we cuddled and fell asleep on top of our luggage.

Before daylight, Papa woke us up from a fitful sleep. "Quickly, a train is coming." Half asleep, we hoisted our packs and picked up our luggage. "Hold on to each other, watch out for ice." The chugging sounds of an engine in the distance grew louder as it approached around a curve. The train was still moving when Papa shouted, "Into position!" Before the train stopped, Papa rushed to a door, grabbed a handle, and pulled himself up. There was a deafening, screeching sound. With a tremendous jerk, the train finally came to a complete halt. Steam from the engine hissed and billowed along the length of the train. Papa had judged well. The door to the car stopped directly in front of us. He had done it again. He had powerful magic. I knew he did. Then came the crush, the pushing, and the jostling by everybody trying to get on. I sensed panic. "Mother and children coming through," Papa shouted, a tone of authority in his voice. He motioned for us to pile into the compartment on the right. He once again counted: "One, two, three, four, five, six, seven." We settled down, exhausted and grateful to be in a warm place.

My feet didn't feel as if they were a part of my body. I took off three pair of socks and decided that the first chance I got, I was going to get rid of those stupid boots. Well, maybe not. Perhaps they were better than nothing—better than the rags old Ivan and Madam Chicowa wrapped around their feet. I rubbed my feet until they were pink and began to tingle. It felt as if one hundred needles were piercing my flesh, but slowly my feet became a part of my body again. Then I rubbed Dagmar's feet, and we played a counting game as she wiggled her toes warm.

The first thing Mutti did was to put the baby to her engorged breasts. While Bärlein nursed contentedly, Dagmar curled up in his carriage. Papa unpacked the bread, sausage, cheese, and apples from a large hamper, and we ate our fill. We unpeeled layers of clothing. Mutti allowed me to hold the baby and burp him. Dagmar and Frank became drowsy and fell asleep, snuggling like puppies. The train moved on.

I climbed into the luggage net strung above the seats and fell asleep. It felt good to be up high, even if it wasn't comfortable. Periodically, I woke up when my legs or arms went to sleep. What I dreaded most of all was the trip to the toilet. After trying hard to put it off by twisting and turning in discomfort, I left the safety of our compartment and pushed open the sliding door to the aisle. I climbed over piles of baggage and passengers asleep on the floor through a hallway reeking of tobacco smoke, sweat, and urine. "Excuse me, please; excuse me," I stammered. People cursed as I made my way to the end of the car. Here I stood in a long line until it was my turn. Even outside, the toilet's overpowering stench hit my nostrils. When it was my turn, I took a deep breath and held it in. I entered, closed the door behind me, opened the seat cover, and stared. There, in a blur, were the railroad ties. I was too scared to sit down for fear of being sucked through the breezy hole. I gasped for air, got another whiff of the stench, and started to wretch. My bladder and bowels were ready to explode, as I hopped from one leg to the other. Squatting, I let go with a sigh of relief.

On my way back to our compartment, I saw a train rushing by with people perched precariously on roofs and clustered like grapes on bumpers and steps. I picked my way around and over grouchy fellow passengers who jammed the aisles, mumbling apologies and fearing that I might not find my family where I had left them. When I found our compartment, I felt weak with happiness.

During our journey, I watched Papa. He did not appear to be afraid. I did not see him sleep. I did not see him relax. He was wily. He was cunning. He was eternally watchful. He was like the animal in the dark forest that he told us about in his stories. He used his instinct and all his skills to evade the hunter, to stay alive, by sensing, listening, smelling, looking, lying low, running, hiding and fighting, if need be, to protect his mate and young. My father vibrated with energy. I was watching the "old fox."

The story of the "old fox" goes back to when I was a little girl, no more than four or five years old. I had been listening to the adults talking among themselves. I picked up three words with which they described my father: They called him "the old fox." I knew what a fox was. I knew the song:

Fuchs, du hast die Gans gestohlen,	Fox, you stole the goose from us,
Gib sie wieder her,	Come on and give it back,
Gib sie wieder her,	Come on and give it back,
Sonst wird dich der Jäger holen	Or else the hunter will come and get you
Mit dem Schiessgewehr,	With his trusty rifle,
Pow, pow.	Pow, pow.

I repeated over and over, "You old fox, you old fox." When my father came home that night and greeted me, I looked up at him, lifted my right index finger, shook it back and forth and said, "*Papa, Du alter Fuchs.*"

Papa grinned, lifted me up and replied, "Remember, no hunter is going to get this old fox."

In the darkness, my fear grew of getting separated from my family and of not doing my job of keeping track of my siblings. Papa was not a patient man. He barked orders, which he expected would be followed without delay or argument. He expected that I be good in school, that I study hard, that I practice my violin, and that I do my chores without complaining. He demanded, he shouted, he reprimanded. Nobody could hurt my feelings the way Papa did. At times, it was quite tiring to be around him. I tried hard to stay in his good graces by doing as he asked. I could tell by the way he looked and smiled at me when he was proud of me. But, what I wanted was to hear him say that he was proud.

As the train raced west past Kattowitz, the engineer continued to blow his whistle at crossings. Air raid sirens wailed somewhere near Gleiwitz. The train stopped. We were trapped in darkness and cold. In the distance was the droning of bombers, followed by the whistling of bombs through the air, and the sound of impact. "Watch out!" someone shouted. More whistling and explosions. The droning of the planes disappeared, and the sirens signaled "all clear." The train started moving again. Brakes squealed, and the hissing of escaping steam ceased. We shunted back and forth on a side rail. We waited and shivered. I finally fell asleep, and I didn't notice when the train started moving again.

In the morning, I heard Papa talking to two men in uniform. Sven, who showed a great deal more interest in soldier's uniforms and their equipment than I, leaned over, and whispered, "SS."

One of the men demanded to know, "Where do you come from, where are you going?"

"From the Kattowitz area. The Russians were on our tail," my father replied. The soldiers puffed on their cigarettes and laughed uproariously as though they had not a care in the world.

More sirens. The train stopped near Oppeln. Total darkness. Sounds from a different kind of plane and the warning, *"Achtung, Deckung!"* I moved closer to feel the warmth of my sister asleep next to me, made myself as small as I could, held my ears and arched my body over hers. The rattling of guns at a distance and the volume increased … *ack ack ack ack ack.* The plane was gone in a whoosh, leaving behind an acrid odor.

Shouting: *"Hilfe!"* accompanied by moaning and whimpering.

Papa's voice: "All clear. Everyone all right?"

Mutti: "It's over, don't cry."

Frank: "I'm freezing."

Sven: "What are we waiting for? Why aren't we moving?"

Dagmar: "I have to pee."

I was thinking, "I don't have to pee anymore."

In the light of dawn, the train traveled through snow-covered countryside. Cities and towns lay in ruins, shrouded by fire and smoke, turned into black smudges in the snow. The roads were clogged with caravans of military vehicles and horse-drawn wagons piled high with household goods, people clinging to them. Other people were on foot, pulling small wagons. They were exposed to the elements, as well as to the rain of fire from above. Like us, they were desperate to keep on moving west.

Papa was alert, anticipating, watching us and the people around us. He walked around in the aisles, talked to people, showed papers to patrols, paid for tickets, asked questions, gave short, precise orders. He herded us, left us, came back, and left us again.

During a moment when Papa was absent, a woman conductor, short, red-faced and robust, her ample body stuffed into her navy blue uniform like a sausage, pushed her way through the crowd to check tickets. *"Heil Hitler,"* she bellowed, as she entered our compartment. After she had punched our tickets, she pointed to the baby and addressed my mother: "You should have left that baby behind. It's going to die anyway." It sounded as if she was talking about a piece of bulky luggage to be discarded. Mutti looked as though someone had slapped her face. Both of her hands went to her breasts. I believed that I knew what she was thinking: as long as I have milk, as long as I can keep him warm, he is going to stay alive. Then I watched her make a move that I had observed a dozen times since we left home and started walking in the snow. She inserted her right hand between the pillows and blankets, under which the baby was sleeping, and caressed him, to reassure herself that he was warm. She grabbed the handle of the buggy tightly with one hand and motioned the rest of us to come closer. Was she trying to pretend that she had not heard the woman? Was she too exhausted to argue with her? After the conductor left, I noticed the vacant stare appear in her eyes, the one I had seen after our sister Ute died. I thought that if Papa had been present, the conductor would not have dared to say what she did. Leave our brother behind, indeed. I should have told that woman off. I was the eldest, after all, and I was going to be twelve years old. But a good girl didn't talk back to adults, did she? I kept my mouth shut and hugged my anger tightly.

When the train stopped in Dresden and Papa left the compartment, I was terrified that he wouldn't come back, and relieved when I heard the compartment door open and saw his face. Papa brought water, which he had made from melted snow in a metal cup. It was for Mutti. Her milk was the only nourishment for the baby. He left once more, returned with more water, only one cup. We each took a few sips. I felt safe when I was close to him, to my mother and to my siblings. The Dresden railroad station was jammed with refugees, who attempted to claw their way onto our train. A few succeeded. Others were left behind.

*   *   *

Exactly one month later, Dresden was bombed into oblivion. It is impossible to know just how many refugees were in Dresden at the time. The most reputable historians disagree on the number of residents and refugees who perished in the firestorm. Their estimates range between twenty-five and forty thousand killed and thirty thousand injured.

*   *   *

My siblings and I rarely quarreled during our flight. When we did, Papa shouted brusquely *"Schluss!"* Once, when one of us whined, he promised, "If you hush, I'll tell you the story about my ride on top of a tank." He revealed that a few days ago he had closed the glider camp in Libiaz and had sent the boys home. He told us that he stood in the middle of the road and flagged down a tank on its way east. He told us that he hopped on and clung to it as it rumbled and churned on the snowy road toward Krenau and home. He told us of getting dropped off not far from our house, just in time to pick us up and catch the train. What he didn't tell us was that, when he and another officer signed the young boys' discharge papers, they were disregarding a direct order. All military and paramilitary units were expected to stand, fight, and repel the Russian invasion. The transfer papers Papa carried had not been properly authorized either, but they must have looked official enough, because during our flight not a single patrol challenged their authenticity.

At a huge railroad station—my mother told me later it was Leipzig—crowds were everywhere, mostly young and old women, children, and a few old men. People shouted, "This is the last train. I have to get on it." People laden with baggage pushed and pleaded, "Any room left for us?" and "Push, push."

We were changing to a train, which would take us south to Gera, west across the province of Thuringia, then north toward Kassel and our destination, Münden. But first of all we had to get off of this train. Papa shouted, "Children through the window." Papa pushed out of the compartment. Mutti followed him with the baby carriage. People cursed, cried, grumbled, and muttered. Papa appeared outside at the window and helped Dagmar, Frank, Sven and me climb out. He ordered us to hold on to each other. In the melee, Frank was torn from us.

Mutti screamed, "*Um Himmels Willen*, where is Frank?"

We could hear him yelling, but couldn't see him. After we shouted as loud as we could, "Fraaank!" we heard his voice somewhere in the crowd.

"Papa! Mutti!"

Papa pushed people aside. "Coming through, coming through!" He shouted, "Frank, Frank!"

"Papa! Papa!" Frank answered.

When Papa discovered him, he put him on his shoulders. Mutti sighed, "*Gott sei Dank.*"

Frank told of people pushing him, of being frightened, of a woman telling him to shout as loud as he could. When he got to ride on Papa's shoulders, he made a face at Sven and me, and bragged that he was the tallest. "Troublemaker," Sven muttered under his breath.

"I told you, hold on to each other," Papa scolded, his face drawn and ashen.

Frank asked Papa for water. "Wait until I melt more snow," Papa replied.

"I'm hungry," Sven groaned.

"I'm sorry. Only a few apples left," Mutti replied.

We all felt better when Sven discovered a woman with a red cross on her cap, who served us each a mug of warm tea. During the night Mutti took her youngest children to her breast. Two days later, our family returned to the heart of Germany. Most of our luggage was lost or stolen somewhere on the way. All we had left is what we could carry on our backs and in our hands. We were exhausted and hungry but alive. The banners welcoming us read, *"Räder rollen für den Sieg,"* wheels are turning for victory.

"The Lair of the Fox." Auschwitzer Strasse 36b, the author's family residence, became a safe haven and temporary hiding place for Jews between 1941 and 1943. Krenau, Poland. In January, 1945, during the family's flight from Poland, much of their luggage was stolen at the end of their journey. After rifling through the content, the thief threw one of the cases into the Werra River. A kind soul fished it out and restored the waterlogged papers and photos to the family. The photo above is one of those saved.

The author's mother. Krenau, summer, 1941.

The cottage on Auschwitzer Strasse 36b before renovation. Krenau, summer, 1941.

The rear entrance to the cottage on Auschwitzer Strasse 36b before renovation. Krenau, 1941. On the right is the corner of the hay barn, one of the two barns where the author's father hid over one hundred Jews during a night in the early spring, 1943. In the summer of 1944, it served as a shelter for the author and her siblings, during an air raid.

Auschwitzer Strasse 36b during renovation. Krenau, winter, 1941–42.

Auschwitzer Strasse 36b. Krenau, winter,1942–43.

Anita Tudela Crespo with the author's sister Dagmar. Krenau, summer, 1942.

The author with brothers Sven and Frank and Maria Crespo. Krenau, summer, 1942.

The author's hiding place, the linden tree, in the garden at Auschwitzer Strasse 36b. Krenau.

Madam Chicowa, Gela, and Ivan making hay. Krenau, 1944.

The author (front row right) with a small group of her fourth-grade class. Jürgen Helms on the far right. Krenau, 1942.

The author's father, Karl Laabs, in Luftwaffe uniform, 1943 or 1944. During the spring of 1943, shortly after he saved over one hundred Jews from Auschwitz, he was indicted for conduct unbecoming a German civil servant. He was fired from his job as County Architect by his Nazi bosses, drafted into the Luftwaffe, and narrowly escaped arrest by the Gestapo.

The author's mother with her four children. Krenau, summer, 1943 or 1944.

The author trying out wings. Libiaz Glider Camp near Auschwitz, October, 1944.

Map "Norddeutschland," Diercke Schulatlas für höhere Lehranstalten, Grosse Ausgabe, 81. Auflage, Westermann Verlag, 1942, pp. 153-154.

The map shows the annexed territories and extended borders of the German Reich under the Nazis. It is reprinted here with permission (Nr. F072-40) from the Schulbuchverlag Westermann Schroedel, Braunschweig, Germany, with the specific stipulation that it not be used for Nazi propaganda, which is against the law in the Federal Republic of Germany. Marked in black is the route the author's family traveled during their flight from the advancing Russian army from Poland in the east to central Germany in the west, between January and April of 1945.

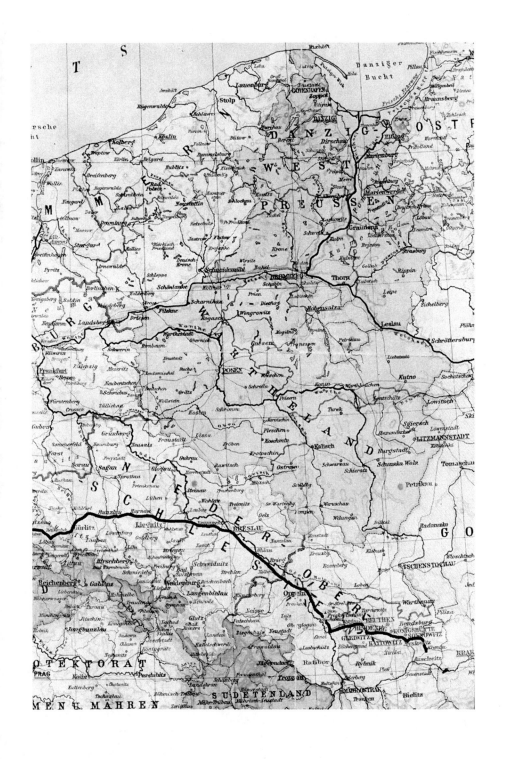

PART III

Return to Germany:
The Collapse of the Third Reich and the Liberation
1945–1946

Back in the Heart of Germany

When we got off the train in Münden, the ladies from the Nazi Social Services ushered us into the waiting room and served us hot tea and bread from the top of a baggage cart. Exhausted, we slept on the floor of the waiting room alongside other travelers. Papa walked up to his family home on Kattenbühl Lane to alert his mother of our impending arrival. The white stucco house, with its green shutters and high-pitched red tile roof, overlooked the medieval town where Papa was born almost fifty years earlier. Three rivers embraced the town, with its castle, ancient churches, narrow streets, and quaint half-timbered houses.

The next morning, feeling dirty, hungry, fatigued, and disoriented, we struggled up Kattenbühl Lane, carrying our knapsacks and bundles. What was amazing is that I still had my violin and my knapsack. Somehow, I had been able to keep track of them during our flight. It was January 18, 1945. Unbenown to us the Russian Army would take the city of Krakau, located 18 miles northeast of Krenau, the next day. At the railroad station in Münden, someone stole much of our luggage, rifled through the suitcases for valuables and then tossed them into the Werra River. A kind soul retrieved one of the cases from the water and returned it to us along with some waterlogged documents and photographs.

Mutti worried about moving in with her mother-in-law, with good reason. There had been friction between the two of them ever since my father left his first wife and their three children to marry my mother. When we arrived, Grossmutter Laabs threw up her hands and cried out, "*Um Himmels Willen,* where are we going to put all of you?" Papa was too tired to respond. He threw himself on a cot and slept through the next two days and nights. When he awoke, he went to the authorities and registered our family members as refugees. The authorities assigned us one bedroom and kitchen privileges at grandmother's, and a second bedroom in the house next door. We received ration stamps for food, and coupons for kitchenware. For one Reichsmark each, we bought plates, cups, and cooking pots.

Also living in the house were my father's sister, Irmgard, her husband, who was stationed nearby and their four-year-old daughter, whom we called "the princess." Irmgard, a tall, attractive woman with a head of curly, ash blond hair, had a constant frown on her face. She and her daughter lived behind closed doors. Our cousin guarded her toys like *Rheingold*. Irmgard prepared and ate her meals with her daughter. She rarely spoke to us children. During the two and a half months we lived on Kattenbühl Lane, Irmgard's husband, Kurt, came home a number times. He wore a uniform, highly polished black riding boots, and argued noisily with his wife.

In a garret lived Frau Stanislavski, a widow whose home had been destroyed by bombs. I didn't mind the crowded conditions as much as the tense and miserly atmosphere that permeated the house like hoarfrost. Papa's mother, a petite and slender woman, dressed in dark garments that covered her swollen ankles. She wore her long graying hair combed back, braided, and wound into a large bun. The skin on her narrow face appeared pallid and wrinkled. Like Papa, she had bushy eyebrows, but that is where the resemblance stopped. Her gold-rimmed glasses sparkled in the light and were the only bright thing about her person. Her most distinguishing feature was a growth on her neck the size of a small egg. My brothers speculated about what it contained. I wondered why she continuously shook her head. We gathered that her head shaking probably meant "no, no, no," and so we scurried out of her way. Our grandmother muttered about the impending *Zusammenbruch,* while she puttered about the house and garden. This was the first time I heard the word "collapse" in connection with the loss of the war.

Grossmutter Laabs, who had wholeheartedly supported Hitler, still displayed his portrait on her living room wall, and she continued to wear her party insignia on her lapel. I remembered when she threatened to disown Papa when he told her what he thought about Hitler, and when he predicted, after the defeat at Stalingrad, that Germany would lose the war. Throughout the day, while listening to the radio, peeling potatoes, and going about her chores, she muttered, "I can't believe what is happening. The Führer promised us a thousand-year Reich."

The Führer wasn't the only one who had disappointed our grandmother. It wasn't really surprising that she preferred Papa's children from his first marriage to us. I figured the reason was that they most likely had better manners than we did. An example of our bad behavior was an incident that had happened on one of grandmother's visits. It began when I noticed that mischief was brewing from the way Sven and Frank huddled. I wasn't sure exactly what the two of them were planning when I heard Sven call out, "Dagmar, Frank and I are going to teach you how to greet Grossmutter properly, and maybe she'll give you some chocolate."

Dagmar looked up into the grimy, grinning faces of her two big brothers. Without hesitation, she asked, "How?"

With a wicked smirk on his face, Sven instructed her. "All you have to do is: go up to Grossmutter, curtsey, smile, and in your sweetest voice say '*Arschloch.*' Can you do that?" Dagmar twisted one of her braids and nodded.

I warned, "*Junge, Junge*, you boys are going to get into deep trouble."

"Aw, stay out of it," said Sven and waved me off. He turned his attention back to Dagmar.

"Go ahead, and show us how you are going to do it. Let's pretend that I am Grossmutter," Frank the co-conspirator coaxed her.

"Silly. You don't look like her," Dagmar said.

"You can pretend, can't you? Come on." He promised, "I'll let you play with my toy horses."

"Honest?" Dagmar walked up to him, curtsied, took his hand, smiled, and said, "*Aschloch.*" Sven ignored the fact that Dagmar had mispronounced the word. He praised her instead and told her that they would be watching.

When I saw Grossmutter coming up the walk with Papa closely behind, it was too late to do anything about the plan Sven and Frank had hatched. Besides, I was curious what would happen next.

Dagmar, in her prettiest white dress, ran toward her grandmother, took her outstretched hand, curtsied, and chirped in her sweetest voice, "*Aschloch.*"

The smile on grandmother's lips faded at being called an "asshole." Her expression quickly changed into one of scorn as she turned to her son. "Karl!" she said in a cold voice, "Is that what you teach your children?" After a pause, she added, "Why should I be surprised?" Papa tried to cover his mouth with his hand to hide a wicked smile. Unlike Mutti, our father regularly indulged in salty language himself. He had bragged often enough about the fantastic and brilliant deeds of mischief he had pulled off when he was a youngster.

"Sorry, Mutter," he replied. "I'll get to the bottom of this." He swept his daughter up into his arms and shook his head at her, trying hard not to smile while he stroked her soft hair, "That's a naughty word, dear, and you mustn't say it anymore."

"But, Papa, what about the chocolate? The boys said …" She didn't get any further. Papa had placed the tip of his index finger on her lips.

"Bad children don't deserve treats," our grandmother huffed. Dagmar pushed out her lower lip and looked as though she was about to cry.

The boys grinned, nudged each other, and quickly disappeared behind the house. Papa didn't sound very stern when he called after them, "No supper for you two tonight." Later, I overheard Frank betting Sven that Grossmutter didn't bring chocolate anyway.

Red with embarrassment, I waited for my grandmother to approach. "Good afternoon, Grossmutter" I stuttered, as I curtsied and waited for her hand. She slowly walked past without looking at me. I started to cry but felt better when Papa made a funny face behind his mother's back and pulled one of my braids, as he followed her into the house. I felt sorry for Mutti when she had to apologize for the appalling behavior of her children.

Although it was deep winter when we arrived in Münden, my brothers and I spent as much time outside the house as possible. We tried to stay out of everybody's way. When Papa discovered two old sleds in the attic, the boys and I pulled Dagmar up a hill and raced down the narrow lane. We yelled and landed on top of each other at the bottom. We stayed outside until dusk, and we returned home cold and ravenously hungry.

While we lived on Kattenbühl Lane, I got the answers to some of the questions that had plagued me. I remembered when Mutti had pleaded with Papa not to take her to Münden. Instead, she had wanted to join her friends, Frau Doktor and Frau Seif, on the southern escape route from Poland through Czechoslovakia toward Bavaria. Mutti had suggested that we stay at a refugee camp until we could figure out where we were going to settle. Papa insisted that he had designed, built, and still owned part of the house on Kattenbühl Lane, and that is where we were going to live. "*Aus, Punkt, Schluss,*" end of discussion.

Later we heard that our friends who had taken the southern route first encountered hostile Czechs, who mistreated them horribly. Some were unable to continue west, when Russian soldiers caught up with them, killing some and wounding others. Papa had been right. He had chosen the safer route. Relieved and grateful, I felt like dancing and singing, "My Papa has magic."

Dagmar had found a new friend in Frau Stanislavski. They spent days together in Frau Stanislavski's garret. Frau Stanislavski told us stories while she sat bent over, endlessly knitting gray woolen socks for the "soldiers at the front." She and Mutti became friendly as well, and, from time to time, they shared a cup of *Ersatzkaffee* under the eaves. When Frau Stanislavki asked Mutti how our family survived the war and the flight from Poland, Mutti folded her hands, closed her eyes and answered solemnly, "We were protected by a higher power," and added, "For the duration of our flight I was in a trance-like state." The needles stopped clicking for a moment while Frau Stanislavski crossed herself. Mutti talked about some of the terrible things that had taken place in Poland. Once she hinted that Papa's activities had put our family in great danger, and once again, she emphasized that our survival was a miracle.

When I heard Mutti say out loud for the first time that Papa had done things that put him and us into terrible danger, I left the room to hide my tears. I sat on the stairs and sobbed, as I came to realize that Mutti's revelation confirmed that the anxiety I had lived with during the past three years had been justified, and that the veil obscuring the mysteries which had plagued me was beginning to lift a little at last.

Sometime around the middle of March, we heard rumors that the Allies had crossed the Rhine. All during the war, I had heard the word "front." To me the front was the place where the fighting and most of the killing took place. If a soldier went to the front, it meant that he might not come back. Mutti's brother, Fritz, had fought on the Russian front, where he was seriously wounded and lost a leg. Mutti didn't stop worrying about her brother Willi, who was still at sea. "Nobody has heard from Willi in months. I hope that his luck holds out." She reminded us once again that two of his ships had gone down. One of them, the Bismarck, sank without him on board because he had missed the ship's departure. When she heard the news, Mutti rejoiced, "Our Willi must have been born under a lucky star." The next time when one of his ships was torpedoed and sunk, he was equally lucky. He survived by floating in the water for twenty hours, was rescued, and reassigned to another ship.

I never got used to the sounds of wailing air raid sirens. Every time we heard the first signal, the pre-alarm, we started looking for a place to take cover. The second signal meant that the planes were close and that the bombing could start anytime. The third signal let everyone who lived through the raid know that all was clear. While other cities had been destroyed during years of relentless bombardments that killed hundreds of thousands, Münden had been spared. It did not have any heavy industry and the only *Pionier*, Corps of Engineer, installation was located north of town. For that reason most of the time when the sirens sounded, the bombers droned overhead on their way to distant targets.

Papa believed in being prepared. He knew it was impossible to get five children dressed and ready to descend into the basement before the full alarm signal sounded. We slept in our clothes. We knew the drill. Get out of bed as soon as the pre-alarm sounds, put on your shoes and your coat, and grab your blanket. Help your sister get dressed, grab her blanket, put on your knapsack, and carefully descend the steep stairs. We settled in Grossmutter's air raid shelter. It had a thick concrete ceiling, walls, and a heavy, steel plated door with a rubber seal to prevent smoke and gas from seeping in. The shelter had cots and benches along the walls. It had shelves filled with apples, canned goods, fruit syrup, and glass jars of preserved fruit and vegetables. As I deciphered the old-fashioned German script on their labels, my mouth watered and my stomach growled. We waited for the radio announcer to tell us where the bomber formations were headed. Papa was proud of the way the shelters he had designed were constructed. He lectured, "I knew that Germany was headed for war. All of the houses I designed after 1935 have air raid shelters." Even Tante Marianne grudgingly gave Papa credit for the construction of a well-built shelter in the house he designed for her and Onkel Wütt.

On March 30, 1945, the day before Easter, American planes bombed Münden for the first time during the war. Papa estimated that some of the bombs had exploded three blocks from us near the railroad station. After the sirens signaled the "all clear," we raced down the hill and explored the smoking craters. They were exactly where Papa had predicted they would be. We collected jagged splinters of iridescent, gray metal and rubbed them until they were hot. Closer to the center of town a bomb destroyed three houses and killed a family.

We heard rumors about a plan to blow up the bridge across the Fulda River. That rumor made Papa decide that "the ground was getting too hot." Some time ago, Mutti had contacted her friend, Annie Blankenburg, in Vaake. Annie agreed to give us refuge. The village was located twelve kilometers north of Münden. The question was, "How do we get there?" We had no car, and the bus didn't run any more. Papa lectured us, "We'll have go on foot after sundown."

"Walk all the way to Vaake in the pitch dark?" I asked.

Papa ignored my question. Instead, he asked, "Remember the burned-out cars and wagons we saw on the roads during our flight from Poland?" We nodded.

"How are we going to get through?" I asked Sven after Papa left the room.

"Papa will manage. You'll see," my brother answered matter-of-factly.

The Trek

The word Papa used for acquiring things was *organisieren*. It meant borrowing, trading, sometimes paying, or if need be, stealing, to get a job done. The *Handwagen* Papa acquired after the air raid to transport our few possessions was too small for our knapsacks, blankets, pots, and pans, but it was all he had been able to scrounge. Seven-month-old Björn would travel in his carriage, Dagmar and Frank would take turns riding on top of the luggage, and the rest of us would walk. "Fight 'till the last drop of blood? Indeed," Papa ranted, as he wiped the perspiration from his forehead.

Mutti leaned toward him and whispered, "Karl. They could hang you for saying that." The image of Papa strung up on a tree made me feel sick, but I, too, was relieved that we would soon be moving on.

Papa paid no attention to Mutti and cursed the idiots who might blow up the Pionierbrücke over the Fulda River before we could get across. He tied another bundle on top of the load, caught his breath, and raged on about the stupidity and futility of such an attempt. We knew that he didn't expect anyone to answer him and that we had better not interrupt. "Nothing can stop the *Amis* and *Tommies*," he fumed.

We were terrified by the American *Tiefflieger,* who not only were shooting up military convoys but were strafing civilians who crowded the roads and farmers who worked in their fields. That is why Papa had decided to wait until early evening, to have us line up before him. We nodded dutifully as he counted, "One, two, three, four," pointed to the baby, "five," to Mutti, "six, and with me that makes seven. Ready?" We had become used to this ritual since the day we almost left Dagmar behind. Our goodbyes didn't take long. I thought I detected an expression of relief on my grandmother's face.

Glorious spring weather with unseasonable warm temperatures had arrived early that year. The air was still balmy although it was late in the day. Papa and Mutti took the lead, held onto the handle of the wagon tongue, and pushed against its weight as we descended Kattenbühl Lane toward the underpass near the railroad station. Sven placed a sturdy stick between the spokes of one of the rear wheels to act as a brake. I gripped the handle of the baby carriage tightly while I kept an eye on Frank and Dagmar, who had been told to hold onto the carriage. We made it down the hill and took a breather. We walked past the bomb craters and under the railroad tracks before we started to rattle over cobblestone streets toward the Fulda River. Papa and Mutti pulled the cart. Sven pushed. The streets were empty, except for a few pedestrians, who scurried along with their heads low as if they wished to make themselves invisible. The air seemed saturated with apprehension.

We stopped at the Rotunde, a tower built during the Middle Ages as part of the encircling fortification to protect the town from marauders. During the Thirty Years War, General Tilly's army beleaguered the town for three days. He then crossed the moats, breached the walls, sacked the town, and massacred most of its inhabitants.

"Hört zu, Mund zu, Augen auf, Füße hoch," listen up, keep your mouth shut, your eyes open, and watch where you're going, Papa ordered when we got to the second tower, the Hagelturm. The sun had set behind the Tillyschanze on the bluff to the west. A motley unit of very young and very old *Volkssturm* soldiers in ill-fitting uniforms allowed us to pass, after Papa showed them our papers. They ordered us to hurry across the bridge, with the warning that they were getting ready to "blow'er up." The wagon wheels made a hollow sound as we crossed. On the other side, more soldiers urged us to move along. We took a turn to the right onto Mündener Strasse and walked first along the Fulda and then along the Weser River. I got tired pushing the carriage over the rough cobblestones. Dagmar and Frank took turns bouncing up and down on the handcart. When we passed through the new part of town, Papa pointed at a villa with low-slung dormers. "Your Onkel Otto designed it before he went to war," a tone of admiration in his voice. After we left the town behind, we noticed that the bomb craters created by the recent raid were already filled with water. It was too dark to detect the damage done by the bombers to the Corps of Engineers installation on the other side of the river.

Papa told us that the night was our friend. My eyes had adjusted to the dark, and I recognized the outline of the forester's house on the left and the youth hostel on the right. When the baby began to whimper, we pulled off the road and rested while Mutti nursed him. He was a good little boy who cried rarely, whimpered only when he was hungry or needed to be changed. Dagmar and Frank stretched their legs, and we all had a drink of water.

Out of the dark, an air raid warden emerged. He was wearing a helmet, an armband, and was carrying a bag over his shoulder. It was his job to patrol the neighborhood at night to make sure that every house had its windows blacked out. "Leaving town, hey? I would if I could." He pointed in the direction of the craters. "Too close for comfort. What are things coming to?" He lowered his voice, "The end I guess. Never mind. Didn't hear me say that, right? Better watch out for trucks. They drive as if the devil were behind them." He paused for a second and cackled, "Heh, heh, he may be at that."

Papa nodded, "*Ja, Ja,*" as the old man limped off into the night. But before I could feel too comfortable, Papa warned us about *Tiefflieger*. "If you hear a plane, move into the ditch at once, cover your heads and do not get up until I tell you to. Understood?" We understood. Then he did something strange. He handed Sven the baby's white blanket and asked him to wave it at passing trucks and cars to keep them from running us over. We moved on. Pushing the carriage on the blacktopped road was easier than over cobblestones. Papa and Mutti took the lead. Dagmar lay curled up on the cart. Frank held on to its side. I was glad that we had left our grandmother's house behind. The mild night air felt like velvet on my skin. I was happy that we were going back to Vaake, a peaceful, beautiful place I had missed during our years in Poland. Papa and Mutti pulled the cart shoulder to shoulder. They whispered, they laughed, and kissed. We were together. We were alive.

When military trucks rumbled passed us, Sven waved the white blanket. The trucks were enormous, their headlights painted black with only a narrow slit to illuminate the way. Around the curve and to our left I made out a guardhouse. "Soldiers are targets," Papa mumbled and urged us to quicken our pace. We passed the military base and after five kilometers reached a large agricultural estate, the Gut Hilwartshausen. Here, the road curved sharply to the west and away from the river. We kept on walking, pushing, and pulling. Surrounded by an expanse of fields, I smelled freshly plowed earth. A covey of quail took off with an eerie, whirring sound from the ditch in front of us and startled me. We moved away from the river and approached the last big bend in the road toward the north and Vaake.

Frank was allowed to join Dagmar once again on the wagon. The road made its sharp curve to the north as it carved out the rocky hillside on one side with a steep drop-off to the river on the other. Where the narrow road ran between the hill and the river it was blocked by rows of concrete structures that looked like huge, jagged dragon teeth. Papa investigated. When he returned he warned, "*Vorsichtig!* It's a tank trap. There must be troops nearby. Remember the rabbit, children?"

Sven answered, "It keeps its eyes and ears open. It runs, makes quick turns, and hides from the fox."

"Right you are, son," Papa praised. After we slowly zigged, and zagged around the trap, we turned north and continued walking high above the river. The baby slept blissfully. It was then that we heard voices. I felt a twinge of fear when Papa walked ahead to reconnoiter and was swallowed up by the night. I was relieved when he returned a few minutes later to tell us that the voices we had heard were those of other refugees making their way north.

We walked until Papa suddenly stopped. Sensing something, he admonished us to be quiet. I perked up my ears and detected the faint roar from a single plane. "*Deckung!* Into the ditch, now!" Papa commanded. We worked like a well-oiled machine. I pushed the carriage off the road, Papa snatched Dagmar and Frank off the wagon, Mutti and Sven pulled the cart into the ditch. Disobeying Papa, I pressed my back into the mossy hillside, and stared into the night determined to get a glimpse of the plane.

At that moment, I saw a light glimmer ahead of us. My father had seen it, too. He shouted "Put that cigarette out, you *Arsch* ..." The rest of his expletive was drowned out by the engine of a plane, as it thundered by at our eye level, so close that I thought I could touch it. Afterwards, I couldn't resist bragging to my brothers that I that I had seen the pilot.

"Yeah, sure you did," Sven snickered.

Everybody, including the baby, was wide-awake as we pulled ourselves out of the ditch. For a while, we moved fast until we reached a small waterfall, which spilled over the side of the steep hillside. We rested and drank its cool water from our cupped hands. Once we were refreshed, it didn't take us long to reach Steinerwehrberg, a sandstone quarry blasted out of the hillside on our left. There we slowed down once again.

In past years, this was the place to which we came each spring to gather the wild *Himmelsschlüssel*, said to be Saint Peter's legendary keys to heaven. These were the yellow primroses that had pushed their way toward the sun through layers of rotting leaves. I planned to come back here once the war was over. Frank would want to join me. Whenever he wandered through the woods and fields, he carried a box and a small trowel under his arm. When he found a flower or a plant he liked, he dug it up gently so that most of the soil clung to its roots, took it home, and planted it in the garden, where he tended it with care.

After the quarry, the road went uphill. I was getting very tired and my feet hurt. Another two miles and we would arrive at the barrel factory. From the factory it was only a little further to the parish house in the center of the village. I imagined how nice it would be to sleep. We rested one more time before we reached the cobble-stoned road leading through the village. The rest of the way I must have walked in my sleep, for I only dimly remember our arrival at the parsonage. I do remember waking up—warm and snug under a snow-white featherbed, next to my friend Brigitte, on a luminous Easter morning. It was April 1, 1945.

The Americans Arrive in Vaake,
April 1945

Our arrival at the parsonage was like entering a beehive. The queen bee was my mother's friend and Dagmar's godmother, Annie Blankenburg. While her husband, the local Lutheran pastor, was away at war, she opened wide the doors of their home to refugees. Thus, we joined Annie, her mother, her daughters Brigitte and Christiane, sons Dietrich and redheaded Martin, and Annie's sister Ulla, with her three children. Rounding out Annie's household was Leon, their French housekeeper, whose response to every misfortune was *"so ist das la vie,"* that's life.

Our hostess, an energetic, competent, somewhat prickly yet generous woman rummaged through her cupboards and drawers for kitchen utensils and clothes for us. She offered our family a room overlooking the river, as well as the laundry cottage next to the main house for use as a kitchen. Eighteen people were now in the household, but soon more would join us. On April 2, nineteen-year-old Dorothea Weimann—we called her Putti—and her fourteen-year-old brother, Albrecht, and two cousins arrived on bicycles. They were fortunate and happy to have survived the flight from their hometown, Martin Luther's Wittenberg. Their mother, Häns, joined us a day later. So did a number of others whose names I can't remember. Eventually, by the time the Americans arrived, the total number of occupants was somewhere around twenty-six.

In the midst of this crowd, we made ourselves as comfortable as we could. After we burned Papa's air force uniform, he had only one set of second-hand clothes. When Mutti decided they desperately needed laundering, Papa had to stay in bed until they were dry. On these days, when he could not get up, he told us more stories about the rabbits, deer, the wild boar, the wolves, and the foxes in the forest. Across the river, we watched a feathery mist drift and dissolve like a gossamer veil into mysterious shrouds between tall spruce trees, a sign, Papa claimed, that the foxes were brewing their coffee. None of us doubted Papa, for we, too, believed that strange and wondrous things happened in the deep, dark forests surrounding us.

When Papa had to stay in bed, we gathered around him on cots and pallets. One of the stories he told us was "The Princess of the Outhouse," about Mutti's brother Willi, and his daughter:

Once upon a time, on the edge of the woods, stood a small cottage, where a man, his wife, and their little daughter found refuge after a terrible war had ravaged their homeland. Food was scarce, and the little girl helped her parents gather berries and nuts in the forest and plant potatoes and cabbages in their garden. She was a pretty little thing with brown hair and rosy cheeks, and she was happy except when she needed to go to the privy. "Papa," she wailed. "I have to go, and I'm afraid."

"Aw," her father answered with a smile. "What's worrying you?"

"I am scared of falling into the hole, and I don't like the bad smell and the cold wind up my bottom."

"There is no need to be frightened, but I'll tell you what. How about playing a game of pretend?"

"A game? Will it help?"

"Why don't we give it a try?" Her brown eyes looked trustingly into her father's, and she nodded. "This is what we'll do. You'll be a princess, and I'll be your devoted servant."

She looked down at her shabby dress and bare feet, "But, Papa, I don't have pretty clothes like princesses do."

"We can take care of that quite easily. You see, when we pretend, we can have anything we desire."

"Really?" she asked her eyes wide in wonderment.

"What's your favorite color, Your Royal Highness?"

"Blue like the sky, and ..." she hesitated a moment, "gold like the sun, and silver like the moon and the stars."

"Ta da ... and look what I have here for you." The servant raised both hands to hold up an imaginary dress. "Just what you wished for, Your Highness. Isn't it the most beautiful dress you've ever seen?"

"It is, it is." The princess clapped her hands, "Blue all over with pretty flowers in gold and silver. Please, help me get dressed."

"You'll have to stand still, Your Highness." The princess nodded, smiled, and lifted both arms. The servant gently pulled the imaginary dress over her slender body and fluffed out the folds. "Your Majesty," he said, "your radiant beauty will delight the sun."

The little princess twirled around and chirped, "Thank you, thank you. What shall I call you, my good man?"

"My name is Willi, and I am at your service, Your Royal Highness," he answered with a bow and a flourish.

"But haven't you forgotten something, Willi?" asked the princess.

"Pardon me, Your Highness. What is it you desire?"

"My golden crown, of course."

"Oh, pardon me once again. I'll take a look. Your handmaiden was polishing it only this morning. Here it is, Your Highness, all shined up. Aren't those rubies and sapphires sparkly?" Willi bowed low and handed her the crown. She carefully placed it on top of her curly hair.

"Is it on straight?" she asked, turning left and right so he could see.

"Yes, Your Highness. Indeed it is. Are you quite ready, Your Highness?"

"No, not yet. It's a bit chilly today. I believe I'll wear my royal robe. You know, the one made of white fur and decorated with little black tails."

"At your service, Your Highness." Willi swirled the robe over his head. "Allow me to drape it over your shoulders." He bowed deeply, opened the front door, and flourished his hat in the direction of a small house at the end of the path, under the tall spruce trees. The little princess, her head high, turned toward her trusted servant and nodded graciously.

"I'm ready. You may pick up my train." Willi did as he was told, and they walked with slow and measured steps until they reached the small house. The princess pointed to the heart-shaped cutout on the door. "Very pretty."

Willi opened the door of the privy and waved away a fly with his hat. "Your Highness, if you please," he pointed toward the three holes, two big ones and a small one. He lifted one of the lids, "The small one was made especially to fit your royal bottom." The princess put her hands to her mouth and giggled. "May I hold your cape while you …?" The princess blushed, nodded, and handed it to him. Then she pulled down her drawers, hopped onto the small hole, and cast a worried look in Willi's direction. "No need for concern, Your Highness. Nothing bad can happen. Would you enjoy some entertainment while you …?"

The princess nodded graciously as she squeezed her nostrils with her left hand and held on tightly with her right. "Yes, Willi, please leave the door open, and tell me a story and sing me some songs," she naseled.

"As you wish, Your Royal Highness." While the princess sat on her throne, Willi entertained her with stories about the animals that live in the forest. He sang a song about the birds that planned a wedding, and he danced for her to the tunes of an imaginary orchestra.

To show her pleasure, the princess let go of the seat and her nose long enough to clap her hands. When she was finished, she pulled a square of newspaper off a hook on the wall, and wiped her royal bottom. She hopped off her throne, pulled up her drawers, and held her hand out to Willi, who helped her out the door. She straightened her imaginary crown, nodded, and, with her pert nose up in the air, commanded, "My robe, please, and thank you, my dear Willi. I am ready to return to my castle."

He answered with the deepest bow he could manage as he flourished his hat, "I am your devoted and faithful servant, Your Royal Highness."

The End

Once Papa's clothes were dry, there was no more time for storytelling. He quickly got dressed, barked orders and rushed around once again to take care of urgent matters in preparation for the imminent allied invasion.

During that first week in April, the villagers prepared to surrender to the Americans. They hung white sheets from their second story windows. We heard rumors that the Nazi flags had either been burned or were hidden under the potatoes in basements. Sven proclaimed, "Boy, am I going to be glad to see the *Amis.*" When I asked him why, at first he wouldn't say. When I didn't stop pestering him, he told me that it would mean the end of the war. I thought about it and agreed that he had a point. At the same time, I could tell that Papa was wary of our liberators. He painted two large signs in neat black letters that read in Oxford English:

VICARAGE
OFF LIMITS

"This may keep some marauders out or slow them down," he grumbled, a hammer in his hand and two nails in the corner of his mouth, as he attached the signs to the front and back doors. Our mothers moved benches, blankets, and supplies into the basement. Meanwhile, we children roamed. Each time the rumblings of artillery reached our ears, we ran back home and reported excitedly, *"Die Amerikaner kommen."*

Papa looked odd in a faded shirt, baggy pants cinched at the waist, and oversized jacket, and Mutti told Annie that she was hoping his age and his white hair would keep the Americans from taking him prisoner. I also heard her say for the hundredth time that we had been in "the hands of a higher power during our escape from Poland." I, on the other hand, had decided that we would have perished if Papa hadn't guided and protected us during that perilous journey.

At one point, a heated argument ensued between Nazi leaders and some villagers, who objected to a barrier of tree trunks, which the Nazis had erected across the main road into the village. In the end, the sensible citizens prevailed, and Papa helped dismantle the obstruction. Soldiers and Nazi officials burned or buried their uniforms, papers, and medals, and some of them hid in the forest. The farmers, who had stopped working in the fields for fear of being strafed by American fighter planes, clustered in courtyards and exchanged dire predictions. Our parents speculated whether the Allies would come as *Sieger*, conquerors, or as *Befreier*, liberators.

On Friday afternoon, April 6, when the first shells began screaming low over the parsonage, we rushed into the basement. To the west of us, heavy American artillery positioned at the edge of the Reinhardswald shelled two small German artillery emplacements. The German batteries were located a few hundred yards directly across the river from the parsonage. Instinctively, we ducked and held our ears. We shook with fright every time a shell roared over our heads. After we got used to the noise, we took turns peering through two small windows in the stone foundation. We watched shells explode, and fountains of soil and metal spew into the air and clatter to the ground near and on the German batteries. Clouds of black smoke billowed, slowly drifted to the north, and dissipated. From a distance, we couldn't tell if any German soldiers were killed or injured. After a while, we saw some of them retreat in single file and disappear up the steep hillside into the trees of the Bramwald.

After the battle, an eerie calm spread over the village. We settled down on benches and blankets, and resumed our quarrels and games while munching on shriveled apples from last year's crop. I begged to be let upstairs, but Papa, who had taken a look around, shook his head. An errant shell destined for the German guns had hit a house down the street, killing an old man. Down river, Frau Henze, the midwife who attended Mutti at the births of Sven, Frank, Ute, and Dagmar, was riding her bicycle on the way to another birth, when she was killed by American artillery as well.

Papa lined all the children up and lectured, "One more thing. The *Amis* will be looking for soldiers and weapons. They will point their guns straight at you with their fingers on the trigger. I want you to be *mucksmäuschenstill*, quiet as a mouse." He turned to the boys and asked, "What does it sound like when a rifle is put on safety?"

Sven answered quickly before anybody else could, "It goes 'click.'"

"Exactly. When you hear the 'click' it means that the soldiers no longer consider you a threat. Understood?" We realized that what he said was very important and nodded obediently.

We did not have to wait long before the earth shook with the rumbling, clanking and grinding of tank tracks. I don't know why it was much scarier than the sound of bombs exploding. We heard the roaring of trucks on the cobblestone road that ran through the middle of the village. I shivered when I heard the clanking of metal on metal approaching the basement. Seconds later, we heard heavy pounding, then voices. We watched as the door opened slowly and saw the silhouette of a soldier in full battle gear loom against the blue sky. He wore baggy pants, a helmet, carried a pack, an ammunition belt, and had a drawn rifle. He crouched down and peered into the semi-darkness. There we were: a bunch of children between the ages of seven months and fourteen years, sitting shoulder to shoulder on benches, staring back at him with big eyes. The youngest, baby Björn, squirmed in my arms. Albrecht, who was tall for his age, knelt on the ground between Sven and Frank, with a blanket pulled up to his waist. This had been Papa's idea, because he was concerned that the Americans might take the boy prisoner. I wasn't sure how a blanket would make a difference, because once Albrecht got up, the soldiers would see how tall he was, but I kept these thoughts to myself.

The American shouted something about, "a nest of little Krauts," and motioned to someone behind him. Naturally, we knew that *Kraut* meant cabbage, but why they called us cabbages puzzled us. We discovered much later that it was their nickname for us Germans. Annie and Albrecht's mother, a gray-haired, confident, and imposing lady who taught high school English, climbed the stairs. We heard her ask in flawless Oxford English. "How do you do?" I caught the words, "No soldiers," "vicarage," and "children."

With guns still pointed at us, one of the soldiers cautioned, "easy" and motioned us to ascend. The bigger children pulled, nudged, and carried the smaller ones. I still hadn't heard the 'click' of the safety. We squinted as we moved into the light. When all of us had gathered in the courtyard, I heard the first 'click,' followed by another. In spite of what Papa had said, I did not relax until the soldiers smiled after they had counted all fifteen children. We were surprised and relieved that the first wave of fighting units that captured the village did not fit the picture that the Nazi propaganda had painted of the enemy. I was especially grateful that they hadn't bothered Papa, and I was glad that they hadn't taken Albrecht prisoner, for I had developed a secret liking for this handsome boy. Our parents herded us into the house after the soldiers had searched it, the laundry cottage, and the barn. Papa believed that the German artillery positions across the river remained a danger to us all. He pointed them out to the Americans, over the opposition of some of the parsonage residents.

The Americans decided that they needed the house for an observation point. They ordered us to vacate. Häns explained to them that this would be a hardship for the twenty-six occupants, more than half of whom were children, as well as for one of the women who was in her eighth month of pregnancy. After Häns pleaded with them to allow us to stay, they assigned us one room and the use of the kitchen.

Papa had injured himself while cutting firewood. Mutti bandaged the profusely bleeding head wound. While he was resting, we sneaked through the garden toward Mündener Strasse. The tanks and trucks pulling artillery, halftracks with mounted machine guns, big white stars painted on their hoods and doors, rumbled along the narrow road in clouds of diesel fumes. Jeeps and trucks crammed with soldiers followed. We stared at the black truck drivers, who flashed their gleaming, white teeth, waved, and threw small packets to us. The one I caught had HERSHEY printed on it. I sniffed it, jumped up and down, and squealed, *"Schokolade!"* It had been years since I tasted chocolate. I let it melt on my tongue, while I savored every morsel of its velvety sweetness. We picked up other packages that contained thin strips of something that smelled minty or fruity. We found out later that the strips wrapped in silver paper contained gum, which one chewed and spit out after the sugary taste was gone.

My brothers and their five little friends were thrilled by the sight of speeding scout cars on the far side of the river. They hung over the fence and sang, *"Panzer Spähwagen, Panzer Spähwagen,"* to the tune of puppet Kasperle's *"Tra Tri Tralalla."* For hours, they amused themselves by counting and naming each piece of equipment that moved north towards Hemeln.

That night our parents calmed our fears by leading us in song as we settled down on wall-to-wall mattresses in the living room. When the German positions did not fire another shot, the Americans decided against occupying the house and left. Once again, however, we feared for our lives when the shelling of targets beyond the Bramwald resumed during the night.

After the sudden departure of the American fighting units, people crawled out of their basements and ventured forth in search of water, food, and news. We had been without electricity since the bombing of Münden the day before Easter. We knew little of how the war was progressing. This had created an atmosphere in which rumors and speculations flourished. The only reliable source was Gärtner

Becker, who lived up the Ahle Valley. He generated his own electricity, using the water from the creek to run a radio.

The question people continued to ask themselves and each other was, what would happen next? The fathers and sons of our friends and neighbors, who had been at war for years, were dead, injured, or missing. Some of the people who had found shelter in the parsonage began leaving to search for family members in the ruins of their hometowns. Postal and telephone service, and food distribution had broken down completely. When we ran out of our mainstay, potatoes, Annie handed us a basket and sent us off to make the rounds of the village farms. She instructed us to say that, "Frau Pastor sent us," and as a result we returned home with a full basket until supplies ran out.

The End of the War,
May 1945

Sometime in May, while Brigitte, Christiane, and I were sitting under a Japanese magnolia in bloom, we heard the adults talking about Hitler's suicide and Germany's surrender. Although we were afraid what was in store for us, we breathed a sigh of relief that day. We bowed our heads to thank God that the war was finally over and to ask for His continued protection.

For a while, we lived in a kind of limbo until a second wave of American troops arrived in the village. They requisitioned houses and settled in. Papa ordered us to "stay in the compound" and "out of their way." The presence of the Americans fascinated us so, that at times we disregarded these orders. We were astounded when we peeked through the kitchen door and saw two soldiers talking to Leon, who was busy shaking a frying pan with fat snails we had gathered in the garden that morning. The men leaned back in their chairs, rested their boots on the table, chewed, puffed on cigarettes, and talked as though they had marbles in their mouths.

When Papa turned his back, Sven and Frank ventured down to the river, where Frank discovered a metal object that looked like a large egg with knobs. Sven yelled, "Idiot, leave it!" Frank had already picked it up and was examining it. When he began handling a small ring, Sven screamed, "Pitch it." Frank threw the object as far as he could into the river, where it blew up, creating a fountain. The boys threw themselves on the ground as Papa had taught them. Silvery fish started floating belly-up on the surface of the water. After the explosion, we saw soldiers running toward the boys, yelling "Hell!" and "Little shits." The boys dashed home, leaving the cursing soldiers behind.

The Americans may have let Sven and Frank off easy, but there was more than a scolding to come from Papa. "What did I tell you?" he raged.

"We're not supposed to leave the compound," Sven replied, his head hung low.

Usually punishment was swift. When Papa took his time, I knew that the boys were in big trouble. Later that day, after Sven and Frank each got a spanking, they hung over the fence with the rest of us to watch the Americans. We were amused by the way the American soldiers marched back and forth, turned right and left, on the meadow in front of the parsonage. Their sergeant yelled, "hop, hep, hep, ho, hop, hep, hep, ho," for hours on end. The soldiers strung telephone wires and dug holes in the sandy loam of the riverbank. They unwrapped crackers and cheese, opened cans and ate their fill. They boiled water, brewed coffee, and threw their leftovers into holes, poured gasoline over everything, and set it on fire. When we asked Papa why the *Amis* burned food, he thought about it before he replied. "Remember. We're their enemy, and we've lost the war." When we examined the holes the next day, all we found were charred cans and silver paper. Years later, I read that the reason the soldiers burned their leftovers instead of sharing them was that during and immediately after the war, their orders were not to "fraternize" with Germans.

The Americans who were quartered in the village were young, healthy, and attractive. They cleaned their weapons and polished the brass buttons on their uniforms. They smoked, they laughed and joked with each other. A few smiled at us and threw chocolate and chewing gum. Once, as my friend Margret and I walked along Mündener Strasse, a soldier threw a colorful packet. Thinking that we would find candy or gum, we picked it up, hurried home, and opened it. We were disappointed when we discovered instead small individually wrapped rubber bags. Margret's older brother, Oskar, grinned and asked what we were doing with *Pariser*. Margret didn't answer him, and since I didn't want to appear ignorant, neither did I. Once we were alone, she explained, "Men wear them when they sleep with women." I pretended that I knew what she was talking about, but I wondered how come Margret was so much smarter than I.

What I did understand is that the American soldiers weren't all that different from German soldiers. They liked to flirt and spend time with women. Although they spoke little or no German, they had no trouble communicating their wishes. One day, as my mother walked on the main street, a soldier whistled and called out to her, "Hey, baby."

As Mutti later told the story, "I turned around to see a boy, who didn't look to be older than twenty, following me. I stopped, smiled and addressed him, 'Young man,' I said in my best school English, 'You should know that I am old enough to be your mother.'"

The poor boy blushed, stuttered, "Excuse me, Ma'am," and quickly went on his way.

Each morning we opened our windows to the ringing of a brass bell. We watched as the town crier slowly proceeded down the street. We listened to him read the new rules and regulations of the military government: All weapons and ammunition had to be surrendered, a 7 p.m. curfew was established, and to our puzzlement, the clocks had to be set back two hours. The next day the crier ordered us to keep our doors unlocked at all times. This order was of particular concern since bands of Polish and Russian POWs and other displaced persons, who had been released from forced labor camps, roamed the countryside and were taking their revenge on the German population by robbing and murdering them.

One morning, around five o'clock, the crier awakened us with the urgent ringing of his bell, "By order of the American commander, every one is to get out of bed, get dressed, and remain inside until further notice." A sense of panic electrified us. We had heard about the atrocities being committed by the Russians, and we were afraid of what might happen to us if the Americans left and the Russians moved in.

We huddled all morning, but nothing happened until the afternoon, when two heavily armed American soldiers appeared at the front door. One of them entered and began to search for weapons. The other remained outside on guard. Putti, who was taking her bath in the attic, heard the commotion, panicked, and, instead of pouring the bath water onto the roof into the gutter, threw the water out the window in one big swoop and drenched the guard below. As expected, he took the deluge to be a deliberate attack on his person and stormed up the stairs, cursing and shouting threats, when he ran into Putti's mother, who barred his way with her arms raised high and quickly explained that the downpour was an accident. "I am so sorry, pardon us, please," she said, as she toweled his helmet and uniform dry and offered to have her daughter launder his clothes. From then on, Putti washed and ironed uniforms for a number of soldiers, under the strict supervision of her mother, of course, in exchange for a bar of soap, or coffee or C rations. All of these items were highly prized at a time when our stomachs were often empty and the shelves at the village store were bare.

Eight-year-old Frank was a skinny little fellow, who liked to hang around the Americans. One of the men befriended him, took him along to the field kitchen, and gave him a mess kit. There, he motioned Frank to stand in line between two soldiers. When Frank's turn came, and he stretched out both hands, one with a cup and one with a plate, the soldier passing out the food refused to serve him. But as Frank told it, then followed a heated discussion between his friend and the cook. In the end, Frank's mess kit was heaped high with potatoes, beans, and sausage. His cup was filled with hot coffee. Without taking a bite, Frank carried his treasure carefully before him. He brought the food home to share with Mutti and told us that a soldier named "GI" had given it to him. From that day until he left a few weeks later, Frank's GI saw to it that the scrawny Kraut received a daily serving of a nutritious meal.

The River Gave and the River Took

From the time my siblings and I could walk, our parents had warned us not to go near a river without supervision. We had heard many stories of children drowning in the Weser's swift waters. Those stories did not keep us from sneaking off to watch fishermen set their eel traps, boats ply their trade, and log rafts drift toward the sea. We made paper boats and sent them downstream. We threw sticks and rocks and cooled our toes. During floods, we watched the muddy waters inundate the meadows and the houses along the river's banks. When the waters receded, they left behind fine gray silt, which enriched the soil and made the meadows lush. That is how I learned that the river gave and the river took.

Many battles were fought during the last months of the war. The dead floated down stream until finally the bodies got caught in one of the eddies, where they circled around and around in one last, macabre dance. In time, the eddies gave up these bodies and gently deposited them between the rocky jetties protruding into the river. On one of our expeditions, we discovered the body of a German soldier, as it lay with its head in the silt, partially in the water, bloated and very still. But I did not dare to look too closely. I did not want to see his face. As long as I could not see his face, I reasoned, he would not become real, for if I allowed him to become real, I would not be able to stop crying. The boys ran home shouting, "There's a dead man in the river!" We were not allowed to watch the adults retrieve the body and bury it. That is how I learned, that in times of war, the river mostly took.

Where the river curved, jetties protruded into the water and made the water curl against its tips. They had been built to keep the Weser from eroding the fat bottomland. The safest place to bathe was between two such jetties. Before we learned how to swim, we splashed in these shallows, under the watchful eyes of adults.

During the early summer of 1945, when I was almost twelve years old, I awoke one morning to a river that was only half its normal width. I had wanted to get to the "other side" since I was six, when we moved to the valley for the first time. When our parents saw how low the river was, they allowed Brigitte, Christiane and me to swim across, admonishing us to be careful. My friends put on their bathing suits, and, since I did not own one, I stripped to my underwear. We entered the water between two jetties. The instant I passed the calm, crescent-shaped cove, I felt the swift current tugging at my legs. It pulled and forced me off my feet. I was frightened for one moment, but I began to move my arms and legs froggy style, with my head above the water, the way I had been taught. There was no turning back now, for the river had me in its power. Brigitte and Christiane had plunged in and were moving ahead of me. I allowed the river to carry me, moving my arms and legs, at first rapidly, then slowly and rhythmically, when I realized that if I continued this way, I would never reach the other side. I had noticed that my friends were swimming against the current on a diagonal line. I decided to follow their example. Every once in a while, I put down my feet to test the depth of the river, and to my surprise, I felt its rocky bottom. In the middle of the river I tried again, but this time I had to dive into the bottle-green water to touch the rocks below. After I surfaced, I strained against the current and reached the other side, out of breath and a good distance downriver. I waded ashore to join my friends, who lay panting and sunning themselves in the high grass.

We talked about the last battle that we had watched from the basement window, and we decided to look for the remnants of the German artillery posts. Near the edge of the woods, we came upon the craters, the twisted remnants of guns, empty shells, and a partially burned boot. I shivered, despite the warm sun on my body.

On the way back, I plunged into the water, with more confidence, and after swimming against the current, splashing and shouting, we arrived downriver, near the church, where Brigitte and Christiane's father used to preach every Sunday before the war.

Later that summer, after heavy rains, the river spilled over its banks and flooded the valley as it had done for centuries before the Eder River Dam was built to control the flooding: first the meadows, then the fields, and finally it crept up the wall surrounding the parsonage. It licked at the foundations of the half-timbered sixteenth-century farm houses on the banks of the river. It looked like nothing could stop such a mighty stream, intent on completing its journey to the sea. Its awesome power drew us to its banks. The swirling, chocolate-brown torrent mesmerized children and adults alike, as clumps of bushes, trees and portions of wooden fences floated by.

Frau Götte—I thought of her as *Hutzelweiblein*—was an old shriveled-up woman who lived a few doors down. She joined us and observed, "This is nothing compared to the time during the war when we thought that God was sending us a second flood." She wiped her brow with her dirty apron, sighed, and went on to explain that one night a British plane had torpedoed and destroyed the Eder River Dam. Without warning, the rushing waters had inundated river valleys for hundreds of miles. We listened in awe as she described in detail how the debris of houses, barns, uprooted trees, corpses of humans, and bloated animal cadavers floated by in the swirling waters for days. With a crooked finger, she pointed to the high water mark carved into the corner post of a house down the street, reminiscing, "That was the worst flood in over 200 years." When the water finally receded, it left behind another layer of rich silt and all kinds of debris high up in the willow trees and shrubs.

In a recurring dream, I found myself struggling in panic, with all my strength, against the river's swift, black current, never gaining an inch, until one night, I gave in to the river's powerful pull. As I floated on my back, I allowed it to carry me gently, it seemed forever, toward the sea.

The river gave and the river took.

Praise the Lord

There was cause for joy, even in those days. One was the birth of Ulla's fourth child, a little boy, who was born in the parsonage at the end of May. Another one was Björn's baptism. My parents had asked Putti, who cared for and had fallen in love with the little fellow, to be his godmother. On a glorious Pentecost morning, when the bells started ringing, everyone who had found refuge in the parsonage walked along the river to the old church. The girls wore wreaths of daisies in their hair, and Dagmar and I wore white dresses that we had borrowed from the Blankenburgs.

Eight-month-old Björn was a challenge for his young godmother. He amused the congregation by drowning out the pastor's sermon with his babbling. During the service, we praised the Lord with every breath:

Lobe den Herrn,	Praise to the Lord, Oh, let all
Was in mir ist, lobe den Namen.	That is in me adore him.
Alles was Odem hat,	All that hath life and breath,
Lobe mit Abrahams Samen.	Praise Him with Abraham's seed.
Er ist dein Licht,	He is your light,
Seele, vergiss es ja nicht.	My soul will never forget.
Lobe ihn und schliesse mit Amen.	Praise him and end with an Amen.

Even Papa, who had grown up in a devout Lutheran family, but hadn't worshiped in a church in years, lifted his voice in praise. A photo taken that day shows Papa and Mutti—thin, pale, and care-worn—with their five children, Annie's four children, and their three cousins on the steps of the parsonage.

I was happy because I had never had so many friends to play with. Brigitte, Christiane, and I rummaged through the attic and found a trunk with costumes and gowns fit for a queen. We decided to put on weekly plays. With fourteen children and our friends, Margret and Marlis, we had more than enough actors. During good weather, we staged our plays in the garden, and, when it rained, in the living room or down the street in the Gasthaus. We sold tickets for ten pennies apiece. Everyone in the house attended our performances. Annie's imperious mother, Frau Weber, lent a touch of elegance to the occasions by wearing her mink stole and carrying opera glasses.

Brigitte played the role of the emperor in "The Emperor's Clothes," which was a big hit with our parents. My favorite role was the witch in "Hänsel and Gretel." I tried not to let it bother me when Sven let everyone know that it was the perfect part for me. In "Snow White," Dietrich played the king to his queen, the much older and taller Marlis. Three times the queen told the king, "I want a child." Three times the king solemnly nodded his head. The adults roared with laughter when her wish was swiftly granted by one of us shoving a doll carriage with a baby doll onto the stage. For the tower scene in "Snow White," we upended the carriage and used it as a spinning wheel. Our brothers clowned around as the seven dwarfs. We girls took turns playing princesses and queens. I perched high in the branches of the magnolia tree, in the role of the bird that grants Cinderella's wishes.

Albrecht, who thought our performances were silly and childish, wrote a script based on Friedrich Schiller's Ballad, "Der Taucher." In this narrative, a brave young man survives a dive from a high cliff to the bottom of a raging sea, to retrieve a golden goblet cast there by an evil king. Upon his return, the diver exclaims:

> Da unten aber ist's fürchterlich,
> Und der Mensch versuche die Götter nicht.
> Und begehe nimmer und nimmer zu schauen,
> Was sie gnädig bedecken mit Nacht und Grauen.

> For below all is fearful,
> Let no man tempt the gods.
> Let him never desire the things to see,
> That with night and terror they veil graciously.

When the king promises him the hand of his beautiful daughter, the hero tempts fate a second time and perishes. The rehearsals were a disaster, because, with the exception of Albrecht, none of us had memorized our lines. He finally gave up his attempt to bring some sophistication to our theatrical repertoire.

During the summer, a few German men and boys began returning from American, British, French, and Russian prison camps. My parents worried about the fate of the Hartmanns, but they had no way of finding out if any of them had survived the war. One day, a wild-eyed, emaciated man arrived at the door. Annie promptly escorted him to her husband's study and locked him in. We heard that the man was a former Nazi judge, who had been incarcerated by the Allies for ordering and signing an execution during the war. While he was a prisoner, he had lost his mind. Then, one early morning, Annie's husband Walter, the village pastor and Bach scholar, returned as well. He was shoeless, covered in rags and had been walking for weeks.

Elisabeth Bengen, who, with her husband and children, had fled Kassel and lived in a small cottage outside of the village, came to the parsonage to give Putti voice lessons. At first my friends and I stood outside the door, clowned, and mimicked Putti doing her warm-ups and scales. In time, I learned to listen and to love Putti's beautiful voice. On warm summer evenings, after the day's work was done, we gathered in the garden to sing folk songs until the sun set behind the Reinhardswald.

Annie came up with the idea for bi-monthly musical evenings, to which she invited anyone who wished to play or listen to classical music. Twice a month people arrived with their instruments from as far away as Kassel, to rehearse and present programs of Beethoven and Mozart. Musicians and guests crowded into the living room and the hallway.

Soon after, Hans Weimann, a magnificent bass, was released from a Russian POW camp. From then on, J. S. Bach's cantatas, concertos and masses filled the house and lifted everyone's spirits. I learned to appreciate and love Bach's music while sitting on the stairs of the parsonage. Annie later remembered, that "for many who experienced these evenings, they created a flicker of hope, a hope that there was more to life than the misery they had to endure … something that was comforting, something that was not of an ephemeral nature, but something that was like a bridge that lead out of the depths of hopelessness to a future."

The Brandenburg concertos were the high point of the performances. For the occasion, a cembalo was barged up the river. In Veckerhagen, it was loaded on a wagon pulled by a cow, and was accompanied by a crowd of hooting children all the way to the parsonage.

There were times during that summer when I was not afraid, and I began to agree with my mother that God had been watching and continued to watch over us.

At Pawa's

On October 1, 1945, the mayor's office assigned us lodgings in the half-timbered house two blocks down from the parsonage. The house was known as, *"die Post,"* because it housed the village post office. It was owned by Wilhelm Wallbach—known as Onkel Willem in the village—a great-uncle of my mother's. My mother was a member of the Wallbach tribe, who had settled in the Weser Valley after the Reformation. Close to a dozen large families, all descendants of Christof Wallbach, who died in 1648, still lived in the area.

Willem must have been in his eighties or nineties and suffered from the effects of a stroke. With him lived his daughter-in-law, Pawa, and her daughter Irmgard. Our living quarters consisted of a small, dark kitchen at the rear of the house and a tiny bedroom on the second floor. Once again, we packed our meager belongings on a handcart, and with the help of Putti and Albrecht, moved from the parsonage to the *Post*. Papa, Mutti, and the baby would sleep in the kitchen. We placed Björn's crib in the corner, between the window and the stove. We piled Papa and Mutti's bedding on the daybed, underneath one of the small windows. Besides the big iron cookstove and the daybed, the kitchen held a cupboard for pots and dishes, a stone sink with a cold-water pump, and a table surrounded by rickety chairs and stools.

Sven, Frank, Dagmar, and I moved into the bedroom at the top of the dark and narrow stairway. We stuffed sacks with straw from Pawa's barn, put them on pallets that Papa had scrounged from the abandoned Flemish work camp, and stashed our belongings underneath. The walls of the room were papered with garish pink flowers on a dark blue background. Some of the paper was torn and hung in long strips. The only natural light came from a small window. One naked light bulb hung from the ceiling. By stepping on one of the pallets, I could look down into the barnyard, where a flock of chickens cackled and scratched around the dung pile. There was the familiar sound of a cow mooing and stomping about in the stables below us. A roof protected rabbit hutches, farm tools, sacks of feed, and firewood. The pungent odor of manure permeated the house. Fat flies covered the walls and window. The drafty outhouse—with not one, but three holes of different sizes—stood at the far end of the barnyard, past the manure pile and an open septic pit, the *Jauchegrube*. Sven succeeded in scaring us by telling horror stories about the Thirty Years War, when conquering armies drowned their victims in such pits.

Onkel Willem was the much beloved patriarch of a large clan. For many years, until his retirement, he had served as mayor and postmaster of the village. He was tall, slender, with a shock of white hair surrounding his long, narrow face and thick eyebrows. His mustache twisted and curled up at each end, but his most prominent and impressive feature was his wavy, long beard. Snow white and parted halfway down the middle, the beard reached to his waist, in the fashion of Kaiser Wilhelm II, after whom he was named, and of whom he was the spitting image.

Willem had ten children by two wives. I only got to know Willi and Luischen, the mother of my friend Margret. Willi grew up to be a gentle man, a dreamer with a yearning for foreign parts and adventure. In his youth, he had gone to the circus in Münden. What he saw enthralled him: the tents, the colorful performers, the beautiful horses, and, especially, an exotic, dark-haired and dark-skinned woman a few years his senior. She was different from the village girls he had grown up with. Her name was Pawa. She was a member of the circus, a dancer, and we heard that she was born in Turkey of gypsy blood. It was expected that Willi would marry a local girl, settle down, and work at the post office. Instead, he fell in love with Pawa, left home, and joined the circus to ride the great Arabian horses and to be near the alluring and intriguing Pawa. When he and Pawa married, they moved back home to live with his father, now a widower. Since Willi and Pawa were unable to have children of their own, Pawa decided to adopt a girl and named her Irmgard. She turned into a bright, kind and gentle girl, who loved playing her piano for us.

Young Willi adored his wife and daughter, but the villagers were scandalized by Pawa's ways. This wasn't surprising, for they were suspicious of anyone outside their little village. They considered the inhabitants of Veckerhagen, two miles down river, as *Fremde*, strangers. The Veckerhagians responded in kind. They called out, "*In Vooke do gibbet vill gequoke, in Vooke do sittet de Düwel up den Dooke*," in Vaake one does a lot of squawking, in Vaake the devil sits on the roof. The Vaakers countered, *In Veckerhoogen do sittet de Düwel up den Woogen,*" in Veckerhagen the devil sits on the wagon. The men from the two villages showed their mutual dislike for each other during the annual harvest festival and during occasional Saturday night brawls at the Gasthaus.

After Willi married Pawa, he started working in the post office, first as a mail carrier, then as postmaster, after his father retired. During World War II, Willi was drafted into the army as an infantry soldier, and his father filled in for him as postmaster, until he suffered a stroke. When our family moved into the *Post*, Pawa's Willi had not yet returned from the war.

Our family's only source of heat was an old, black, cast iron cookstove in the kitchen. We obtained a permit from the forester to collect firewood. My brothers and I helped Papa pull the handcart up the hill into the forest, where we gathered fallen branches and twigs, piled them high onto the wagon, and tied them down with a rope. Papa held onto the tongue of the wagon and uttered strings of expletives as we made our way into the valley. Sven stuck a stick between the spokes to slow the wagon down, while the rest of us tried to keep the teetering load from tipping over. Sometimes, Sven, Frank, Dagmar, and I foraged for firewood on our own and took turns riding on top of the wagon. When the load shifted and the cart got away from us, we ended up in the ditch, laughing and crying.

By far our most serious problem continued to be the lack of food. "I'm hungry," Sven complained.

"Me, too," chimed in the rest of us. I never stopped thinking and dreaming of food. Sven, who cried himself to sleep at night, fainted on a number of occasions.

"Mutti, is he dead?" Dagmar wailed, as she knelt beside him.

"No, dear, he is not, just passed out." Mutti tried to calm Dagmar, as she busied herself to revive her son. She looked up at Papa and lamented, "Where are we going to get food for the children?" When we gathered around the table for our bowls of watery potato or turnip soup, I noticed that Papa and Mutti ate little. They waited until we had our fill before they consumed what was left over. That had to be the reason why Papa's pants seemed to be getting bigger, and Mutti's dress hung in loose folds about her.

Sven, Frank and I stood on the cot one day, looking out of the window into the kitchen of the farmer next door. Our noses pressed against the windowpane, we stared at the neighbor's family sitting around a kitchen table, laden with bowls of potatoes, vegetables, meat, and tall glasses of milk. I was ready to burst into tears, until I saw a big grin on Frank's face. He pushed Sven and me in the ribs and went through an elaborate pantomime, as he chewed, smacked his lips noisily, rolled his eyes, and groaned with pleasure. He pretended to swallow, rubbed his stomach, and proclaimed that the food was "delicious." For a finale, he gave a loud burp. Sven and I imitated his theatrics, our mouths empty, except for the saliva that pooled in them.

By fall, the regular postal service had resumed. Every chance I got, I would slip across the well-worn wooden floor into the post office, which was a busy place, cozy and warm. I sat quietly on a bench in the waiting area, which was separated from the inner office by a wooden balustrade. I watched the postmaster sort, stamp, and bundle the mail, receive and send telegrams. Through the office passed the good and the bad news from and to all those who lived in and near the village. Early each morning, the mail carrier gathered the letters and postcards from wooden cubbies. He stashed them into a leather satchel, swung himself on his bicycle and pedaled from house to house to deliver the mail, starting on one side of the main street and working his way up and down each side street and along rutted dirt roads leading to outlying farms. But I missed the old days, when Onkel Willem was postmaster and the air was filled with swirling clouds of blue smoke from his Dutch pipe, with the fancy lidded ceramic bowl.

Another place I liked to visit was Pawa and Irmgard's parlor, which doubled as their kitchen and was located directly across the hall from the post office. Here, Pawa prepared their meals and received her customers. Since Pawa's services as a fortuneteller were highly valued by the people of the village and those of the surrounding countryside, there was a stream of clients. "Eycke," said Pawa one day, "I'll read your fortune if you take a lunch tray to Onkel Willem." I was curious what the future held in store for me. The first time I watched Pawa do her magic, she planted her ample buttocks on a chair behind the kitchen table and invited her client, an old woman, to sit across from her. Pawa pushed a strand of her short, greasy hair from her forehead, lowered the glasses on her nose, and put on her serious face. After politely asking her customer if she were comfortable, Pawa engaged her in a bit of small talk. Without being obvious, she elicited random information, while she shuffled her cards and looked at the old woman over the top of her glasses. It seemed to me as though she were reading the woman's mind. Pawa held the deck of cards face down in her left hand. She closed her eyes for an instant, licked her thumb, and then ever so slowly, turned over each card with a sharp snapping sound, and placed them in rows on the grimy kitchen table.

"I haven't heard from my boy," the woman said, her face taut with anticipation. Pawa bent forward and studied her customer, then her cards. She shook her head, sighed, and pointed to this or that card.

"He's surrounded by darkness," Pawa lifted a finger without looking up. "But, you will hear from him soon. You can tell your husband his rheumatism will improve."

I soon learned that the queen of hearts meant love and that one of the other cards, the *schwarze* Peter, signified misfortune, danger, darkness, or death. Snapping the cards on her kitchen table, Pawa talked to her customers about love with dark-haired strangers. She rattled on about reunions and good times ahead, of riches, of marriages, of births, and she warned of possible sickness and danger on the road ahead. Some of Pawa's customers paid her with foodstuffs. In this case, the old lady had brought a chunk of butter. Some exchanged cigarettes and small valuables for her services, while others offered a few Reichsmark. The money she tucked into the left cup of her brassiere, smiled to herself and gave it a gentle pat or two.

One day, a man wearing dusty clothes and holding his cap in his filthy hands came to see her. He sat down at the kitchen table across from her and listened intently as she read the cards. I knew him to be a man who sold "brown coal," a low-grade fuel that was dug at the Garenberg Mine in the hills above the village. The kitchen was quiet and dark, except for the light from the lamp over the table, casting its glow in a circle on the two of them. Pawa placed the cards on the table. As she read them, she smiled in a seductive way and stroked his hand, while pointing to the queen of hearts. She looked straight into his eyes and slowly began to rub her left breast. I blushed with embarrassment but kept on watching. Pawa glanced in my direction and whispered something into the man's ear. The next day a load of coal went down the shoot into the cellar.

Delighted by Pawa's promise to have my fortune told, I hurried to take the tray upstairs to Onkel Willem's room, careful not to spill anything. When I opened the door, I was overwhelmed by the pungent stench of urine. With his eyes closed, and his magnificent beard spread out on top of the white featherbed, Onkel Willem lay in the unheated room on a high narrow bed near the window. His pale hands covered with parchment-like skin lay at his sides. Dear God, I thought, he's dead. I had the urge to turn and run, but remembered my promise to Pawa. On his bedside table stood a glass urinal with a long narrow spout, filled with dark yellow urine. I put the tray on the floor, approached the bed warily, and touched his arm lightly. I whispered, "Good day, Onkel Willem, I brought you your *Mittagessen*." Without opening his eyes, he pointed to his bedside table.

I hesitated for a moment, but then I remembered how kind the old man had been to me years ago, when I ran errands to the *Post*. He would smile and glance at me over his glasses, point the long stem of his pipe at me, and say, "You must be Tutti's girl. How grown-up and pretty you are. What's your name?"

I liked being called grown-up and pretty, and replied, "Yes, Tutti is my mother, and my name is Eycke."

But on the day I brought him his lunch, he didn't look at me nor did he speak. I quickly moved the urinal under the bed, wiped my hands on my apron, placed the tray on the table, touched his arm lightly, and tiptoed out of the room as fast as I could.

Pawa was waiting for me in our kitchen. Björn was asleep in his crib next to the stove. The rest of the family was out gathering wood. Pawa made herself comfortable at the kitchen table. She opened a small, greasy leather pouch, from which she extracted a pinch of tobacco, carefully placed it onto a shred of newspaper, rolled it up, and used her tongue to moisten the paper along one side. She then glued the whole thing together, tapped each end lightly, and asked me for a light from the stove. I watched her inhale deeply, close her eyes, and blow out a cloud of acrid smoke. After she opened her eyes, she shuffled the deck, licked her thumb, and started snapping down her well-worn cards. She studied me closely, concentrating. Her eyes took in my face and shifted to my flat chest, before she started examining her cards.

"You're going to marry young," she said, taking another puff from her cigarette. "You're going to go far away, and you're going to become rich." All that sounded good to me, but I was puzzled at her next prediction, which she delivered with a mocking smile. "You know," she added, "sexual intercourse would do wonders for your skin." I was twelve years old, hadn't even started menstruating yet, and the last time I looked into the mirror, my skin looked just fine. But what about this ... sexual intercourse?

My friend Margret had mentioned about men and women sleeping together, and I had heard from Mutti that men and women held each other close when they loved each other. She called it *"eine Umarmung,"* an embrace, but she hadn't explained what that was, not exactly. Later, I told Mutti, "Tante Pawa read my fortune today, and she said that I would get married young, move far away, and become rich."

I decided to wait to tell her what Pawa had said about my skin and intercourse. As it was, I could tell that Mutti was not pleased, and when I asked Pawa some time later to read my fortune, she hissed, "Your mother won't allow it. Leave me be."

Pawa was proud of her days in the circus, regaled us with her stories, and showed us albums with photographs of herself as a young woman in the fancy costumes that she wore for her acts. She continued to express her love for the theater by producing and directing the children of the village in a colorful pageant of the flowers, for which she made our costumes. We recited verses, flitted, and danced about the stage, carrying garish garlands of crepe paper flowers.

By the time we moved into the *Post*, Pawa was in her late forties and no longer the beauty her Willi had fallen in love with. She wore ankle-length skirts, felt slippers, and sometimes dribbled blood on the floor as she walked. Her daughter Irmgard was nineteen years old and in bloom. American soldiers came to visit her day and night. They were friendly fellows who brought coffee, Hershey bars, C rations, and cigarettes. I thought that Irmgard must have liked one of the fellows especially well. Once, I walked into the kitchen during the middle of the day, and found them cuddling under a blanket. When they heard me come in, they pulled the covers over their heads. I left in a hurry with burning cheeks, my head filled with questions about what it was that men and women did under the covers besides embracing. Years later, when I told Mutti about Pawa's introducing the subject of intercourse during our fortune-telling session, Mutti revealed to me that it was Pawa who had arranged the trysts between her daughter and the American soldiers.

We, too, experienced Pawa's dark side when something happened that made me dislike and mistrust her intensely. One day two men knocked on our kitchen door. They introduced themselves as criminal investigators and asked to talk to my parents and Sven. I was not allowed to listen, but when the interrogation was over, Sven told me, tears streaming down his face, "The old witch Pawa accused me of stealing her husband's stamp collection." I knew that Sven could not have done such a thing. My parents were outraged. Papa said that Pawa probably was afraid of what Willi would say when he found out that his prized stamp collection was missing. They suspected that Pawa had sold or traded the collection herself, then tried to make it look like it had been stolen. Mutti said that it was loathsome of her to accuse a child. Sven was eventually found to be innocent. From then on, I felt awkward around Pawa. If we could, we would have moved, but we had nowhere else to go.

The war had been over for months, and all that time Pawa worried about her husband. "I wonder what has happened to my Willi?" she lamented, bent over her cards. *Swish, swish, swish,* she shuffled and snapped them on the table. "He is still alive, I can feel it in my bones, and look," she pointed, "the cards agree." She rolled a cigarette "to calm my nerves," she said, puffing as she searched for answers in her cards and in the curls of the rising smoke.

When Pawa received a tattered postcard from her beloved, the news was good and bad. Sweet Willi was alive, but he was a prisoner of war, incarcerated in a former concentration camp, and was in big trouble. It turned out, that a few months before the end of the war, Willi's infantry unit was ordered to guard a concentration camp. They abandoned their prisoners before the Americans liberated the camp. Willi stayed behind to aid the sick and helpless. The Americans assumed, quite naturally, that he was one of the monsters who had killed, tortured, and mistreated the inmates. He became a prisoner himself in the camp he had guarded and was waiting to be tried.

From the minute Pawa found out where Willi was, she mounted a formidable campaign to free him. Pawa mailed packages with food and clothing. She enlisted the help of anybody who could be a character witness for Willi. Papa dictated and Mutti typed petitions to the commandant of Willi's camp. Then Pawa decided to go and see Willi for herself. She collected affidavits, food supplies and as many cigarettes as she could get, packed up a suitcase and took off in the *Postauto*. When she returned from her trip weeks later, she told us that when she was barred from entering the camp, she stationed herself at the front gate for days. She waved to Willi, smuggled food in to him and generally made a nuisance of herself. Finally, the commandant granted her an interview. She informed him that she, a Gypsy, and Willi, a Baptist, had suffered discrimination under the Nazis and that Willi wouldn't hurt a fly. She spread out the documents before him. After the commandant promised that Willi would get a speedy hearing if only she would stop hanging around the gate, she returned home.

While Pawa anxiously waited for her husband's return, she consulted her cards daily. I walked in on her as she sat hunched over her kitchen table with her back to me, alternating between shuffling cards and taking puffs from her cigarette. "Tante Pawa, Mutti sent me ..."

She held up her hand, "*Shshshsh* ..."

I stopped in mid-sentence and walked around to watch her pick up each card and gently place it on the table. She sighed, took another puff, and hesitated before she looked at the last card. A look of utter horror clouded her face. She closed her eyes. What sounded like an oath in a language I did not understand escaped her mouth. She quickly turned her head, spit over her shoulder, and, without looking at me, asked me to leave.

Months later, an emaciated Willi returned home. With devotion and patience, Pawa nursed him back to health. Although he recovered physically and eventually returned to his old job as postmaster, his eyes retained a far-away look. Although gentle and quiet, he was never again the happy and friendly man we had known.

Back to School

For the primary students, the Vaaker *Volksschule* remained closed during 1945, but during the fall of that year, the boys, and girls' high schools reopened in Münden. From then on, we rode an old bus, which picked up and discharged passengers along with the mail in front of our door. It was fueled with smoldering sawdust and so overcrowded that the driver had to get off the bus, go around and push the passenger door closed from the outside. The bus ran from Veckerhagen via Vaake to Münden, and back. On the way to and from Münden, it had to pass through two military checkpoints, one American and the other British. The road-bed had been heavily damaged by tanks and trucks, and where parts of it had slid into the river, only one-way traffic was possible. Every time we passed within three feet of the abyss, we could see the river one hundred feet below us and prayed that the bus would be able to stay on the roadway. Since the big bridge in Münden had been blown up by German troops earlier that year, we had to walk across the Fulda River over a narrow suspension bridge, and from there walk to our respective high schools, the Gymnasium for boys and the Lyceum for girls.

Teachers came out of retirement, and young men and women with little or no experience replaced those who were deemed unsuitable to teach because of past Nazi party membership. Eventually, all adults over eighteen underwent denazification, a legal process during which their past political activities and affiliations were examined and judged.

Since my school records were lost during our escape from Poland, I enrolled with girls my age. Although German, history, geography, botany, sports and especially music were subjects I loved and did well in, I was behind in English, French, mathematics, physics and chemistry. Since the Allies prohibited the use of all books and materials printed during the Third Reich, teaching without books was a challenge for our instructors. When we were able to obtain scraps of writing paper, we copied our lessons from the board. Most of the time the teachers lectured and we listened.

With an empty stomach, I found it almost impossible to concentrate on my schoolwork, and I don't remember much about the lessons. What I do recall with profound gratitude were the daily distributions of a cup of delicious, thick, sweet soup—we called it *Quäkerspeise*—and a soft white roll, which the American Quakers provided for children who were sickly and underweight. I was one of those children, and I gratefully received their life-saving gift.

School was over at noon, but there were times when school let out early because there weren't enough teachers to go around. For lunch, I had an apple and two thin pieces of bread spread with margarine. I was overjoyed whenever Margret shared with me one of her tasty sandwiches spread with butter and smoked sausage. Because the bus didn't leave until 4 p.m., some days my friends and I stayed at my grandmother's, with whom I had made peace. Sometimes, we waited for hours at the bus stop, tossing a ball, playing hopscotch, and fighting with the boys. When the bus arrived, the adults cursed at us and pushed us aside, the boys elbowed their way onto the bus, and, on occasion we girls were left behind to wait for the next one, which left two hours later.

As an alternative to the overcrowded bus, Margret's grandfather, Herr Tichy, the owner of the local Gasthaus, talked the American commander into transporting us home on the way back from one of their beer runs. For a few months, three times a week, we climbed onto the back of an open truck and rode home with a load of beer barrels. Sometimes, when it wasn't raining, we hiked the three hours from school until my shoes wore out, or I was too weak from hunger to walk the distance. It was during one of those walks that a girl explained the facts of life to me. My initial reaction was one of disbelief. The sexual act she described didn't make any more sense to me than when my mother couched her explanation in poetic instead of graphic terms.

Once, I borrowed a bicycle and ended up getting a flat on my way home. An American soldier passed me in a Jeep, stopped, and exposed himself. This frightened me so that I got back on the bicycle and pedaled on rims to get away from him. He passed me once more and waved a limp penis at me before he sped off. From then on, I never traveled that road by myself again. When the cold weather set in, there wasn't enough fuel to heat the school. My clothes did not keep me warm, and I was embarrassed, because they were worn and no longer fit me properly. When classes were canceled, I didn't really mind.

Instead of going to school and doing homework, I helped with household chores and the care of my younger siblings. During the late fall, we received permission to cut down a whole tree deep within the hills of the Reinhardswald. With the help of friends, we sawed, hauled, chopped, and stacked the wood. When we grumbled about the hard work or whined about anything at all, Papa shook his finger and thundered, "Wait 'til the Russians come, then you'll have something to complain about."

By the time the snow started falling, we had stored enough firewood for the winter. I don't remember much about those dark times, except that we crowded into the dingy kitchen to stay warm. We ventured outside only when we had to. We survived mostly on thin potato or turnip soup and black bread laced with ground-up wood fiber. We did not have a party for my twelfth birthday, and, on Christmas Eve, there were no presents. We gathered around a tiny tree in the kitchen to sing of Jesus born in a manger and to thank God for our survival. Mutti heated bricks and wrapped them in rags to warm our beds. We wore sweaters over our nightclothes, and by kicking our feet, we tried to quiet the rustling mice that had taken up residence in our straw mattresses. On Christmas morning, the contents of the chamber pots were frozen solid.

Heidehügel,
1946

Papa once again took up his profession as an architect. He rendered architectural drawings of houses, additions to houses, barns, and outbuildings. In exchange, he sometimes earned a sack of potatoes, some brown coal or a few Reichsmark. When I pleaded with him to let me watch him draw, he agreed gruffly on one condition, "Not a peep out of you, understood?" I understood perfectly, breathed as quietly as I could, and watched as he placed the table in the middle of the kitchen, under the lamp where the light was bright, unfurled a roll of yellowed wallpaper, turned the pattern toward the table top, and tacked it down. He pulled out his pocketknife and slowly and methodically sharpened his pencils. "Nothing to it," he said, "all you have to have is a sharp knife." He pulled a small pin on the side of a beaten up leather case and opened it with a snap. On a cushion of dark blue velvet, each in its special space, nestled his gleaming architect's tools. Papa placed his ruler, a T square, a triangle, and compass on the table beside him, pushed his glasses onto his forehead, leaned forward, and began to draw. In awe, I watched him create on paper structures where moments before there had been nothing but a blank sheet.

In the spring of 1946, we bought five acres on a bluff covered with heather. We named it *Heidehügel,* heatherhill. The land had belonged to the village gun club and lay in the embrace of the Reinhardswald to the west, fields and meadows to the south, and the Weser River and the Bramwald to the east. In the distance to the northeast, across the Ahle Valley, we could see the red-tile roofs of Vaake, Veckerhagen and the winding Weser River.

The first thing we did, was to scout out a secluded spot between two saplings for a toilet. We nailed an old board between them and dug a hole. Next, we cleared the land for a garden, planted vegetable seedlings and carried water from a nearby creek to keep them moist. Then we tore down the dilapidated shed that had been used by the local gun club, chopped down trees, and hacked at brush and brambles. Frank and Dagmar made offerings out of clay for the *Wurzelmännlein* and *Weiblein* that—they believed—lived in mossy crevasses under tree roots. I was beginning to feel weak when Papa called out, "Let's eat." We quenched our thirst with creek water. Mutti unwrapped a round of dark sourdough rye bread, hard-boiled eggs, and the apples we had gathered from under the trees lining the path on the way. She held the bread against her chest and, with her right hand, cut it into long, oval slices, let them drop into her lap, and passed out equal portions. Papa gave a brief blessing, *"Gesegnete Mahlzeit. Amen,"* and added irreverently *"Macht's Maul breit,"* Blessed be this meal, Amen, and open your mouth wide.

After lunch, Papa asked Sven and me to help Mutti gather brush and brambles, and promised a bonfire and a sing-along as a reward. Sven spat into his hands, as he had seen the men of the village do just before embarking on a hard job. *"Hau ruck, hau ruck,"* he shouted, as we pulled the heavy brush onto a pile. Thorns bloodied our hands, arms, and legs and tore more holes into our already frayed clothes. Mutti got trapped in the middle of a patch of brambles and Papa had to rescue her, which reminded me of Sleeping Beauty being rescued by the prince. Mutti and Papa laughed and put their arms around each other, and for a moment, I forgot how hungry I was. The sun had begun to set behind the Reinhardswald and the air had cooled. Dark spots stained Mutti's blouse, where her milk had leaked. I was glad when she decided that it was time to go home and nurse her youngest, who was being cared for by his godmother.

Chanting, *"Dornröschen war ein schönes Kind"* at the top of our voices, we descended the steep hill into the valley. We crossed the footbridge over the Lange Ahle. We walked along the meandering creek through meadows, around the cemetery and the new school before entering the village, where families sat in front of their houses to rest at the end of a hard day. The women chatted with neighbors, knitted, and kept an eye on the children at play. The men smoked their pipes or homemade cigarettes stuffed with tobacco gleaned from American cigarette butts. We wished each other *"einen guten Feierabend,"* and went on our way.

The farmers grew grains, beets, and potatoes in their fields, and vegetables in their gardens. They milked their cows, kept chickens, rabbits, and slaughtered livestock. When we offered money for food, they shook their heads with disdain. They refused our money, but they were willing to trade with people called *Hamsterer*, who carried large knapsacks and roamed the countryside. The farmers offered cured hams, hard sausages, flour, butter, milk, and eggs in return for cigarettes, jewelry, silver, and fine china. There were those who joked that some farmers covered the floors of their cowsheds with oriental rugs. Since we had nothing to trade, we looked for food elsewhere. For a five-Mark fee and with a permit from the *Bürgermeisteramt,* the mayor's office, we picked apples from one of the trees lining a *Feldweg,* to fill our empty stomachs.

In exchange for picking potato bugs off vines for hours on end, I was allowed to glean rye and wheat fields and dig for potatoes after the farmers had harvested their crops. I walked to Wallbach's *Mühle,* which had been in my mother's extended family for three hundred years. There, for a few pennies, the miller ground up the grains into flour between two large stones, put into motion by a creaking water wheel. I picked wild blueberries, blackberries and elderberries with my friends and siblings, "One for the pot, one for me," I counted as purple juice stained my hands, and I gorged myself on the sweet, wild fruit until my stomach hurt. I traded ten pounds of tiny beechnuts that I gathered on the forest floor for one cup of oil. We picked nettles for soup, and dandelion and sorrel leaves for salad. But, no matter how hard we worked and scrounged, hunger was our constant companion. It followed us into our dreams and tormented us wherever we went, whatever we did.

The Last Crust of Bread

Besides the Gasthaus, Margret's family owned the only grocery store in the village. The Tichys depended largely on shipments of American surplus food: yellow cornmeal, oatmeal, flour, dried milk, and egg powder. With long lines of customers outside their store, everything was sold out within an hour or less. Since Mutti was busy and disliked shopping, Sven and I took turns going to the grocery store, the bakery, and the dairy. Mutti awakened us early each morning. We dressed and hastily wolfed down the sticky oat bran, containing slivers of husks. Sven, who loved the gruel, boasted that eating it would make him as strong as a horse. I ate it only because I was hungry. From Mutti we received our instructions: a list, ration stamps, money, a basket for me, a milk can for Sven, and a reminder to mind our manners.

I ran to the store and took my place in the queue, which had formed long before the store opened. Carrying shopping nets, bags and baskets, the women greeted each other. They jostled, cackled, fussed, and gossiped about the elderly Frau Tichy's purported habit of cheating her customers. Sometimes they waited patiently, and at other times they quarreled with each other over who was first in line. Women pushed ahead of me. I knew how to stand up for myself with my siblings and other children, but I detested confrontations with adults, and I kept quiet the first time it happened. Later, after I noticed that supplies were gone by the time I got to the counter, I started defending my rightful place, with red cheeks and a pounding heart. When it was my turn, I greeted Frau Tichy, Margret's paternal grandmother, and curtsied. I had hoped that Tante Luischen, my mother's distant cousin and Margret's sweet-tempered mother, would wait on me. Luischen always had a kind word, a smile, and something extra for her cousin's children. Best of all, after Margret and I did our homework at their kitchen table, she would invite me to share a plate of fried potatoes or a bowl of nourishing soup. That morning, Luischen was nowhere to be seen. I handed Margret's grandmother my list, and I watched as she deftly rolled newspapers into cones, placed them upright into the gleaming copper bowl of her scale, and added iron weights for counter balance. She scooped up corn meal and oats from wooden barrels, and measured until the scales balanced perfectly. To my relief, she did not put her thumb on the scale to add a bit of weight. I handed her the ration stamps, the exact change, thanked her, curtsied and quickly left the store, hoping that Mutti would be pleased with the purchases.

Early one morning—it was my turn to get milk—I joined a long line in the courtyard of the dairy, where Frau Dolle measured out milk from large cans. Each adult, each child, each baby, received his or her daily share. It was mostly *Magermilch*, a light-blue watered-down milk, from which all the butterfat had been removed. The wooden handle of an aluminum can firmly in hand, I stood in line among the chattering women and children until it was my turn. Happy that I had arrived early enough, I kept careful count of the number of liters she poured, making sure that each measure was full. I handed over my ration stamps and money, thanked Frau Dolle, and started for home. Just before reaching the *Post*, the handle on the milk can broke, and the can fell to the ground, spilling every drop. I burst into tears. There was only one thing I could do, as much as I dreaded it. Clutching the broken can in my arms, I backtracked to the end of the street and knocked on a farm door. When a woman answered, I curtsied and explained what had happened. I asked politely if they could spare a few cups of milk, enough for my mother and baby brother, and I promised to pay later.

"We have no milk left," was the curt answer from the rotund woman.

In all I knocked on five doors and received the same answer: "We have no milk left."

One woman called me a *"verdammter Flüchtling,"* a damned refugee, and she slammed the door in my face. It wasn't until that moment I realized that, even in our own country, my family was considered to be part of the despised "gray horde of refugees," the millions who had lost everything except their lives during that cursed, bloody, and senseless war. I returned home sobbing. Mutti was unable to console me.

"Eycke," Papa whispered one fall evening. "I need your help tonight."

Eager to please Papa even before he had explained, I answered, *"Na, klar,"* of course.

"We're going on a raid."

"A raid?"

"Scrounging for sugar beets and turnips." He explained that the farmers had harvested their root crops and stored them in long, dirt-covered mounds.

"But, Papa, you said yourself that they have guards posted in the fields."

"Ach, don't worry," Papa grinned. I swallowed hard but nodded.

The slender sickle of the moon hid behind clouds, as Papa and I crept into the fields, across the freshly plowed clods of dirt, under cover of darkness. I could hear the blood pound in my ears. After Papa was satisfied that there were no guards in our immediate vicinity, we got on our knees to root for beets and turnips from underneath thick layers of straw and dirt. We stuffed our knapsacks and refilled the holes with straw and soil. In an attempt to cover our tracks, we kicked around dirt clods before we left the field. We breathed hard under our heavy loads and stumbled back to *Heidehügel*. Here, we hid our loot under a pile of brush. For the next week, to avoid suspicion, we carried home a few turnips and sugar beets at a time. Mutti prepared turnip soup for our noon meals. We shredded and boiled the sugar beets in a large laundry vat, heated by a wood fire. We stirred the beets for hours on end to keep them from burning. After the beets turned into a thick, brown, earth-flavored syrup, we drizzled it on our bread and oatmeal.

While I was terrified of being caught during our raids, I got a sense that Papa didn't seem concerned. I came to believe that he actually enjoyed our forays. He liked to tell stories of his World War I soldiering adventures, and he boasted how he kept himself and his comrades fed by scrounging. During the coming months, I accompanied Papa several more times. I was scared every time, but I noticed that my conscience began to bother me less each trip.

Dagmar was busy mixing clay and water to make furniture for the root people. Sven, Frank, and I were helping Mutti collect fieldstones in preparation for the next day's work, when a German soldier, wearing a tattered uniform, unshaven and hollow-eyed, approached slowly on the narrow path leading to our place on *Heidehügel*. By that time, we had gotten used to people wandering about the countryside, trying to get back home, looking for food or a place to settle. I could tell from his worn boots that the man had been walking for a long time, but I thought it odd that, as he walked toward us, he continued looking over his shoulder. When he reached Mutti, he lifted his cap and stretched out his left hand, palm up, and pleaded, *"Bitte, haben Sie etwas zu essen?"* Please, do you have something to eat? Then he collapsed next to a tree.

Mutti supported the small of her back, groaned as she straightened up, wiped away the beads of perspiration from her forehead with the back of her hand, and went to her basket and took out the heel of a loaf of bread. She walked toward him, carrying the *Knust* in both her hands, like an offering. I felt like shouting: "You can't do this! I'm hungry, all of us are hungry! I heard Sven crying himself to sleep last night. Why do you give away our last crust of bread?" Instead, I choked back the words and turned away to hide my anger.

I heard my mother say, *"*I am sorry. This is all we have.*"* As I turned around, I saw him hesitate for a second before he greedily stuffed the bread into his mouth, chewing and swallowing as he held both hands cupped under his chin to catch every crumb. He licked his fingers and asked for something to drink. Mutti answered, "Water is all we have. I am sorry."

He drank his fill, struggled to his feet, and thanked her politely, "*Danke, gnä-dige* Frau," doffed his cap and walked off, looking all around, as he disappeared through the fields into the forest beyond.

I desperately wanted to ask Mutti right then why she had given away our last crust of bread, but many years passed before I told her what I had felt that day. I listened to her answer: "Child, how can I explain? Those were desperate times. I did not know from one day to the next where the food would come from to feed you children. Chaos all around us."

"But ..." I tried to interrupt.

She continued, "Whenever I despaired, something mysterious occurred. From somewhere, enough food for a meal appeared. Sometimes a few potatoes or beets for a soup, other times a basket full of apples, a few eggs, anything. I'll never forget the day Albrecht came to me with a sandwich he had earned working for a farmer. He, a growing boy of fourteen, hungry himself, offered the bread to me, '*Bitte*, Tante Tutti, for you.' I refused, but he urged, 'You need it to nurse.' I accepted his gift gratefully. You remember, I nursed Björn for two whole years." She touched her breasts, as her thoughts trailed off. "Otherwise, he might have died like so many infants those days." She folded her hands and continued, "I came to understand that I had to trust in God. You remember the story in the Bible about how God takes care of the birds in the sky and the lilies in the field, don't you? Faith sustained me. But if you had asked me at the time, I probably would not have been able to explain why I gave away that crust of bread."

A Wild Ride

School was out during the harvest season, and Mutti and I were alone in the kitchen at Pawa's. She was rinsing the dishes in a chipped enamel bowl when she turned to me, "I want to talk to you." She removed the dishtowel from her left shoulder, handed it to me, and announced that her sister Loni was coming to take me to Kassel the next day. Mutti seemed surprised that I didn't answer her right away, "What's the matter? I thought you would be excited."

In a barely audible voice, I replied, "I would rather stay home."

"But, why?"

"Don't know," I lied. I was hesitating to tell her that being cursed by fat farmers, living in two dingy rooms, begging for and stealing food, wearing threadbare and ill-fitting clothes was bearable as long as I was with my family. Being with them was the only thing that made me feel safe in this scary world.

"You've always loved visiting Tante Marianne," Mutti reminded me. She pointed out that since my aunts were able to supplement their rations with leftovers from an American field kitchen, she would not have to worry about me getting enough to eat.

"I'll go if I have to," I replied, without enthusiasm.

That night, when I tossed and turned, Sven asked, *"Hast du Reisefieber?"* I admitted to having travel fever. I was afraid to travel the thirty kilometers through the woods. We talked about the recent murder of our neighbor, Herr Beck, who had chased some robbers and ended up lying in a pool of blood on the road to Münden. Sven offered to accompany Tante Loni and me. I was moved that my brother, the kid who pestered me, called me names, and pulled my braids, the brother with whom I rarely exchanged a civil word, should care about my safety. My last thought before I fell asleep was that Loni might decide that the journey would be too arduous and dangerous. But the next day, as promised, she arrived on her bicycle. Instead of taking the level road along the Fulda and Weser rivers—where she would have had to pass through several American and British military checkpoints—Loni had chosen a route through the forest instead.

Loni—short, wiry, and athletic—could be loving, or as prickly as an ill-tempered porcupine. That day she was in a good mood. "I see you have your

knapsack ready. We'll have to take off soon if we want to get home before dark."
After she refreshed herself, we took our leave. Mutti thanked her sister for coming
to get me. She kissed and blessed me by making the cross on my forehead with
her thumb, and asked me to be a good girl. I wiped away my tears.

We left the village and the school behind, turned onto the path along the
creek, crossed the bridge at Becker's Nursery, and walked up the hill toward *Heidehügel*, where Sven and Frank ran to greet our aunt. She made them turn
around. "Let me take a look at you. You've grown. Scrawny, rascally, and filthy,
as usual."

"I got muscles," Sven bragged, flexing his biceps.

"Me, too," Frank piped up.

The boys tagged along, as I showed Loni around. With a lot of good-natured
me-first-shouting-and-shoving, my brothers and I took turns describing in detail
how our family, including Björn, had collected fieldstones for the foundation.
We described how Papa and friends felled the trees for the frame and siding, how
we helped dig clay, mixed it with sand and straw to form adobe bricks, and how
Papa dug coal for the firing of the roof tiles. I bragged that none of my siblings
was as skillful at hammering rusty nails straight as I was.

Frank added, "You should have seen Papa. He looked like a black *Ami* truck
driver, after mining coal all day."

We proudly showed off rolls of barbed wire and a pile of building materials,
which Papa, the boys, Albrecht and I had looted from the abandoned military
installation near Münden, and which we piled on a handwagon, and dragged to
Heidehügel.

"We are going to have a home again," I pronounced. I kept to myself my fantasies: of a garden, where dragonflies flitted over the black pond that was dotted
with white water lilies, of a linden tree, where I hid when I was sad or had been
bad, and of a hay barn, where I learned to fly.

Papa came over to greet Loni and advised her to take a little-known shortcut
through the forest back to Kassel. He turned to me and asked, "You know the old
logging roads, don't you?" Eager to show off how clever I was, I explained, "We
have to cross the meadows and fields, pass through the gate at the *Hexenhaus*,
turn right and continue uphill toward Garenberg Ridge, past Kaufmanns Born,
the Round Bench and the Finken Ponds."

Papa nodded, "You'll gain a lot of time that way. Once you get to the ridge,
it's down hill most of the way." Papa wiped his sweaty brow and offered us a
drink of creek water. Then Papa said something to Loni I couldn't hear. She nodded. I kissed Papa and waved to the boys, and we started on our way. "Don't let

the big, bad wolf eat you up," Papa shouted with a big grin. He waved his dirty handkerchief, until we took a turn onto the path toward the woods and disappeared out of his sight.

For the next half hour, Loni pushed the bicycle as we made our way through meadows and fields, without talking. The sun shone. The sweet scent of *Grummet*, the late summer crop of hay, filled the air. Farmers piled hay into cone-shaped stacks to dry, or forked the dried hay high on top of horse-drawn wagons. At the edge of the forest, the broad branches of beech trees provided shade from the sun. I carefully opened and closed the gate leading into the woods, as Papa had taught me. We stepped into the enchanted forest of the brothers Grimm, the setting for Sleeping Beauty, Frau Holle, Little Red Riding Hood, Hänsel and Gretel, and all the other fairytales. This was my favorite part of the forest: quiet, cool and suffused with the fragrance of pine needles warmed by the sun. We walked uphill along a logging road lined with spruce trees to Kaufmanns Born, where we took a drink from the spring, and Loni filled her water bottle. We skirted the Round Bench and arrived at the Finken Ponds, brackish pools surrounded by larch trees. According to Papa, this was a magical place, a place where a colony of tiny root people lived and played on moss cushions under toadstool mushrooms. We sat on the soft ground, and my aunt unpacked rye bread spread with butter and hard sausage. I hadn't tasted anything so delicious since the last time Margret had shared her *Wurstenbrot* with me. Upon leaving the Finken Ponds, I followed Papa's advice and spread a few crumbs as a gift for the root people.

*   *   *

As we neared Garenberg Mine, the highest point of the Reinhardswald, I was reminded of what happened near here the year before. Sven, Frank, and I had accompanied Papa and his helpers on a tree-felling expedition. Papa had yelled at us for getting in the way and ordered us to gather kindling on the ridge. "Work, work, work," fretted Frank.

"You, work? Don't make me laugh." Sven lowered his voice, knitted his brow, and imitated Papa shaking his finger. "Just wait until the Russians come, then you'll have something to complain about."

Frank stretched out his tongue, picked up pine cones, and lobbed them in Sven's direction. "You can't hit me, you can't hit me," Sven chanted, thumbing his nose and stretching out his tongue. A fierce pine-cone fight ensued, until the boys ran out of ammunition.

"We'd better gather some wood, or we'll get into trouble," I warned.

Frank yelled at Sven, "I'll get you later."

"Promises, promises." Sven waved his brother's threats off, like one would a fly.

We trudged up the hill, both boys keeping an eye out for pine cones. When we reached the ridge, we came upon a small clearing. It was a circular meadow covered with high grasses, dotted with daisies and delicate harebells, and surrounded by a grove of tall fir trees. A light breeze danced in waves through the grass and wild flowers in the warm afternoon sun. Except for the sawing and chopping noises in the distance, it was quiet and peaceful.

"Look, over there," Sven whispered, as he pointed to a cluster of wooden crosses, crowned by helmets, at the far end of the meadow.

"Graves," Frank replied, and covered his mouth with his right hand.

We approached the graves. "Helmets with shrapnel holes," Sven observed.

I ran my fingers over one of the sharp edges and recalled Papa telling us how his brother had been killed by a grenade while the two stood shoulder to shoulder in a trench at Langemarck. Every time Papa recalled the horror, he mentioned *zu viel schwarzes Blut,* too much black blood, and wiped his eyes. I thought of my friend, Jürgen, the redhead I had a crush on in fourth grade. During the last month of the war, at the age of twelve, he was drafted into the *Volkssturm* and was killed while delivering messages to an anti-aircraft position. I suddenly felt a chill, and when I suggested to the boys that we start gathering firewood, they agreed.

*   *   *

During my journey with Loni, I felt uneasy and glanced over my shoulder from time to time, to make sure that we weren't being followed. When we came to the crossroads, I wondered out loud why we hadn't seen a soul since we entered the forest.

"Be grateful," my aunt answered and explained that we were going to turn south and make our way toward the southwest through Holzhausen, Espenau, Wilhelmsthal, and the Habichtswald to Schanzen Strasse and home. When we got to the highest point of the forest, she smiled, "From now on we ride." With her hands on the handlebars, and her legs firmly on the ground, she invited me to hop on. Being accustomed to riding on the rear baggage rack, I pulled myself up, put my arms around my aunt's waist, ready to travel the last fifteen miles to Kassel. "Here we goooooo," she called out. The wind was in our faces and our hair was flying as Loni leaned forward and peddled hard. It was a wild ride, as she skirted potholes and rocks, until we abruptly veered to the right, tumbled off and landed in the ditch on a carpet of grass. Dazed, we looked at each other.

"What happened?" I asked.

"I don't know. Are you all right?"

I felt my legs and arms, "I think so."

"Good." My aunt brushed the grass off and examined her bicycle. "The fork that holds the front wheel is broken."

"Can you fix it?"

She shook her head, "I'll be able to push, but we are going to have to walk the rest of the way."

We emptied Loni's water bottle and resumed our journey through several villages. We passed farmers driving hay wagons, pulled by cows or teams of horses. We watched women fork manure onto steaming dung piles in the front of their houses. Children chased geese, chickens, and each other. Dogs yapped at our heels. My aunt tried in vain to find someone to repair the bicycle. My stomach grumbled, and I wished I had the courage to ask for a piece of bread from one of the farmers, but I remembered what had happened the last time I begged.

The sun disappeared behind the woods. Mist rose from plowed fields and dusk settled on the land when we entered the Habichtswald. My legs and feet hurt, and I was weak from hunger. When we arrived at Schanzen Straße 103, it was dark and way past curfew. Tante Marianne embraced me warmly. After she gave me a drink of water and a bite to eat, I fell into bed.

Begging

The next morning, I took in my surroundings and asked Marianne, "Why are we sleeping in the basement?"

"Didn't Loni tell you? I had to move down here when the Americans confiscated the house last year and turned it into their regimental Information and Education Center. We are permitted to live in the basement and the railroad coach.

"The coach? Didn't it belong to a prince?" I asked.

"He was only a duke." Marianne quickly changed the subject. "I want to ask you a favor. Loni is going to need your help today. I would like for you to accompany her to the field kitchen that the *Amis* set up in the abandoned Café Hessenschanze. Can I count on you?"

"You may," I answered quickly.

"I knew I could," she smiled and gave me a hug and a kiss on each cheek.

I hadn't seen my aunt Marianne in over a year. Petite, with a small waist and full bosom and dressed in a pair of tan trousers and white shirt, she looked as radiant and vivacious as ever, in the dingy and dank surroundings of her basement. After I splashed cold water on my face, pulled on my gym pants and an old shirt, I followed her around, the way I did when I was little girl. I watched as she swept the concrete floor. I poked into the different nooks of the basement and noticed that the mattress I had slept on lay near the foot of the stairs, leading to the main floor above. My aunt saw me looking up. "Don't worry," she said, "The door is locked."

She talked about the invasion, during which the American soldiers ransacked the house, took everything valuable—her jewelry, Leica camera, and furs—and when they couldn't get the cookstove going, made a fire on the parquet floor in the middle of the living room.

"Weren't you furious?" I asked.

"Naturally. It was sort of ironic, wasn't it? Here we and the house had survived three years of bombing raids, and then …" She didn't finish the sentence, and she hesitated before she added, "So many dead."

"Papa said that there weren't enough coffins to bury the victims."

She nodded and reminisced about the RAF raid on October 22, 1943, when more than 10,000 people were burned to death or asphyxiated during a horrendous firestorm. My aunt shook her head, as if to get rid of these disturbing memories, put her arms around my shoulders, smiled and said, "It was a miracle that we survived."

*   *   *

Years later, I read that Kassel burned for ten days after that raid, leaving 150,000 people homeless. When the Americans invaded, on April 5, 1945, only 50,000 of a prewar population of 250,000 still lived among the ruins of the town.

*   *   *

I explored the concrete shelter, where we had huddled during a vacation. At that time, it was furnished with cots and shelves that held rows of preserves and fruit, layered on beds of straw. Marianne, who rarely spoke well of Papa, mentioned that it had been his idea to add the shelter, when he designed the house. "Long before anybody else, he was convinced that we were going to need it, and he was right. We felt safe in our own shelter until the British and the Americans started bombarding us with heavier and more destructive explosives."

My aunt and I left the basement by ascending a flight of stairs that led into the garden. The garden with its ornamental trees, lawns, flowers, and vegetable beds was as I remembered it. Apple and pear trees lined the gravel paths. In the forest across the fence arose a fire tower. Hidden among pine trees stood the former field hospital barracks, now crammed to overflowing with the homeless.

Marianne led me toward the coach—a vestige from the days nobility traveled the world in their private railroad cars. Weathered with age, its slate roof covered with moss, it sat on a vine-covered foundation. We climbed the wide staircase leading to a veranda, and we entered a galley appointed with mahogany cabinets. My aunt spread two slices of snow white bread with strawberry jam and offered them to me. I was taking my first bite, when, Loni, crackling with energy, swept through the door. "Do you like it?" she asked. I smiled and nodded eagerly. Both aunts watched as I tasted the soft bread and felt the sweetness of the jam explode on my tongue. While I chewed and wished that this moment would last forever, my aunts looked at each other and smiled.

I licked my fingers and asked, "From the *Ami* kitchen?"

"Yes, and it's time to leave," Loni replied. She cinched a military belt around my waist and commented, "You are as skinny as a rail, but don't worry, we'll fatten you up." She hooked two mess kits onto my belt and handed me two metal milk cans, strapped a belt with assorted containers around her own waist, and picked up two more containers. We walked through a combination bathroom-dressing area into the sleeping compartment, with its comfortable daybeds. From there, we passed through the Salon furnished with couches covered in gray velvet, with a mahogany table bolted to the floor, and walls adorned with gleaming brass sconces. We left the coach through a heavy metal door and stepped onto the veranda.

Three-year-old Brita and two-year-old Heiko came tumbling out from behind a berry patch, their hands and mouths smeared with juice. Marianne's yapping dachshund, Hexe, accompanied them. "Eycke, play with us," Brita pleaded.

"Play," Heiko echoed, as he got his legs tangled up with the dog, tripped, fell, picked himself up and continued toddling in our direction.

Loni laughed, "Been snacking on berries, have you? Eycke will play with you later." She called to her sister, "Marianne, please see to it that they don't escape through the loose board in the back fence." Pots and cans clanking, we skirted the house and stepped into a scene of devastation. Loni pointed to a yellow mansion. "A woman and her son died there, and dozens of people further down the street perished during one of the carpet bombings. Once we realized that we would not survive a direct hit on the house, we ran to the bunkers in the forest every time the sirens wailed." My aunt and I continued along a path carved out of the rubble. Hollow skeletons of ruins with smoke-smudged walls reached toward a blue sky. Collapsed walls exposed intimate living spaces to the eyes of strangers. A carpet of purple *Trümmerblumen*, fireweed, bloomed among the ruins. I observed men walking around with their eyes cast down searching for cigarette butts the American soldiers had thrown on the ground. We joined a line of emaciated women, youngsters, and old men dressed in ill-fitting clothes, who emerged from basements, shacks, and temporary shelters. Their blood appeared to have been drained out of them and been replaced by despair.

Our destination was the courtyard of the damaged Café Hessenschanze, where American troops had set up a field kitchen and mess hall. Here, young, robust, gum-chewing soldiers with short haircuts, wearing boots, baggy pants, white undershirts and beanies joked with each other as they hauled about immense kettles of leftovers. They ladled and spooned food into containers held by outstretched hands.

In my mind's eye, I saw myself at the Café before the war. I was dressed in a light blue summer frock, and sat at a table under a shady tree. The table was covered with snowy white linen, and I feasted on a raspberry tart, topped with a mound of whipped cream.

"Hold out your mess kits, Eycke," Loni urged, nudging me with her elbow.

I kept my eyes down as I held out each container to receive dollops of mashed potatoes, chipped beef, vanilla pudding, and tea. The food odor filled my nostrils and made me feel faint. Loni garnered white bread, portions of beans, and what looked like a yellow soup, plus two cans filled with moist coffee grounds and tea leaves. On our way home, I assuaged my hunger pangs with a hand full of mashed potatoes. My cousins peered through the slats of the gate and stomped their feet. Brita called out, "Hungry, Mama, hungry."

Heiko joined her, "Hungry."

My aunt wrinkled her nose and exploded at her son, "Get away from me, you stink." His sister fled in the direction of the coach, calling out for Marianne, "*Tata*, come quickly."

Her face contorted with rage, the veins on her neck swollen thick, Loni got rid of her load and pushed her son toward the basement stairs of the big house. She ordered me to follow them to the laundry room. Marianne came running and called out sharply, "Loni, stop." Loni paid no attention.

We carried the food to the coach, listening to Heiko's wails and Loni screaming at her son, "When are you going to learn not to crap all over yourself?"

"Do I have to obey Tante Loni?" I asked Marianne.

"Yes, you do. I have to keep Brita away from her. Quickly, see what you can do." I hurried to the laundry room where Heiko was standing naked, in the middle of the concrete floor, his eyes closed, wailing. From a hose, his mother was pointing a stream of ice-cold water over his tiny body to dislodge the feces clinging to his bottom and legs.

"Here," she handed me the hose, "You finish up."

"Tante Loni, no."

"What did you say?" she spit out, and without waiting for an answer, she glared at me, "Do as I say, or I'm going to box your ears so hard you won't be able to hear or see. Moreover, from now on it's your job to clean him up when he shits all over himself."

Reluctantly, I redirected the spray at my cousin's feet. My aunt turned, muttered, "I am going to kill that kid one of these days," and stormed out. As soon as she was gone, I turned off the water, grabbed a towel from the clothesline, wrapped up the hysterical, shivering boy, and folded him into my arms.

Sobbing, I whispered into his ear, *"Ist gut, ist gut,"* as I gently dried and hugged him tightly. Then I picked him up, carried him to my mattress, covered him with a blanket, and patted him until his sobs subsided into little hiccups, and he fell asleep.

After a while, Marianne came and sat on the edge of my mattress.

"What is the matter with her?" I asked.

"Years of running to the bunker with two babies every time the sirens wailed, the fear, the devastation and the stench of death—all this has made her crazy. There is no reasoning with her once she gets in one of these states. And now … she so abhors begging and fighting for scraps from the *Amis.*" Here my aunt's voice trailed off. She shook her head, as if this would help her forget, recovered, and offered to prepare a meal for me.

"No, thank you, I've lost my appetite," I replied.

"Come on, *Mäuschen.* It's late. Let me make you some pancakes. The batter is going to spoil if we don't use it up. You needn't worry about Loni. She'll calm down." Loni was nowhere in sight when Brita crawled out of her hiding place, Marianne picked up the sleeping boy and put him to bed in the coach. Marianne's kind words had melted the tension I had felt since the row in the laundry room. I watched her pour a stream of silky batter into a frying pan, to form small circular pancakes, which she fried to a light golden brown. She served Brita first, and then set a plate of three pancakes in front of me. After the first taste, I got caught up in a frenzy. I cut off large pieces, brought them to my lips, chewed and swallowed, chewed and swallowed.

As soon as I finished, my aunt served me another plate full. Satiated, I breathed "thank you," and fell asleep on one of the beds next to my cousins. Later that evening, I awakened with excruciating stomach pains. "Tante Marianne," I screamed, "I'm dying."

My aunt came running and muttered, "Oh dear. It's my fault. You aren't used to rich foods. I'm sorry." She proceeded to rub my bare stomach with slow circular strokes.

For the next two or three hours, she continued rubbing. When she stopped for a minute, I moaned, "I'm dying," and I begged for her to continue. She assured me that I wasn't dying, calmed my fears, and soothed my pain until I fell asleep in her arms.

When I opened my eyes at dawn, I remembered the effects of my gluttony during the previous night. Brita and Heiko lay curled up on the bed next to me. Loni was asleep on the couch in the Salon. Still clad in my wrinkled shorts and the stained shirt, in which I had fallen asleep, I quietly slipped out the door. I ran barefooted through the early morning dew to the big house, down the basement stairs, crept past Marianne's bed on tip toes, crawled into bed and pulled the covers over me.

Around noon the next day I found myself once again in line at the field kitchen waiting for the soldiers to finish their lunch and for the kettles with leftovers to be hauled into the courtyard. I wondered just how I had gotten there. That morning, Marianne was vigorously shaking out our featherbeds, when she told me that Loni had bicycled to Simmershausen to help with the harvest in exchange for potatoes and beets. "This means that you'll have to go to the field kitchen. You don't mind, do you?" she asked. My first thought had been: "Hey, me? Go up there by myself? It was bad enough yesterday with Loni at my side." Instead, I heard myself say, "I don't mind." I was lying, of course, and perhaps Marianne sensed it, but I also knew that I couldn't say "no" to my favorite aunt. I hadn't forgotten how upset Loni had been the day before, and I knew that Marianne sympathized with her sister, because she herself would probably rather starve than beg.

When I arrived at the Café, it seemed that the entire neighborhood was looking for a handout. I joined a line that snaked up the driveway and into the street. People shuffled, bickered, and worried aloud if there was going to be enough for everyone. A woman cut in front of me. A second and a third followed her brazenly. It was as though they hadn't noticed my standing there. When somebody pushed me from behind, I stumbled and nearly fell. One of the soldiers saw the commotion, "You there!" he shouted at the woman who had pushed me, "Cut it out!" He pointed with a large spoon and waved me to the front of the line. With downcast eyes, I passed people who objected, "Look at that, will you?" The soldier winked at me and without another word pointed me in the direction of the kettles. I went from vat to vat and ladled cocoa, moist tea and coffee grounds, pickle relish and pancake batter into my mess kits. I leaned into a pot, scraped macaroni and cheese off the bottom, and was tempted to taste it. Sneaking food when nobody was looking was one thing, but in front of all those people?

I hooked my mess kits onto my belt, picked up the milk cans and was walking past the line when a woman hissed, "*Amiliebchen!*" an insult reserved for the German girlfriends of American soldiers. I felt a confusing mix of shame and pride as I carried the containers filled with food to my aunts and cousins.

Marianne thanked and praised me for a job well done. When we sat down to eat she gently reminded me, "Sometimes our eyes are bigger than our stomachs." Still, I found it hard to resist the urge to stuff myself while thinking, eat all you can today, because there might be none tomorrow.

Amiliebchen

I stayed with my aunts and cousins through that fall into the winter of 1946. When I asked Marianne about school, she answered, "You'll catch up with your school work. Right now it is more important that you get enough to eat." The Americans gave us permission to use the kitchen in the house. In time, I got used to going to the field kitchen by myself. Loni was content to leave the job to me. My cousins and I befriended a sergeant who was quartered in my aunt's house. We tried to teach him German, and he taught us English. He entertained us by clowning around, wearing a brassiere he had taken off the laundry line, and by dancing the hula.

I helped care for my cousins and tried to clean up Heiko's "accidents" without his mother's knowledge. From time to time, Loni lost her temper, yelled at her sister, her children and me. On the other hand, never again in my presence did she treat her son as harshly as she had that day in the laundry room. There were also many times when she was lighthearted and funny. Loni, who was a kindergarten teacher by profession, played games with her children, entertained them with her guitar, sang, told them stories and rolled around the floor with them. I continued to stay on my guard whenever I was around her.

On October twenty-first, we celebrated Marianne's fortieth birthday. We congratulated her and presented her with homemade gifts and a bouquet of the last roses from the garden. Loni's husband Seppel, who had returned from a POW camp by then, exchanged some American cigarettes for two bottles of wine on the black market. We pooled our ration stamps, and I baked a cake. I hoarded enough food from the field kitchen to help put together a modest spread for the party that evening. Later, I watched Marianne get ready, as I had done on many occasions when I was a little girl. She slipped into a black evening gown, twisted her hair into a chignon and applied pink lipstick, powered her face and dabbed a drop of her favorite perfume, Tosca, behind each ear and on her wrists. She twirled in front of the mirror, smiled at me, and asked, "How do I look?"

"Beautiful," I answered and clapped my hands. "Just like before the war. I remember how Onkel Wütt would compliment you, kiss you on the cheek, and help you into your coat."

A wistful look softened my aunt's features. "I wonder if he is still alive?" she said. It appeared that she didn't want to dwell on that and quickly changed the subject. "Do you remember what happened next?" she asked.

"He would have the Mercedes already warmed up, he'd wrap me into a blanket, put me in the back seat, and open the car door for you. You'd get in, he'd close the door, and off we would go into the city."

"You remember?"

"As if it happened yesterday. You would walk up the wide stairs to the opera house, turn around, and throw us kisses with both hands. We'd watch you disappear through the doors, and only then would we drive back home. I'd be long asleep by the time Onkel Wütt picked you up late in the evening. The next morning, you would sing the arias from the opera you had seen the night before."

"Amazing," Marianne laughed.

"Papa says I have a good memory, and that I can hear the fleas cough," I bragged.

"He is right." She glanced into the mirror one more time and declared, "It's time to receive my guests. Do you want to come and say hello?"

I looked at my aunt in her finery and then at my baggy pants and wrinkled shirt, but I was too curious to turn down the invitation. Everything was ready in the Salon. A record with Marlene Dietrich's sultry voice played on the gramophone. Loni looked lovely in a dove-blue dress, and her husband was handsome in pressed trousers and a white shirt. The guests arrived: the tall, dark and beautiful Fräulein Hilde, wearing a green dress to match her eyes, and two handsome young surgeons whom Marianne and Hilde had met when they were stationed at the Wehrmacht field hospital next door.

"A toast to the lovely Marianne," said one of the doctors, who had fastened his eyes on my aunt from the moment he entered the Salon. After everyone lifted their glasses and sang, *"Hoch soll sie leben,"* long shall she live, I excused myself and returned to the big house. Before I went to sleep, I thought, when I grow up, I am going to be as beautiful as Marianne, I am going to wear long gowns, dab Tosca perfume on my ear lobes, go to the opera, and have lots of parties and admirers.

Some time during the night, I was awakened by loud and insistent pounding on the door above my head. I made out, "Open up this ... ing door. Open up, or I'll break it down." The rest was unintelligible. Oh, dear, I thought, an angry *Ami,* and I am all alone. What am I going to do? Without turning on the light, I slipped back into my clothes and felt my way to the back door leading into the garden, when I heard someone retching above. I ran up the flight of stairs and heard something splash on the steps behind me. Doubling my speed, I fled across the lawn toward the lights of the coach. Strains of flamenco music came from the Salon, and a man's voice said, "Please, Marianne, dance for us."

Through the open door, I saw my aunt rise from her seat, bow and smile. She closed her eyes, threw back her head, gracefully lifted her bare arms, snapped her fingers like castanets, twirled around once, and abandoned herself to the music. Her hips began to sway slowly and rhythmically, and she stamped her feet, as I had seen Spanish dancers do in the movies. I slipped into the Salon and watched in awe. When the music stopped, she bowed to the applause. Her cheeks were flushed, and her eyes sparkled. When she noticed me, she smiled and asked, *"Mäuschen,* can't you sleep?"

I whispered in her ear. "One of the *Amis* is pounding on the basement door, and another one is vomiting out the upstairs bedroom window."

She gave me a hug and whispered, "You can stay in the next room with Heiko and Brita." I fell asleep to music and laughing in the next room.

The next morning, on the way to the basement, I walked by the living room picture windows and saw a young woman, nude from the waist up, sitting on a stool while a soldier sketched her. This made me wonder, if the women who hissed at me at the field kitchen would have called her an *Amiliebchen* too.

The Homecoming

Shortly after Marianne's birthday, my aunt and I were already in bed when there was a knock on the basement door. My aunt put on her bathrobe and slippers and walked into the hallway. "Who is it?" she asked.

"It's me, Wütt."

I heard the door creak, as my aunt let in her husband. The moment I heard my uncle's voice, I jumped out of bed, but then I remembered that he was coming home to his wife, not me. I crawled back into bed, where I remained in the shadows.

"Eycke, look who is here," my aunt waved for me to come greet my uncle as he emerged, limping, from the basement hallway, supporting himself with a tall walking stick. I ran and threw my arms around him.

"My goodness, girl, how you have grown. How did you get out of Poland?"

"Papa got us out on the last train during the middle of January last year," I replied.

"Come, you should get some of those clothes off," my aunt urged her husband. I helped my aunt relieve Wütt of a smelly blanket, which he wore draped over his shoulders. We helped him take off his knapsack, a filthy greatcoat, and a fur cap. His boots were padded with layers of tattered newspaper, which protruded from several holes. The right boot had been cut open at the toes and tied together with a string.

My aunt handed me my uncle's clothes held between two fingers and asked me to discard them in the laundry room. He collapsed in a chair. As Marianne slowly and gently unwrapped the rags from her husband's foot, she fired off one question after another, without waiting for an answer. "What happened to your foot? Where were you all this time? How long have you been on the road? Haven't heard from you in over a year. I was afraid that you had died somewhere in Russia." She stared at his right foot, "Oh, dear. You're wounded."

Wütt leaned back, exhausted, "Janchen," he said in a hoarse voice, "I've been in a POW camp. Since my release, I've been walking forever. Don't even know what date it is. I'm tired, and my foot hurts." My uncle took in his surroundings for the first time since he had entered the basement. He shook his head, "What are you doing living next to the coal cellar?" He continued, "We had heard rumors that Kassel was completely destroyed, so I didn't hold out much hope that you had survived. I was so relieved when I saw that the house was still standing, but then I noticed the big sign, UNITED STATES ARMY, INFORMATION AND EDUCATION CENTER, on the front lawn. I almost made a mistake and knocked on the front door. Didn't have the strength to go any further, so I decided to sneak in through the driveway gate and head for the coach. Loni told me that you were alive."

Marianne explained, "A few incendiary bombs fell in the garden, and one penetrated the roof, but we put the fire out with buckets of sand." She touched her forehead with her hand, "Oh, dear," she cried out, "you must be hungry and thirsty, and we haven't any food down here."

"Loni served me a piece of bread and a hot cup of tea before I came over here. Right now, I need to get cleaned up a bit."

After my aunt and uncle disappeared into the laundry room, I prayed, "*Lieber Gott,* thank you for bringing Onkel Wütt home safely." As I fell asleep, I conjured up an image of my uncle the way he used to look: wavy hair combed back meticulously, gray at the temples, dressed impeccably in muted tones of light gray and creamy white, his round face clean-shaven and smelling of Birkenwasser aftershave. But the man who had returned home that evening, and whose voice I had recognized instantly as that of my favorite uncle, looked like a vagrant.

Later that night, I was awakened by the sound of my aunt and uncle's voices coming from the air raid shelter. I caught snatches of my aunt's accusations: "… another woman … pictures … letters … Krakau … unfaithful …"

And my uncle's muffled replies: "Sorry … lonely … make it up … promise."

And my aunt's angry reply: "I am counting on that."

I put a pillow over my ears and thought about what I had heard. I knew that letters addressed to men in the field were returned to their next of kin, stamped "missing in action." I assumed that such a letter written by another woman to my uncle had ended up in my aunt's hands. I was slowly and painfully beginning to understand that relationships between married couples were complicated, and that long separations caused much trouble.

I was angry with my aunt for confronting my uncle the night of his homecoming, and for turning her head every time he tried to kiss her on the cheek. After all, I remembered only too well how she had flirted with the young doctor on the night of her birthday. There were the snippets of conversation between my aunt and her friend Hilde that made me think that the two of them had not spent the war knitting socks, when they weren't dodging bombs. Before going back to sleep that night, I resolved to be especially nice to Onkel Wütt so that he would be happy to be back home.

*   *   *

Many years later, I read in my mother's diary, that before I was born, Marianne and Wütt were having serious marital problems. Both had been present at my birth. My mother and I had lived with them for over a year, and during that time their shared love and devotion for me helped mend their relationship.

Christmas on Heidehügel

For my thirteenth birthday, Tante Loni baked a cake, and Marianne transformed a blanket into a cape and some old dresses into a wardrobe for me. My mother wrote:

> Dear Eycke,
> Happy Birthday.
> Last week we finally moved to *Heidehügel*. The cottage
> isn't finished. We have no running water and no electricity.
> We live, eat, and sleep in the kitchen, but we miss you and
> want you to come home for Christmas.
> Warm regards to everyone.
> Lovingly yours,
> Mutti

The prospect of celebrating Christmas with my family made me glad, but my mixed emotions puzzled me. I didn't want to leave home to come here, and now I wanted to stay. Marianne consoled me, "*Mäuschen*, you won't be leaving until Christmas, which gives us plenty of time to get ready." We unraveled worn sweaters and used the yarn to knit hats, scarves, and mittens for my parents and siblings. We saved up our rationing stamps to buy flour, sugar, powdered eggs, and shortening. Our next-door neighbors contributed a basket of walnuts. The week before Christmas, we mixed and kneaded, rolled and cut out stars, bells, and moon-shaped cookies, until we were covered with flour, our hair was disheveled, and I had tasted enough raw dough to be just short of getting sick. The day before Christmas, we stuffed my knapsack and two shopping bags with my new dresses, homemade presents, cookies, Christmas bread, and leftovers from the field kitchen.

It was bitter cold. A fresh cover of snow blanketed the ground the morning of my journey. I hugged everyone goodbye and hoisted my knapsack. My aunts asked me to give their regards to my family, and they wished me *Fröhliche Weihnachten*. Onkel Wütt carried the two shopping bags, and Marianne waved to us until we climbed into Streetcar Number Three, at the Prinzenquelle stop. "Come back soon," she called after us. I waved back, blinking away tears.

The beat-up yellow streetcar rumbled and screeched downhill, past ruined neighborhoods, toward the center of town. There I saw *Trümmerfrauen*. These were women, who huddled close to open fires, where they cleaned and sorted bricks, which they had picked from rubble piled high among skeletons of burned-out buildings. Although the war had been over for more than a year and a half, there were still blocks where not a single house was left standing. My uncle shook his head and lamented, "I no longer recognize my hometown."

At the bombed-out railroad station, we waited in a long line to buy my ticket for the next *Bummelzug*, the slow train to Münden. The station, once an impressive and stately structure covered by an enormous curved glass roof, was in shambles. Half of the tracks and platforms had been repaired, but more tracks, twisted into weird shapes and damaged beyond repair, remained strewn about. Anxious travelers with pinched faces pushed and jostled each other toward the icy platform, where the train waited, its engine churning, hissing, and emitting clouds of steam. "*Gleis drei, Einsteigen!*" called out the stationmaster.

"Remember to get off at the sixth stop," my uncle counseled, after giving me one of his bear hugs. "Best wishes to everyone and *Fröhliche Weihnachten*," he added, "and we'll see you at Easter." He helped me up the steep steps into the coach and handed me my shopping bags. My uncle had made me feel special from the time I was little. He treated me like a lady by helping me into my coat and opening doors. Unlike other men, including my father, he spoke to me in polite tones, he listened to me with respect, and he never told me that I asked too many questions. That day, as in so many years past, his love warmed me and filled me with gratitude and joy.

The station manager blew his whistle and announced the departure of the train, "*Gleis drei, Abfahrt!*" We pulled away from the station and slowly picked up speed. Through a window, I watched my uncle wave his handkerchief until the train took a turn and I lost sight of him. With no seats left inside the compartments, I sat on my knapsack in the corridor, which reeked of sweat, cigarette smoke, and urine. I clutched my shopping bags tightly.

My thoughts drifted back to my last train ride during January, 1945. The train from Kassel to Münden, like the one during our flight from Poland, was filled with surly passengers who pushed and shoved the old, the crippled, the weak, and the young out of their way. They argued with each other over a spot to stand or sit. But in spite of their lack of compassion for each other, I did not sense the intense desperation and fear that gripped us during the flight from the

Russians. All the while, I kept in mind what my uncle had said about the five stops between Kassel and Münden. I listened as the conductor called out "Niederfellmar, Ihringshausen, Kragenhof, Speele, and Wilhelmshausen." When the train screeched to a halt and I heard "Hannoversch-Münden" over the loudspeaker, I hustled out the door and climbed down the steps to the platform. The crowd swept me along as we headed for the exit. I passed through the lobby, where, during the war, the walls had been plastered with posters proclaiming *Räder rollen für den Sieg*, wheels turn toward victory and *Psst, Der Feind hört mit*, beware, the enemy is listening. Instead of slogans, thousands of photographs and notices about missing children covered the walls. I thought about how we almost left Dagmar behind at the railroad station in Conti, how Frank had been torn from us on a platform in Leipzig, and how fortunate we were that their faces had not wound up on posters in a railroad station.

Because the bridge across the Fulda was still in shambles, I made my way through the old town past the medieval walls and then crossed the Fulda River on a shaky suspension footbridge, which swung with each step I took. From time to time, I put down my bags to catch my breath. Perspiring and exhausted, I reached the bus stop, where I waited for the bus to arrive. The cape Marianne had sewn for me from an old blanket, the woolen socks she had knitted, and the pair of second-hand but sturdy shoes Loni had exchanged for cigarettes on the black market, did not keep the cold from spreading into my body. When the bus finally appeared, rattling and backfiring, it was already full. I thanked the driver when he urged his passengers to make room for me. Wedged in between cranky and smelly men and women, who elbowed each other and me, I let the heat of their bodies warm me. I closed my eyes and wished myself back to a time before we joined the despised ranks of *Flüchtlinge*.

As I rode, I thought of past Christmas seasons. Red candles on the Advent wreath illuminated the dark and ushered in Christmas. Mutti and Papa taught us Advent and Christmas songs, Sven and I scratched out musical selections on our violins, I played my recorder, and we began our secret preparations. We children helped each other fashion homemade gifts for our parents: for our mother crocheted pot holders, a necklace made from smooth, shiny horse chestnuts or apple seeds, and a bright pin cushion; and for Papa a calendar with different pictures for each month, a hand-knitted muffler, a painted wooden box for his cufflinks, and a pretty drawing.

Each evening, from December 6, until Christmas, we placed our houseshoes neatly side by side under our beds in anticipation of a visit from Saint Nicholas. If we had been obedient that day, we discovered a fir branch, a cookie, or a small toy in our shoes. If we had been naughty, we found a piece of coal. When I discovered a coal in my shoes, it was most likely placed there because of fighting with my brothers or talking back to Mutti. Two days before Christmas, Mutti would lock the doors to the living room, and when in the mornings we discovered small fir branches and angel hair on the floor in the hallway, she revealed to us, smiling wistfully, that it was a sign that the *Christkind* must have dropped it.

On Christmas Eve, scrubbed and dressed in festive clothes, we would wait impatiently until we heard the ringing of a bell. Before we entered the living room, we would form a line, with the smallest child in front, and me at the tail end. There, draped with shimmering angel hair, glowing with one hundred beeswax candles and decorated with colorful wooden figures, stood our *Tannenbaum*. It reached to the ceiling. Clear glass balls danced like soap bubbles in the warmth of the candles. Our eyes would widen in wonder as Papa lit sparklers suspended from the tree's branches. Mutti would play her guitar, Papa his violin, and they would lead us in singing Christmas carols.

I willed myself to hold on to those images, as the bus lurched along the slippery, rutted, and pot-holed road toward home. Within an hour, I got off at the *Post* in Vaake. At the top of the stairs, glasses low on her nose, wearing her worn felt slippers and a gaudy, purple wrap across her shoulders, stood Pawa. "Eycke," she called out. "Home in time for *Heilig Abend,* Christmas Eve, are you? Where have you been all this time?"

"Visiting relatives in Kassel," I shouted back. Worried that she wanted to hear all about my stay, I added, *"Fröhliche Weihnachten,* Tante Pawa. I'm in a hurry to get home before dark."

"Run along then," she laughed, *"Fröhliche Weihnachten."* As I made my way on the snowy footpath along the Ahle Creek across a small bridge toward home, I continued my reveries of past Christmas celebrations. I recalled that during the singing, I would cast furtive glances toward the table, where my Christmas presents begged to be examined. My mouth watered at the sight of my *Weihnachtsteller*, a plate heaped high with apples, nuts, cookies, and marzipan. But Papa did not give permission to open our presents until after we had sung, recited poems, and performed our musical selections.

When I was six, I received a *Puppenküche*, a doll kitchen complete with furniture, a cooking stove, pots, pans and dishes. When I turned eight, my parents surprised me with a dollhouse, and I began to suspect that it was they, not the *Christkind*, who had spent hours constructing and furnishing it. I was especially delighted with all the tiny battery-powered light fixtures that Papa had installed. During late night hours before Christmas, Mutti had sewn beautiful dresses and knitted matching sweaters for Dagmar, our dolls, and me. For Dagmar's doll, Papa had built a cradle, and for my family of dolls, a table and four chairs decorated with cutout hearts. Other presents were books, lots of books for everyone, a toy drum, a trumpet, and a xylophone. The boys received hobbyhorses, trains, cars and trucks, and one year from Wütt and Marianne, a bright red convertible, in which they could pedal around.

I arrived at the foot of *Heidehügel* just as a pale winter sun disappeared behind the Reinhardswald. Breathing hard, I zigzagged up a path to the top of the bluff through a stand of scraggly alders, when it started to snow. I heard sounds of wood chopping. At last the house, it's half-timbered and adobe brick walls covered with bark siding, came into view. I admired the bright red tiles, and especially the gable decoration of two carved horse heads and a row of five birds—a symbol of mother, father, and five children—between them. A wisp of thin white smoke curled into the winter sky.

Sven, dressed in an oversized jacket and wearing wooden shoes, stood at the chopping block, splitting kindling. He glanced at me with hollow eyes, slowly lifted a hand in greeting, "*Hallo,* Eycke," and went back to work. Frank and Dagmar, holding loads of firewood, cheered, "Mutti, Papa, Eycke is home." They galloped toward the kitchen door, nearly losing their wooden clogs, and dropping part of their load. They stood and stared, as Mutti poked her head out the Dutch doors, wiped her hands on a towel, threw up her bony arms, and called out, "Eycke." I put down my bags and ran into her embrace. "*Schätzchen,*" she whispered hoarsely, "it's good to have you back home." She looked deep into my eyes to read the things that remain unspoken at such a moment, as she gently stroked my cheeks with her rough hands. She smiled, turned me around, and marveled, "You have put on weight."

I looked past her into the dim kitchen, "Where is Papa?"

"He's quite ill. Onkel Erich came by and operated on him this morning. We are worried about blood poisoning." Doktor Erich Bengen, a family friend, lived across the fields in the valley south of us. "But, come on in, and see for yourself." Björn was playing quietly in his crib, and I could see Papa, ashen and emaciated, resting on a cot in the corner.

He greeted me with a weak voice, "I was hoping you would come home in time for Christmas Eve." Papa tried to lift himself off his pillow, moaned, and quickly sank back, "I have an abscess."

"Yeah," Frank added grinning, "on his behind."

"*Shshsh …*" Mutti admonished. "Go, and help your sister and brother bring in more wood."

I pulled up a wobbly, three-legged milking stool. "Mutti said that Onkel Erich operated on you this morning."

"Yes. Didn't expect that he would have to do any cutting when he showed up. Only carried a small dissection knife in his bag. Your mother sterilized it on the kitchen stove."

I had never seen Papa so weak. I knew that boils were hard to cure. Sven had suffered from a serious bout for months, and Mutti made him soak in a sulfur bath for hours. In an attempt to hide my concern, I tried to assure Papa, "You'll regain your strength, especially after you eat some of the food I brought."

He nodded, "And then we'll finish the house."

Frank and Dagmar rushed in, their cheeks and noses red from the cold. They continued to stare and smile shyly. Sven entered with a load of firewood, which he neatly stacked next to the stove. Dagmar pulled my sleeve, "Did you bring us anything?"

Sven asked, "Any food from the *Amis?*"

"Can we have some?" Frank pleaded.

I unpacked some cookies and watched them devour the content of an entire tin in minutes. "Did you bring any presents?" Frank asked while he was still chewing.

"Wait until we light the candles on the tree," I replied.

"And after we have sung our songs," Papa interjected.

"Where is the tree?" I asked.

Dagmar pointed at a shelf, on which stood a tiny fir tree with five candles. She proclaimed, "Isn't it beautiful?"

Papa explained, "Next year we'll cut one big enough for one hundred candles."

My family watched me as I looked around the tiny kitchen, with its black tar paper walls. Mutti tried to sound cheerful, "It's easy to heat." I wondered how our family of seven could possibly live, eat, and sleep in such a small space. A tea-kettle and a big pot, filled with soapy water and laundry, simmered on top of the black iron stove. Above the stove, from a rack, fashioned out of sticks and twigs lashed together with twine, hung an assortment of socks and clothing to dry. I glanced at Papa, "One of your inventions, I suppose?" He nodded.

Along two walls stood a day bed, two cots, a straw pallet, and a crib. There was barely enough room for the table and five chairs. The only light came from a smoking carbide lamp. Mutti saw me taking it all in. "It's crowded in here, but we are glad to have our own place at last. If I only knew where to get food for our next meal." She held her cracked and bleeding hands in front of her face, then wiped her eyes and turned to Sven, "Do we have enough kindling for tomorrow morning?"

"Yes, Mutti, we do." He was only fourteen months younger than I, but my brother's calloused hands told of the hard work he had performed clearing the land, putting in a garden, and helping build the cottage, as well as chopping wood and fetching water from the creek.

Mutti lit a piece of kindling in the stove and handed it to me. Sven extinguished the lamp, and by the faint glow of candlelight we sang, "*Oh Tannenbaum,*" "*Oh du Fröhliche,*" and "*Stille Nacht,*" followed by the song Papa composed as a young man in the trenches during World War I:

Leis auf gold'nen Engels Schwingen,	Gently on golden angel wings,
Höre ich ein Liedlein singen,	I hear a song through the quiet winter night,
Leis und süsse, leis und sacht.	Gently and sweetly, gently and sweetly.
Und der Mond mit seinem Scheine,	And the glowing moon,
Und die lieben Sternelein,	And lovely stars,
Stimmen ein mit ihrer Pracht.	Join in with glorious voices.
Leis und süsse, leis und sacht.	Gently and sweetly, gently and sweetly.
Und mein Herz fängt an zu singen,	And my heart begins to sing,
Leise und süsse, leis und sacht.	Gently and sweetly, gently and sweetly.
Weihnachtsglocken hör ich klingen.	Bells for Christmas I hear ringing.
Leis und süsse, leis und sacht.	Gently and sweetly, gently and sweetly.

Our only presents that Christmas Eve were those I had brought. My family appreciated their warm hats, scarves, and mittens, but they marveled at the tins of cookies and Christmas breads. Prized above all were the chocolate bars and chewing gum, all treats from a friendly American sergeant. Mutti was ecstatic at the sight of all that food, the moist coffee grounds, and tealeaves, and especially the taste of the sweet and sour pickle relish. She quickly prepared and served a soup made with flour, dried eggs, dried milk and beet syrup. For dessert, we shared slices of *Stollen.* Before bedtime, Sven helped Mutti place a large beam across the entrance. "To keep the bandits out," Papa whispered in my ear, followed by a more cheerful, "*Fröhliche Weihnachten.*"

"*Fröhliche Weihnachten,*" we replied. Mutti put another log on the fire and blew out the candles. To keep each other warm, Dagmar and I cuddled in spoon fashion on our pallet. Our family never celebrated another Christmas in the years to come when we felt as close to one another as we did on that cold and snowy night on *Heidehügel.*

Vaake/Weserbergland, Hesse, Germany.

The parish house where the author's family found refuge and awaited the end of
World War II. Vaake.

On Pentecost, the author's family and friends celebrated her brother Björn's baptism at the parish house. Vaake, May, 1945.

The *Evangelische Kirche* in Vaake, dating back to the eleventh century, where the author's brother Björn, was baptized and the author confirmed.

In 1946, the author's parents purchased land in Vaake on a hill covered with heather. On it, they built a small cottage with their own hands and named it *Haus am Heidehügel*.

The family home that the author's father designed and built in the late 1960s on the site of the cottage *Heidehügel*. Vaake.

The author's parents on the day German President Gustav Heinemann awarded the author's father the *Verdienstkreuz Erster Klasse,* Cross of Merit, First Class, for rescuing Jews during the Holocaust and for helping rebuild a democratic Germany after World War II. Kassel, 1974.

The author's parents. Vaake, summer, 1978, one year before her father's death in
March, 1979, at the age of eighty-three.

The *Diplome d'Honneur*, issued by Yad Vashem, the Holocaust Memorial for the Martyrs' and Heroes' Remembrance Authority. It "conveys upon Karl Laabs, who, at the risk of his own life, saved persecuted Jews during the Holocaust in Europe, the honor of the Award for the Righteous among the Nations, and authorizes the planting of a tree in his name on the Avenue of the Righteous on the Mountain of Remembrance in Jerusalem. January 6, 1981."

The author planting a tree in her father's honor on the Avenue of the Righteous. Yad Vashem, Jerusalem, Israel, May, 1983.

The author's mother reading and critiquing the unabridged manuscript of *Eyes are Watching, Ears are Listening*. Berlin, Germany, summer, 2000, four years before her death, at the age of one hundred.

Epilogue

"If we are to head into a sane future, as humans we must come to terms with our past, individually and collectively. If we keep others from reconciliation with their past, we have separated us and them from healing. If we keep others from forgiveness and deny their suffering, we have denied ourselves as well."
—Alice Derry, *Strangers to Their Courage.*

More than sixty years have passed since the end of World War II. After our flight from the advancing Russians to Germany, my family survived the chaos of the postwar years, first as refugees, and later, on *Heidehügel*, where we built a small cottage with our own hands. There, in March of 1948, my mother gave birth to her seventh child, a daughter, as she gazed at the stars through a hole in the roof.

The years between 1945 and 1950 were marked by hunger, deprivation, and sickness. Yet, the memories I cherish are of the many acts of generosity and kindness. Those who were themselves in need, extended helping hands and hearts to us. There was the joyous reunion with Fanny Hartmann and the gifts of food and clothing from her and her family, all of them Jewish survivors who owed my father their lives. Over time, I watched my parents open our home to men, women and their children, who had lost their homes, lost their way, or were alone in the world. They included people from different backgrounds, nationalities, religious affiliations, and political persuasions.

My father was exonerated during lengthy denazification proceedings, due to the testimonies by many Jewish survivors. He resumed his career in architecture, first working in Kassel, and later as Stadt Baurat in Frankfurt am Main. In 1972, the Federal Republic of Germany bestowed upon him the Distinguished Service Cross First Class for his active resistance to fascism, for saving Jews, and for helping to rebuild a democratic Germany. He did not think of himself as a hero. He said on that occasion, "I accept this award to honor those I was unable to help." In a letter to Bundespräsident Gustav Heinemann, he wrote, "My activities during those tragic and dangerous years were for me (and my wife) only a natural act of humanness and a Christian duty! Therefore, basically *nothing* special! It is an indisputable fact that not all Germans were passive witnesses to the Nazi terror. It was absolutely possible to resist, if one had the will and the ability to do so."

As my parents wrestled with the past, they passed on to their children and grandchildren, what my mother called *"die goldenen Eimer,"* the golden vessels. By their example, my parents taught us compassion for the poor, the afflicted, and the persecuted. They taught us the importance of learning from the past, the dangers of silence, indifference, and complacency. They urged us to uphold and defend human rights and justice, freedom of speech, and tolerance, and to strive for peace among nations.

My father retired in 1960, tore down the crumbling cottage on *Heidehügel,* and built a new home in its place. It was his way of atoning for broken promises and for the pain he had caused his wife and family. My parents moved back to Vaake and surrounded themselves with old and new friends, and with their children and grandchildren. They had always shared egalitarian ideals, and they continued to be socially and politically engaged, well into their old age. When they became disillusioned with the Social Democrats, they voted for the Green Party.

In her late fifties, my mother began the study of anthroposophy. These studies, and her visits to the Goetheanum in Dornach near Basel, Switzerland, greatly enriched her spiritual life. A quote on her wall, by Rudolf Steiner, a Swiss physician and the founder of anthroposophy, read:

Unsterblich ist am Menschen-werk	Immortal are the human endeavors
Was aus dem Herzen heraus,	Which spring from the heart,
Voll Liebe, für die Menschheit gedacht	Are filled with love,
Empfunden und vollbracht ist.	Perceived and achieved with the Intent to benefit humanity.

During both the war and postwar years, I treasured the closeness of my family, my father and mother's courage, and their ability to protect us in times of peril. What gave me strength, was the belief—passed on to me by my mother—that during those terrible times, we were protected by a Divine Power. I was awed by my mother's courage, in the face of Nazi bullying, her empathy for our Polish neighbors, and especially her friendship with the Hartmann family, who were cruelly persecuted, because they were Jewish. My mother spoke four languages, and was much loved by her family and friends from all over the world. They gravitated to her, were touched by her spirituality, and mesmerized by her passionate nature and candor. She won their hearts by listening patiently to their joys and troubles, by sharing her home, her life experiences, and her despair, as well her insights into philosophy and literature, and her love of music and poetry.

My husband, Charles, our son, daughter and I remain close to my German family. We visited my parents and siblings often, and they visited us. I still long for the landscape of my childhood, the green forests, the rivers and the ancient towns and villages. And yet, I continue to struggle with a deep ambivalence toward the land of my father and mother.

My parents had passionately loved and fought with each other for the first forty years of their lives together, but during the last ten years they lived in peace. After my father suffered a stroke, my mother nursed him at home for three years. In the end, my father asked my mother, "Tutti, tell me, would you take me again?"

Without hesitation, she answered, "I would, Karl; indeed, I would."

"After all the pain I have caused you?"

She answered, "Yes, I would, and she added, "When God puts your failings and your good deeds on His scale, your good deeds will far outweigh the bad ones." He kissed her hand.

My father died peacefully in 1979, on *Heidehügel*, at the age of eighty-three, in the arms of my mother, surrounded by our family. Among those present was his youngest son, Christian, who was born to Papa's relationship with another woman.

In 1981, Yad Vashem, the Holocaust Memorial for the Martyrs' and Heroes' Remembrance Authority in Jerusalem, posthumously awarded my father the Medal of Honor and named him a Righteous Gentile for saving Jewish lives during the Holocaust. In 1983, my mother and I planted a tree in his honor on a hill overlooking Jerusalem. His name is engraved on the Wall of Remembrance at the Holocaust Museum in Washington, D.C.

My mother survived my father by twenty-four years. She lost her hearing, but continued to live in her own home on her beloved *Heidehügel*, until the age of ninety-four. When asked about my father, she quoted from Goethe's Faust:

Zwei Seelen wohnen, ach! in meiner Brust,	Two souls, alas, dwell within my breast,
Die eine will sich von der andern trennen.	And each wrestles for the mastery over the other.
Die eine hält in derber Liebeslust Sich an die Welt mit klammernden Organen.	The one is in the grip of untamed lust And clings to the world where the senses rule.
Die andere hebt gewaltsam sich vom Dust	The other rises unfettered out of darkness
Zu den Gefilden hoher Ahnen.	To lofty fields beyond.

Another one of my mother's favorite quotes was: *"Wo viel Licht ist, ist auch viel Schatten,"* where the light shines brightest, shadows are deepest. She applied this to her own and my father's life, came to regret her own failings, and asked for forgiveness.

The last five years of her life, my mother spent near Berlin, in the home of my youngest sister, Gesine, who cared for her with tender devotion until her death at the age of one hundred. On her one-hundredth birthday, my mother continued to teach us, to pray, to sing the old songs, and to recite poetry to her extended family and friends who had gathered to honor her. She delivered Christian Morgenstern's words with great urgency:

Allen Brüder sein! Allen helfen, dienen!	Be brother to all! Help them, serve them!
Ist seit "Er" erschienen, Ziel allein!	Is the only goal since "He" appeared!
Selbst der Bösewicht, der Dir widerstrebet!	Even the evil one, who is your adversary!
Auch er ward gewebet einst aus Licht!	Was once fashioned from light!
Liebt das Böse gut! Lehren tiefe Seelen.	By loving, conquer evil, say the wise.
Lernt am Hasse stählen Liebesmut!	Transform hate into courageous love!
Brüder! Hört das Wort!	Brothers! Hear the Word!
Das "Es" Wahrheit werde,	So that "it" may be fulfilled,
Und die Erde Gottes Ort.	So that the earth may become God's place.

Almost fifty years ago, I immigrated to the United States as a young bride, leaving behind my parents and siblings. What may have made it easier for me to start a new life far away from home, was that I had been on my own since the age of eighteen, and that I wrote and spoke English fluently. While working and studying languages in Switzerland and in the United States, I grew to be self-reliant. At the same time, I learned to accept and take advantage of opportunities made so generously available to me. I believe that I would not have developed my gifts, had I remained in the country of my birth.

Whenever my past began to haunt me, I asked for help and received it gratefully. I met most challenges head-on. In the process, I was—and often still am—a step or two ahead of where I feel comfortable. That is when I recall the past ... I see myself as a ten-year-old in a one-hundred-year-old barn, where I spread my arms and jump from the rafters into the hay below. I have been flying ever since.

My husband and I settled in Atlanta where both of us taught at Emory University, he in history, and I in the studio art department. Working with clay, teaching, and writing have been deeply satisfying for me. I have loved, and I have been loved by my wonderful husband, children, grandchildren, and friends. These days—from the windows of our house on the northern coast of the Olympic Peninsula in Washington State we look upon forested foothills and snow-capped mountains to the south, and Vancouver Island, British Columbia, to the north. When, in the evenings, my husband and I sit side by side to celebrate the *Feierabend,* watching the sky turn crimson as the sun sinks into the waters of the Strait of Juan de Fuca, I feel blessed beyond words.

I have told these stories to honor my father and mother, of course, but also out of respect for the victims of war and of the Holocaust. I am keenly aware of the infamous legacy that will forever be associated with the land of my birth, a legacy that was on my father's mind as well. In 1978, seven months before his death, he told me with tears in his eyes, "I am haunted by the fact that I was not able to save more."

From the time I was thirteen years old, my father encouraged me to write. The year before he died, he asked me to tell the story of our family. By completing this memoir, I have taken the first step toward fulfilling the promise I made to him.

Acknowledgements

Most of the memories are my own, the things I saw with the eyes of the child I was. But I have also included the written and oral testimonies stored in the memories of others. I wish here to acknowledge their support and to thank them from the bottom of my heart. They include members of my family: my father, who inspired me to write this book, and my mother, who laughed and cried as she read the unabridged version, approved it and gave it her blessing. I am grateful to my aunt Marianne, who illuminated the early years of my childhood, to my cousin Dr. Uwe Lamprecht for his recollections, and to my sister-in-law Ingrid Laabs, for her thoughtful comments and for translating portions of the manuscript into German. I am deeply grateful to my brothers Sven, Frank, and Björn, and to my sisters Dagmar and Gesine, who shared with me their perspectives and insights about our parents. I am indebted to my childhood friends Margret Tichy Iffland and Brigitte Blankenburg Mundry for sharing their memories of the years in Vaake before and after the war.

Warm thanks go to Dr. Eva Fogelman, whose book *Conscience and Courage* remains the classic about rescuers of Jews during the Holocaust, and for letting me know, "your writing efforts will make a difference for generations to come." I also thank Dr. Mordecai Paldiel, head of the Department for the Righteous at Yad Vashem, for guiding me in the search for men and women my father had rescued, and with whom our family had lost contact. My gratitude goes to Shimshon Schönberg, Fanny and Hava Hartmann (whose names were changed at their request to protect the privacy of their family). Over the years, all three recalled in letters and private conversations with me what my father had done for them and their families. Steven Spielberg's Survivors of the Shoah Visual History Foundation videotaped Fanny and Hava's life stories.

My heartfelt thanks to my son Nils, daughter Kirsten, and granddaughter Hannah for their enthusiastic support, suggestions and unflagging encouragement. A special thanks to my son-in-law Beau Brashares, who gave generously of his time and talent by creating the evocative cover for this book, and for helping me reclaim my past through archival photographic images.

Thanks are due to Peggy de Broux, Dr. Suzann Bick, and the members of the Writer's Workshop for creating an environment where the participants could hone their skills and support each other.

Among those who read earlier versions of the manuscript are my friends—Joanna Erikson, Sandy and Charlie Mays, Mary Roon, and Edith and Dr. Roland Blaich. I am grateful for their astute comments, their wisdom, and encouragement. *Herzlichen Dank* to my friend Alice Derry, for reading the manuscript with the poet's sensitivity, and for believing in the power of my stories. Dale Brown, our oldest family friend, a writer, and former editor for Time-Life Books, has been there from the beginning. He has cheered me on when I needed it most. He has been most generous with his inspired guidance, his insight, and expert advice.

I would like to give credit to the German historian, Dr. Reinhold Lütgemeier-Davin, who unearthed pertinent documents and published numerous articles and a perceptive biographical monograph of my father, "Luftwaffen-Feldwebel und Baurat Karl Laabs, Ein Jugendbewegter als Judenretter im polnischen Krenau," in *Retter in Uniform,* Fischer Taschenbuch Verlag, 2002.

Most especially, I would like to express my profound gratitude to my dear husband, Charles, who after listening patiently to my stories for years, suggested that I put them on paper. Besides reading and rereading countless revisions and sharing with me his professional, historical expertise and insights, he has given me the love, encouragement, and indefatigable support I needed to complete this book.

978-0-595-44704-6
0-595-44704-X

CPSIA information can be obtained at www.ICGtesting.com
Printed in the USA
LVOW071634111012

302461LV00002B/8/P